THE DREAM KING

Naive and immature, Ludwig II of Bavaria had little inclination for affairs of state when he ascended the throne in 1864 aged eighteen. Free now to realise his dreams, he immediately summoned to Munich his idol, Richard Wagner, to whom he wrote: 'You have been the sole source of my happiness ever since I was a mere boy.' Their extraordinary relationship developed with all the fervour of German and mid-nineteenth-century romanticism. Without Ludwig's patronage Wagner might never have been able to produce *Tristan*, complete the *Ring*, or compose *Parsifal*. But Wagner's insatiable greed (which led to his exile) and Ludwig's breaking of his engagement to his cousin Sophie, sister of the Empress Elisabeth of Austria, antagonised the King's subjects. Ludwig withdrew more and more into a dream world, and started to build his fantastic castles. Government was neglected; the Privy Purse was bankrupt. Ludwig's despairing ministers had him certified insane and took him prisoner to his castle of Berg, on Lake Starnberg. There, two days later, his body and that of the alienist, Dr Gudden, were found in the cold waters of the lake. Accident? Suicide? Manslaughter? The truth may never be known.

Wilfrid Blunt is the author of several bestselling books. Formerly senior drawing master at Eton, he is now Curator of the Watts Gallery at Compton, near Guildford. The first volume of his autobiography, *Married to a Single Life (1901–1938)*, was published in 1983 by Michael Russell.

HAMISH HAMILTON PAPERBACKS

The Dream King

LUDWIG II OF BAVARIA

by

WILFRID BLUNT

*With a chapter on Ludwig and the Arts
by Dr Michael Petzet*

A HAMISH HAMILTON PAPERBACK
London

First published in Great Britain 1970
by Hamish Hamilton Ltd
Garden House 57–59 Long Acre London WC2E 9JZ
First published in this edition in 1984

ISBN 0-241-11293-1

Scanned and phototypeset by
Datasolve Information, London
Printed and bound in Finland
by Werner Söderström Oy

TO THE MEMORY OF
FREDERICA MACIVER-REITSMA
WAGNERIAN AND LUDOVICOPHILE
A COURAGEOUS WOMAN
AND A GENEROUS FRIEND

A Louis II de Bavière

Roi, le seul vrai roi de ce siècle, salut, Sire,
Qui voulûtes mourir vengeant votre raison
Des choses de la politique, et du délire
De cette Science intruse dans la maison,

De cette Science, assassin de l'Oraison
Et du Chant et de l'Art et de toute la Lyre,
Et simplement, et plein d'orgueil en floraison,
Tuâtes en mourant, salut, Roi! bravo Sire!

Vous fûtes un poète, un soldat, le seul Roi
De ce siècle où les rois se font si peu de choses,
Et le Martyr de la Raison selon la Foi.

Salut à votre très unique apothéose,
Et que votre âme ait son fier cortège, or et fer,
Sur un air magnifique et joyeux de Wagner.

Paul Verlaine

CONTENTS

ILLUSTRATIONS

Except where otherwise stated, the photographs are reproduced b
kind permission of the Bayerische Verwaltung der Staatlichen Schlösser
Garten und Seen, Munich

PREFACE AND ACKNOWLEDGMENTS

I first became interested in Ludwig II when, more than fifty years ago now, I went to Munich to study singing and learn German. In 1949 I began to collect material for a full-length biography of the King, and received much help and encouragement from that fine and generous scholar, the late Dr Ernest Newman; but other commitments intervened and I was unable to give the time to write a book such as I then had in mind. There is still the need of a definitive biography in English, and I venture to hope that this shorter account may encourage some other author to provide it.

I must thank many friends who have generously given me their help and advice. First and foremost I must record my deep gratitude to Dr Michael Petzet, Curator of the Bavarian Administration of the National Castles, Gardens and Lakes, for his valuable chapter on Ludwig and the Arts, a subject on which he is the leading authority. He read and most helpfully commented on my text.

I must also thank him for driving me out one day to Hohenschwangau, Neuschwanstein and Linderhof, thus enabling me to see them for the first time under deep snow.

In the original hardback edition which was fully illustrated much of the splendid photography was done by Herr Werner Neumeister and I am most grateful to him for giving us permission to use three of his photographs in this edition.

Frau Philippine Schick kindly read my typescript and also made the initial translation of Dr Petzet's chapter. I must gratefully acknowledge, too, the help and advice that I received from Mrs Arthur Harrison, Mr Hugh Haworth and Mr Francis Thompson, and from my brother Anthony. The care and patience of Mrs Caroline Lightburn, who saw the book through the press, cannot be allowed to pass unnoticed. Miss Charmian Young was once again my prompt and efficient typist.

Lastly I would like to record my deep gratitude to my friend Mrs MacIver-Reitsma. Her enthusiasm for my book did much to keep up my spirits whenever they began to flag, and her practical support, which was expressed in gifts that ranged from biographies of Wagner to crates of Corton, was hardly less valuable to me. I am sad that she did not live to see the finished article, for I think it would have given her pleasure.

W.J.W.B.
The Watts Gallery, Compton
July 1984

THE DREAM KING

Chapter One

PRINCE LUDWIG

I want to remain for ever an enigma – to myself, and to others. (Ludwig II)

The palace of Nymphenburg, the summer residence near Munich of the electors and kings of Bavaria, is really a chain of pavilions linked by two arcaded galleries. In the centre block, an Italianate villa built by an Italian architect in the seventeenth century, is the lofty Festsaal, carried up through three storeys and at a later date sumptuously frescoed with scenes from Ovid's *Metamorphoses* – with gods and goddesses, groves and fountains, *putti* and rococo shell-work – by the incomparable Johann Baptist Zimmermann. But it is to a humbler room of the palace – a little first-floor room in one of the southern pavilions with Empire furniture and moss-green wall-hangings – that we must turn, in the very early hours of the morning of 25 August 1845. For here Crown Princess Marie is in labour with her first child, the boy who is one day to become King Ludwig II of Bavaria.

Marie, a Prussian princess before her marriage, has recorded the events of that morning in her family journal:

Ludwig Friedrich Wilhelm was born on Monday 25 August at 12.30 a.m. at Nymphenburg, in a room above that in which Max Josef I died. King Ludwig I was delighted that his grandson should have been born on his birthday, and at exactly the same hour. Besides Max [her husband] and his parents, Aunt von Leuchtenberg and Uncle and Aunt Eduard were in the room. King Ludwig I in his great joy embraced several persons of the household. A hundred-gun salute announced the birth in Munich, and Nymphenburg was decorated and illuminated.

The following day the child was baptized with great ceremony by Archbishop Gebsattel. King Friedrich Wilhelm IV of Prussia and Queen Elisabeth [the child's great-uncle and great-aunt] had arrived from Tegernsee the previous day; Adalbert, Max's younger brother, held the baptismal candle, and King Ludwig I the baby. The King of Prussia and King Otto of Greece [the child's uncle] were the godfathers; the latter was not present, nor was Papa. For the first few days the boy was called Otto; then the grandfather asked that the name might be changed to Ludwig, because he was born on his birthday.[1] So now he is Ludwig.

Everyone was delighted at the child's birth, for two years earlier the

---

[1] Ludwig I was named after his godfather, King Louis XVI of France.

3

Princess had had a miscarriage. As for Max, he was quite overwhelmed; to his brother-in-law, Prince Adalbert of Prussia, he wrote 'It is a simply marvellous feeling, being a father.'

When the boy was two-and-a-half years old, King Ludwig I was forced to abdicate; thus, at the age of thirty-seven, Max became King Maximilian II, and his son Crown Prince.

The strange career of the dethroned King, though it has often been told, must be briefly mentioned because young Ludwig had much in common with his sentimental, art-loving grandfather. It was from Ludwig I, philhellene and creator of nineteenth-century Munich, that the boy inherited his passion for building; from the King, too, came his romanticism. In 1846 the 'Spanish' dancer and adventuress, Lola Montez (alias Mrs Eliza Gilbert), stormed her way into the presence of the sixty-year-old King and bewitched him. Infatuated now, reckless always, he surrendered to her insatiable demands until finally in 1848, the year of revolutions, ministerial pressure forced him to send her into exile, where not long afterwards she was to find consolation in the arms of a twenty-one-year-old Old Etonian, a virile young Guardsman named Heald, whom she subsequently, though in fact bigamously, married. On 20 March 1848 Ludwig abdicated in favour of his son.

Queen Marie records in her journal the tastes and the progress of her boy. He was six when she wrote, 'Ludwig soon showed an interest in art; he loved building [with toy bricks], especially churches, monasteries, etc.;' and the following year she gave him for Christmas a model of the Siegestor, itself a replica of the Arch of Constantine in Rome, which the King had just had erected in Munich. Ludwig I, writing to his son, King Otto of Greece, says that he watched the child making 'astonishingly good buildings in excellent taste. In the future Ludwig II I recognize a striking likeness to the politically-dead Ludwig I.' 'He listened with pleasure when I told him Bible stories and showed him pictures illustrating them,' wrote the Queen. 'He was particularly fond of the Frauenkirche in Munich, loved dressing up as a nun, and enjoyed acting. He was always giving away his toys and his money.'

He now had a brother – the prematurely born Prince Otto, three years younger than himself – to play with, and from time to time other children were invited to the palace to join in their games. They were told not to stand on ceremony with the young Princes; but there were limits beyond which familiarity might not go, and after Graf Tony Arco had been caught boxing Ludwig's ears, these parties were brought to an end. Both Ludwig and Otto were shy and highly strung, but in many ways they were very different. Ludwig was dark, Otto fair; while Ludwig played with his bricks, Otto drilled his tin soldiers. Ludwig

4

never let Otto, who was his mother's favourite, forget that *he* was the Crown Prince, and this sometimes led to quarrels; on one occasion he tied his younger brother up and threatened to behead him, a fate from which Otto was saved by the timely arrival of a Court official. But in general they got on well enough together, and when the two handsome boys were seen walking in the streets of Munich, one on each side of their mother, the people thought that all augured well for the future of their country and its almost seven-hundred-year-old Wittelsbach dynasty.

When Ludwig was nine and Otto six, their governess, Fräulein Sybille Meilhaus, was replaced by their first tutor, Generalmajor Theodor de la Rosée - a snob who spent more of his time in warning his charges always to keep the lower orders at a proper distance than in teaching them their books. Ludwig learned more slowly than his brother; though he came to speak French fairly fluently, he was never to acquire more than 'small Latin and less Greek'. He was devoted to Fräulein Meilhaus (later Baroness von Leonrod) and kept in touch with her until her death in 1881.

In the summer the royal family often went to Hohenschwangau, a little gingerbread castle in the Bavarian highlands which Max had purchased in a ruinous condition in 1832 and renovated in the Biedermeier style - a style which, as here exemplified, has certain affinities with Horace Walpole's 'Strawberry Hill Gothic'. Indifferent artists, working mostly from sketches by Moritz von Schwind, had been employed to decorate its walls with the legends of the Grail, of Tannhäuser, and of the Swan-knight Lohengrin who, according to tradition, had inhabited this very castle. Here Ludwig acquired, through the tastes of his father, his love of the German legends and, as he gazed from the windows of the castle across the blue-green waters of the Alpsee to the Alps beyond, his lifelong passion for the solitude of the mountains. Hohenschwangau was the capital of the Swan Country. There were swans everywhere: live swans on the lake which the Queen and her children used to feed, swans painted on the walls of the royal apartments, vases and innumerable knick-knacks in the form of swans. They fascinated both Max and his elder son, and the latter would often draw them or seal his childish letters with a swan and a cross. He was already an incurable romantic.

Max was an intellectual *manqué* who used to say that had he not been King he would have become a university professor. When in the capital he held weekly symposia in his study in the Residenz, his town palace, where over beer and cigars the Munich intellectuals aired their erudition and exchanged ideas. ('And have you any scientific proof,' Max asked Professor Jolly on one of these occasions, 'that the high-born in this world will receive suitably deferential treatment in the next?')

The Queen rarely appeared at these gatherings, though it is recorded of her that she once proposed that the word 'friendship' should be substituted for 'love' wherever it occurred in poetry. She was an anti-intellectual, confessing to a friend, 'I never open a book; I simply can't understand how people can spend all their time reading.' Ludwig was already out of sympathy with her; he realized that she was a woman with whom he could make no real contact, and used later to say that her 'prose', as he put it, spoiled for him the 'poetry' of Hohenschwangau. She could neither understand nor be admitted into his dream world. She liked Hohenschwangau because, until she began to put on weight, she was a keen mountaineer, and the boys and their current tutor were often made to go with her on quite stiff climbs; for these they all wore Bavarian peasant costume, the general revival of which the Queen did much to encourage. Max, who believed in a Spartan upbringing for his sons, no doubt approved of these expeditions, but there were some who did not; one unfortunate tutor, the epileptic Baron Wulffen, who had pleaded in vain to be left behind because he had no head for heights, climbed an awkward rock in order to pick some edelweiss that the Queen had admired, and fell, injuring himself seriously. The accident made a deep impression on the young Princes, who saw it happen.

Soon after this it was noticed that Ludwig, who was now fourteen, suffered from mild hallucinations; these took the form of hearing imaginary voices addressing him. Otto too, though a gay little boy, had almost from infancy felt 'compulsive urges'. It is said that the Queen was worried, but that the Court doctor assured her that there was no cause for alarm; the boys would soon outgrow these little troubles. But she may well have continued to worry; for though she herself was perfectly normal, she knew that through much inbreeding there was mental instability, and what has now been identified as porphyria, on her side of the family. Max too was sane enough; but he had a strange sister, the highly talented Princess Alexandra, whose whole life was clouded and confused by an unshakable conviction that she had once swallowed a grand piano made of glass. There was genuine and, as events were to show, justified cause for the Queen's anxiety, though for some time to come Ludwig did not really betray symptoms of abnormality other than shyness, hypersensitivity, and a dreamy romanticism.

Max was a strict and not very understanding father, for the most part too busy with his official duties to spare much time for his sons. Franz von Pfistermeister, the Cabinet Secretary,[1] recorded that the King saw

[1] 'The Cabinet Secretaryship was a peculiarity of the Bavarian system of administration. The Cabinet Secretary was a confidential official attached to the person of the monarch.' (Newman)

little of them except at mealtimes, and that when the Court was in Munich, Max could only with the greatest difficulty be persuaded to take Ludwig with him on his regular morning walk in the English Garden. 'What can I talk to him about?' he said to Pfistermeister. 'We haven't a single interest in common.' No doubt their shared love of German mythology could not provide the material for conversation day after day.

The boys were often frustrated for their own good, and Max himself beat them when they were reported to him by one of their tutors. They were made to get up very early. Their food was simple and there was not enough of it, though sometimes a kindhearted lady-in-waiting would supplement their meagre rations with a titbit smuggled from the royal table. Ludwig's pet tortoise was taken from him because it was thought that he was becoming too attached to it. Their pocket-money was minimal; and legend has it that one day, when Otto found that he could not afford to purchase something that he particularly coveted, he went off on his own to a dentist in Munich, whom he unsuccessfully tried to persuade to extract two of his molars because someone had told him that healthy teeth fetched a good price.

An account-book kept by Ludwig survives to show how his money went – much of it on others. Among purchases for himself it is interesting to note (in 1860) a little statuette of Wilhelm Tell and, three years later, a copy of *The Legend of Wilhelm Tell*. He was also reading Scott's *Quentin Durward* and other romantic tales. But over Christmas there were occasional extravagances, and like all children he made lists of what he hoped for in his stocking: a model engine; a knife with lots of blades; a book of prayers entitled *Flowers of Devotion*, bound in ivory and with a lapis lazuli cross on the cover; a picture of Jesus on the Mount of Olives; a picture of the contests of the Swan-knights; a watch, and so on.

Before he was thirteen, the boy had heard from his governess about the production in Munich of Wagner's *Lohengrin*, and the following Christmas (1858) he had been given, by one of his tutors and no doubt at his own request, a copy of Wagner's *Opera and Drama*. Soon he was soaking himself in the composer's prose works and in the libretti of *Lohengrin* and *Tannhäuser*, which before long he knew almost by heart. It is said that he found some of these, including *The Art-Work of the Future* and *Music of the Future*, lying on the piano in the Karl-Theodor-Palais in Munich, the town house of his great-uncle Duke Max in Bayern,[1] a gay Bohemian who was viewed with some suspicion by the very conventional King and Queen.

[1] 'Duke Max in Bavaria' – a title conferred on the family in 1799 by the Elector Max Joseph, afterwards King Max I. Herzog *von* Bayern was a title already held by a senior branch of the family.

But it was not until February 1861 that Ludwig actually heard his first Wagner opera, *Lohengrin*; he was overwhelmed by the experience and gave his father no peace until he had promised that the opera should be given again for him. A special performance took place in the following June, this time with the title-role sung by the young but already corpulent Schnorr von Carolsfeld, who in 1865 was to become the first Tristan; and in December 1862 Ludwig heard *Tannhäuser*. This made an even stronger impression on him than had *Lohengrin*. A courtier who was with him in the royal box spoke of its 'almost demoniacal' effect on the Prince, whose reactions during the performance were at times 'little less than morbid. When it came to the passage where Tannhäuser re-enters the Venusberg, Ludwig's body was so convulsed that I was afraid he was going to have an epileptic fit.'

In 1863 there came into Ludwig's hands a copy of the recently published *Ring* poem. In the preface to this, Wagner had written of the hopeless state of opera production in Germany and of the kind of performances he aspired to bring about. But such productions would be costly, and he saw little prospect of German music-lovers being cajoled into raising the necessary funds. A German prince, however, could achieve them in his Court Theatre. 'Will such a prince be found?' he wrote. Ludwig read these words and pondered on them; if ever it were in his power, *he* would be that prince.

In the middle of August 1863 Bismarck visited Nymphenburg. In his *Autobiography* he relates that at meals he was placed next to Ludwig, who sat opposite his mother. Bismarck shrewdly summed up his neighbour. He had the feeling that Ludwig's thoughts were elsewhere, and that it was only by an effort that he brought himself to make polite conversation; but when he did speak, Bismarck was impressed. The boy was drinking glass after glass of champagne. The Queen seemed to be telling the waiters not to refill his glass so often, but Ludwig defeated her conspiracy by holding his glass over his shoulder. He obviously had a good head, for he was not in the least drunk; but he was thoroughly bored, and he drank to stimulate his fantasy. 'The impression he made on me was a sympathetic one,' Bismarck wrote, 'though I must regretfully confess that all my efforts to entertain him with my conversation failed.'

As soon as Bismarck had returned to Prussia, the royal family went to Hohenschwangau for the Prince's eighteenth birthday and coming-of-age. Ludwig was in high spirits: on the morning of his birthday he rose before dawn and went fishing, to return triumphantly at breakfast time with a 9½ lb. trout; and in the evening there were fireworks and singing. Back in Munich he attended lectures on physics at the University, and on 21 February he was present at a performance of

Lohengrin with the Hanover tenor, Albert Niemann, in the title role. Now for the first time Ludwig saw a Wagnerian hero who, besides being a fine singer, looked the part. He was overwhelmed, and further performances were commanded. Niemann was summoned to the palace, and on 7 March the Prince wrote to a favourite cousin, Princess Anna of Hesse-Darmstadt: 'I had a big bouquet presented to him [Niemann], and gave him a pair of cuff-links with swans and jewels, and a cross, with all of which he was delighted.'

In November there occurred an event which might not at first sight seem likely to affect the course of Bavarian history: King Frederick VII of Denmark died, so bringing the male line of the reigning Danish house to an end. This brought to a head the so-called 'Schleswig-Holstein Question' – the long dispute between the German Confederation and Denmark as to whether or not the two 'Elbe' duchies of Schleswig and Holstein were an integral part of the dominions of the Danish Crown. In February 1864 the joint armies of Austria and Prussia crossed the Eider, and in October, by the Treaty of Vienna, Denmark was forced to renounce all rights to the duchies. From this time onwards the Schleswig-Holstein question, which still simmered, became merged in the larger question of Bismarck's growing ambition for a dominant Prussia, an ambition which was to lead to the Seven Weeks' War of 1866, the Franco-Prussian (or Franco-German) War of 1870, and thus in due course to the rivalry between France and Germany which culminated in the two World Wars.

Max, conscientious always over his duties as a king, fretted at the political situation, which Ludwig found nothing but boring; 'I am sick of this eternal Schleswig-Holstein business. . . . *Please don't show this letter to anybody*!!!' wrote the boy to Princess Anna. The King favoured an independent Schleswig-Holstein, and thus opposed Prussia. He had recently been suffering from rheumatism of the joints, and it was only with the greatest reluctance that he had agreed to follow his doctor's advice and go to Italy to escape the worst rigours of the Bavarian winter. But as the tension over Schleswig-Holstein grew, he had felt it his duty to return to Munich. It was a brave action, though possibly a foolish one: his condition rapidly deteriorated, and on 10 March 1864 he died. He was only fifty-three, the new King not yet nineteen.

Chapter Two

THE YOUNG KING

'Max died too soon.' So wrote the Queen Mother in her journal. She was not referring to her personal loss; she meant, of course, that her son was not yet ready to rule.

The boy was a strange mixture. He was tall, athletic and physically very powerful; a good rider and a strong swimmer; yet the feminine in him showed in his fondness for scents and sweet wines, and in his personal vanity. The curls in his dark brown hair that gave him such a romantic appearance were the daily creation and recreation of the Court barber; 'If I didn't have my hair curled every day,' he said, 'I couldn't enjoy my food.'

He was extremely naive and innocent for his age. 'What is a "natural" son?' he once asked a courtier, and the word 'rape' also had to be explained to him. One cannot help wondering how this 'royal Shelley' (as he has been called) would have developed if he had been sent, as were other German princelings from time to time during the reign of Queen Victoria, to Eton; had he stayed the course there – which is perhaps unlikely – he would at least have ascended the throne with a knowledge of some of the facts of life.

His memory was remarkable even by royal standards. He knew most of Wagner's libretti by heart and would sometimes declaim long passages from Schiller's plays, one or two of which he had seen at the Court Theatre. 'His voice,' wrote Count Lerchenfeld, 'was agreeable and his diction good; but he spoke very pompously and without a trace of humour.' He was a sound judge of character – a valuable quality in a monarch. He had always been devout, and he had always been generous – too generous, some said. Though he was never to forget that he was King, he could on occasions unbend – something that Max had never really been able to do, not even at his weekly symposia in the Residenz. Von Leinfelder, a man who had known him since childhood and who now became a kind of private secretary to him, tells us that Ludwig would himself draw up a chair, pour wine, or peel an orange for him.

Ruling was as it were the family business of the Wittelsbachs, and Ludwig entered upon his new job much as a dutiful but reluctant son might join the family firm. At first he was conscientious and hard-working, and those ministers who imagined that he would be content to remain a mere puppet were quickly disillusioned. Their efforts to bully him failed, and he was soon to make changes in his Cabinet. Each morning, after greeting his mother, he was at his writing-table by 9 o'clock, ready to receive the Cabinet Secretary, Pfistermeister. When some difficult decision had to be taken he would modestly inquire, 'What would my father have done?' But the King could be stubborn. He also had a temper, and those who saw him lose it said that his face became suddenly so transformed that he was barely recognizable.

To the people of Munich, however, who did not yet see these darker moods, he seemed, as a dozen authors have inevitably observed, a fairy-tale Prince Charming, an Apollo, an Adonis, another Lohengrin. During their father's lifetime he and Otto had been seen only infrequently in the capital; when they walked in the funeral cortège with the eyes of the whole city upon them, Ludwig's romantic appearance made a profound impression on men and women alike. The Austrian novelist, Klara Tschudi, thought him

> . . . the best-looking boy I have ever seen. His tall, slim figure was perfectly proportioned. With his abundant and rather curly hair and the faintest suggestion of down on his cheek, he resembled those splendid antique sculptures which first make us aware of what virile Greek manhood was like. Even had he been a beggar, I could not have failed to notice him. No one, old or young, rich or poor, remained unmoved by the magic that he radiated.

Allowance must here be made for feminine 'gush'. Ludwig, with his large and lustrous eyes set wide apart, his finely chiselled features and dark hair exaggeratedly crimped, was undoubtedly striking-looking; certainly he was tall and elegant; but no one could fail to notice the too-prominent ears. His shoulders, too, were very sloping, and his clothes and his boots always seemed several sizes too large for him. The Müncheners, however, accustomed to conventional Max, may well be excused for exaggerating the poetic beauty of their new King and falling in love with him. There was no doubt that on occasions he could cast spells.

While Ludwig dutifully attended to the affairs of State and other such matters for which he had little inclination and in which he had received no training, his thoughts turned incessantly to Wagner, to whom he was now in a position to bring help; he had no idea how desperately Wagner needed it at that very moment.

Wagner, pursued by his creditors and almost at the end of his tether, with his unfinished *Ring des Nibelungen* and *Die Meistersinger*, and his *Tristan* that no opera house could stage, had gone into hiding. To his friend the composer Peter Cornelius he had just written, 'My situation is extremely precarious. It is most delicately balanced: a single jolt – and all is over and nothing more can ever come out of me, nothing, nothing! A *light* must show itself; a *man* must arise who will give me

11

immense assistance *now*. . . .' Curiously enough, Cornelius guessed correctly from where this help was to come. He tells us that he had just been saying to a friend, 'Well, the first Ludwig occupied himself with painters, King Max with scholars and poets; what if the present King were suddenly to become interested in music and infatuated with Wagner?'

Meanwhile Ludwig did not know where Wagner was to be found. It was said that he had recently been seen in Munich; but the King searched in vain for his name in the Munich Strangers' List and finally asked Pfistermeister why it was not there.

'Which Wagner?' asked the Cabinet Secretary; Wagner was not an uncommon name.

Ludwig replied that for him there was only one Wagner – the composer Richard Wagner; he ordered Pfistermeister to find him and bring him to Munich immediately.

So on 14 April 1864, within less than five weeks of Ludwig's accession, the search for Wagner began. Pfistermeister first tried a house that the composer had recently rented at Penzing, near Vienna, but he drew a blank there; Wagner had left a fortnight before, and no one knew, or was prepared to admit that he knew, where he had gone. He telegraphed this news to Ludwig, who replied, 'The contents of your telegram horrify me! My resolution is quickly taken: go after R. Wagner as swiftly as possible, if you can do so without attracting attention. . . . It is of the utmost importance to me that this long-cherished wish of mine shall soon be gratified.'

The search continued, the trail leading poor Pfistermeister through Switzerland to Stuttgart, where on 3 May he finally caught up with his quarry. Wagner was visiting a friend when the card of someone calling himself 'Secretary to the King of Bavaria' was handed to him; suspecting a trick on the part of one of his creditors, he had word sent out that he was not there. But when he returned to his hotel he found that his pursuer had tracked him down and that a meeting the next morning could not be avoided. That night he slept badly, fearing the worst.

But it was no trap. Pfistermeister was the man he claimed to be, and he brought a message from his master that he, Ludwig, was Wagner's 'most ardent admirer', that he knew his writings by heart, that he would provide him with all he needed in Munich, and that the *Ring* would be produced there. He sent Wagner his photograph and a ring, and the command to return at once with Pfistermeister to Munich.

So Wagner had found his prince. That same evening he addressed to the King the first of those many hundreds of letters in which he was to express, in language which, especially in translation, sounds to us

12

today embarrassingly sentimental and unbearably artificial, his gratitude to his benefactor:

> Beloved, gracious King,
>
> I send you these tears of most heavenly emotion, to tell you that now the marvels of poetry have come as a divine reality into my poor, loveless life. That life, its ultimate poetry, its finest music, belongs henceforth to you, my gracious young King; dispose of it as your own.
>
> In utmost rapture, faithful and true,
> Your subject,
> Richard Wagner

Then, borrowing from a friend the money for his (first class, of course) railway ticket, he left for Munich.

The first meeting took place the following afternoon in the Audience Chamber of the Residenz, and lasted an hour and a half. It was an unforgettable moment in the lives of both men: of the shy young ruler of an ancient dynasty and of the embittered, fifty-one-year-old Republican and revolutionary composer. 'He bent low over my hand,' the King later told his cousin the Duchess Sophie in Bayern, 'and seemed moved by what was so natural; he remained a long time thus, without saying a word. I had the impression that our roles were reversed. I stooped down to him' – the King was almost a foot taller than Wagner – 'and took him to my heart with the feeling that I was pledging myself to be true to him to the end of time.'

That evening Wagner wrote to his friend Eliza Wille:

> You know that the young King of Bavaria has been looking for me. He is, sad to say, so beautiful and so gifted, so full of deep feeling and so wonderful, that I fear his life must vanish like a fleeting godlike dream in this crude world of ours. He loves me with the fire and tenderness of a first love; he knows and understands everything about me – understands me like my own soul. He wants me to be always at his side, to work, to relax, and to produce my operas. He will give me everything I need to this end. . . . You cannot begin to imagine the magic of his eyes. Oh, may he but live! It is an unbelievable miracle!

And the following day Ludwig wrote to Wagner:

> Rest assured that I will do everything in my power to make up to you for what you have suffered in the past. I will banish from you for ever the petty cares of everyday life; I will procure for you the peace you have longed for, so that you will be free to spread the

13

mighty wings of your genius in the pure air of your rapturous art.

Unconscious though you were of it, you have been *the sole source of my happiness* ever since I was a mere boy, my friend who spoke to my heart as no other did, my best teacher and educator.

I will repay you everything that I am able to. Oh, how I have looked forward to the time when I could do this! I hardly dared to indulge myself in the hope of being able so soon to prove my love to you.

Julius Hey, who a few days later was received in audience by the King, wrote that he found him in ecstasy over Wagner and the possibility of seeing his operas properly produced in the future. The King said to him:

Have any other composers such sweet, such heavenly tunes? I find the *Tannhäuser* poem and the *Tristan* drama wonderful – incomparably moving. How stirring the music [of *Tristan*] must be! I imagine it as predominantly gloomy, especially the third act. . . . Wagner says that our singers don't understand what he wants, for if they did they would be able to sing it. He doesn't believe there's a Tristan to be found anywhere – certainly not here. But mayn't there perhaps be singers elsewhere who are more at home with his operas? I would so love to give him the pleasure of a performance of his work – his 'child of sorrow', as he calls it. But I daren't let him see how impatient I am for one, because he is so eager to please me and he has hardly been able to find the right singers for his earlier operas, still less for *Tristan*. Oh, how wonderful it would be to hear all his operas on our stage, with him conducting!

Hey added that the King seemed to him 'like a child who is waiting outside the room where the Christmas presents are being put out, and who tries to catch a glimpse of the Christmas tree through the keyhole.' 'Do you really believe it possible,' asked Ludwig, 'that the composer of *Lohengrin* has enemies? It is unthinkable! Who could possibly remain unmoved by this magical fairy-tale, by this heavenly music?'

Ludwig's ministers were for their part content that the King had found this new interest; indeed it has even been suggested – though it seems barely credible – that 'Ludwig, so to speak, had the card they wanted him to draw "forced" upon him by the conjurors'. But there can be little doubt that they believed that Wagner could be so manipulated that he would distract Ludwig from meddling in politics. All kings needed a distraction – provided always that certain bounds were not overstepped: they had not forgotten the first Ludwig and his dancer. Probably it never crossed their minds that the day might come when

Wagner, having gained ascendancy over the King, would himself attempt to interfere in the running of the country.

The Austrian Ambassador in Munich reported on 12 May to his chief in Vienna that 'undoubtedly Wagner will cost the King a good deal of money; but it would be a sad thing if at his [Ludwig's] age he could not sow a few wild oats. Much more serious, it seems to me, is the fact that his entourage has begun telling him how good-looking he is and how good-looking the women find him.' Doubtless 'women' were to be tried if Wagner failed. And if women failed – for the King seemed to show little interest in them? But Wagner did not fail. The first Ludwig had gone too far with his Lola; before many months had passed the politicians were to find the second Ludwig's 'Lolus' or 'Lolotte' – as Wagner came to be called – hardly less of an embarrassment to them.

On Lake Starnberg, about twenty miles to the south of Munich, stands Schloss Berg – a royal toy-castle which, like Hohenschwangau, had been completely renovated by King Max. Ludwig had always enjoyed his visits to Schloss Berg, for across the water at Possenhofen was the country house of Duke Max in Bayern, among whose daughters were the only two women who were to play roles of any importance in Ludwig's life: Elisabeth, Empress of Austria, and her younger sister Sophie. Berg had the further advantage of combining country and privacy with easy access to the capital.

Ludwig, in the first frenzy of his infatuation for Wagner, moved to Schloss Berg and rented for his friend the Villa Pellet at Starnberg, about three miles from the castle, where the composer established himself as soon as he had paid off his most pressing creditors in Vienna. Each morning, and sometimes again later in the day, the royal carriage was sent to fetch Wagner. 'I fly to him as to a lover,' Wagner told Eliza Wille. 'It is a beautiful relationship. Never before have I come across eagerness to learn, understanding, trembling and bashfulness, that were so unreservedly delightful. And then his loving care of me, his charming innocence of heart, his every expression as he tells me of his happiness at possessing me. Often we sit in complete silence, lost in each other's eyes. . . .' And to Mathilde Maier he wrote, 'He is like a god! If I am Wotan, then he is my Siegfried.'

Day after day the two worked on their programme for the realization of Wagner's dreams for the future and for adequate productions of his operas in Munich. In 1865, said Wagner, would come *Tristan* and *Die Meistersinger*, in 1867–8 the completed *Ring*, in 1869–70 *Die Sieger*, in 1871–2 *Parsifal* and in 1873 'my happy death'. Only *Tristan* was to be produced on time, and *Die Sieger* was of course never even written.

History can show many examples of royal condescension to great

15

artists: after all, to pick up a fallen paint-brush or throw down a purseful of gold involves a monarch in little loss of dignity or appreciable financial sacrifice. But the relationship of Ludwig to Wagner was never one of conventional royal patronage, such as that extended to a Mozart. The two men saw themselves as joint creators of great masterpieces: 'When we two are long dead,' Ludwig wrote to Wagner, 'our work will still be a shining example to distant posterity. . . .'

Our work! It was no idle claim: had Ludwig not come to the rescue, the world might never have had the completed *Ring* or *Parsifal*; even *Tristan*, which the Vienna Opera House had written off after innumerable rehearsals as impossible, might never have been performed. But, in addition, Wagner was giving substance to Ludwig's vision of the ideal; as Ernest Newman wrote, 'in furthering Wagner's aims he was really accomplishing his own.' Where money was concerned, Wagner was never shy of making his needs known to the King, who for his part treated the composer with the greatest generosity. Big initial gifts to clear Wagner's back-log of debts and provide him with those luxuries that he always considered necessities, were followed by a rent-free house in Munich and an annual stipend of 4,000 gulden – a salary larger than that paid to the head of a ministerial department after eighteen years of service.

Later in the year a contract was drawn up by which the composer was to receive, in addition to his agreed stipend, an eventual 30,000 gulden for the completion, within three years, of the *Ring*, which would then become the property of the King. To Wagner this expenditure seemed in the nature of a shrewd investment on Ludwig's part; no one, certainly not Wagner, could at that time have foreseen that eight years were to elapse before the great work was ready.

In view of the fact that Ludwig is known to have shown overt homosexual tendencies in the latter part of his short life, it is only natural that our curiosity should be aroused over his exact relationship with Wagner.

First, we must largely disregard the sentimental tone of the letters that passed between them: the undying 'love' that they were constantly protesting must, as Newman points out, 'be viewed in the light of the period, the race, the language of the race, and the peculiar circumstances of the King and the composer'; future generations may well be equally puzzled by our present mode of addressing total strangers as 'dear' Sir. It is significant that Wagner wrote of the Greeks that there was one thing about them 'that we shall never be able to understand, a thing that separates them utterly from us: their love – pederasty.' He saw in the young King a charming, eager, intelligent boy who understood his dreams and ambitions (which very few people at that time did), and who was, moreover, in a position to help him to realize them. Admittedly this was very fortunate, but there was no cunning calculation here. Wagner felt for Ludwig much as a middle-aged married schoolmaster of sensibility might feel for an attractive, lonely, affectionate, well-connected pupil with an unhappy home-life, who chanced to share his interests and enthusiasms. It would have been remarkable indeed if he had been wholly unmoved by Ludwig's charm and hero-worship. The King, for his part, was certainly not physically in love with Wagner – a man considerably more than twice his age. He did not love him: he worshipped him; and what he worshipped was the artist rather than the man, to whose faults, even at the height of his infatuation, he was never blind.

Nor, as is often imagined, was Ludwig really in love with Wagner's music, for the available evidence seems to suggest that the King had little 'ear for music' in the conventional sense of those words. Ludwig's piano teacher admitted that the boy could not tell a Strauss waltz from a Beethoven sonata, and that it was 'a red-letter day in his life' when he gave the Crown Prince his last piano lesson, because his distinguished pupil had 'no talent whatever'.

Though the King appeared, to one who was present, to be listening with rapt attention at a Beethoven-Mozart-Bach concert which Hans von Bülow conducted in the Odeon the following winter, Bülow himself stated that Ludwig showed little desire to study music seriously, and had no real interest in music other than Wagner's. Ludwig was, in fact, the kind of concert- or opera-goer who is so despised by the professional musician: the listener who is content to let the music break over him like a wave and who cares nothing for codas, 'second subjects', and all the technical paraphernalia with which the average programme note is always so generously stuffed. It was the world of fantasy evoked by Wagner's operas, the dream-world in which alone he could fully live, that captivated the King; and possibly it was exactly this that made him the ideal patron, for opposition to Wagner's music came principally from professional musicians, who could not accept the composer's revolutionary technical innovations.

It is true that Wagner said that the King was one of the very few people who really understood him; but he also wrote, on two separate occasions, that Ludwig was 'completely unmusical'. What Ludwig understood was Wagner's ambition to redeem the world through his opera-dramas. The unmusical Wagnerian is still very much with us.

The Berg idyll was interrupted in June by a visit to Bad Kissingen that it was considered politic for Ludwig to make. Kissingen was at that time a recognized summer rendezvous of European royalty, and already assembled there when he arrived were the Emperor and

Empress of Austria, the Tsar and Tsarina, and the heir to the throne of Württemberg and his wife.

Elisabeth, Empress of Austria, daughter of Duke Max in Bayern and thus Ludwig's first cousin once removed, was eight years older than the King and had married the Emperor Franz Josef in 1854. Ludwig had known and admired her all his life, though since her marriage he had seen her only occasionally, usually when she was staying with her parents at Possenhofen. That very spring she had written from Possenhofen to her nine-year-old daughter, Gisela, in Vienna: 'Yesterday the King paid me a long visit, and if Grandmama had not come in he would probably still be here! ... He kissed my hands so many times that Aunt Sophie (who had been watching us through the door) asked me afterwards whether I had any hand left. ...'

Not conspicuously beautiful as a girl, by the age of twenty-six Elisabeth had become one of the loveliest women of her time, and Ludwig, who had intended spending only two or three days at Kissingen, for her sake prolonged his visit to a whole month. But the bond that united the two cousins – and during that month they were almost inseparable – was as much spiritual as physical; they seemed more like brother and sister. Both hated the tedious routine of court life; both were lonely and at heart unhappy. They both loved riding, and whenever they could escape from the monotonous round of entertainment that was designed to fill their days, they would go off together on horseback, he on his Irish hunter and she on her Hungarian grey, into the countryside. She called him 'the Eagle' and he called her 'the Dove'.

Meanwhile the question of a bride for the young King was being much discussed in many quarters; but the royalty at Kissingen that summer could provide nothing more suitable than the ten-year-old daughter of the Tsar. Did it then occur to anyone that Elisabeth, who seemed to be the King's unobtainable ideal, had a much younger sister, the seventeen-year-old Sophie, who might provide the answer? We do not know; but so far as Ludwig was concerned, though he had always enjoyed Sophie's company his thoughts were at that time far from matrimony. He was, in fact, much more nearly in love with Sophie's brother, Karl Theodor, known in the family as 'Gackl'; and one day, petulantly, he cried: 'Oh, these women! Even the cleverest of them is totally incapable of logical argument!' But scheming mothers with pretty daughters felt that the post of royal mistress was probably still vacant; more than one attempt was made to take the King by storm, and it was said that many a lovesick girl 'wore in her locket a few hairs of a horse that the King had ridden, or the petals of a flower that his foot had crushed'.

During the month that he was at Kissingen, Ludwig, preoccupied as he was with Elisabeth, did not write a single line to the Friend at

Starnberg. Wagner, though not ungrateful for a brief respite from the exhausting hero-worship of the young King, was feeling in need of company – but of company less rarefied. To his friend Frau Wille he wrote complaining of his loneliness, and added, 'It is only on the highest mountain-tops, as it were, that I can associate with this young King.' However, his friends – and he approached a number of them – had their own lives to lead; they knew only too well that in Wagner's company this was something that was never possible, and with one accord begged to be excused the honour. But at last it was agreed that Cosima and Hans von Bülow, Liszt's daughter and her musician husband, should come.

Cosima and her two children arrived on 29 June, but Hans did not appear until 7 July. Probably Cosima had already become Wagner's mistress in the previous November; but it was in this week alone together that their fate was decided. The child, Isolde, who was born to Cosima nine months later, was Wagner's.

Chapter Three

WAGNER

During the summer of 1864 Wagner composed a *Huldigungsmarsch* – a *March of Homage* – which was to have had its first performance at Hohenschwangau on 25 August, Ludwig's birthday. But at the very last moment – the band of eighty players had actually got as far as Füssen, only two or three miles from the castle – the unexpected arrival at Hohenschwangau of the Queen Mother (or some say her sudden illness) resulted in the cancellation of the concert. The March finally received its première at a concert of Wagner's music in the courtyard of the Residenz on 5 October.

Between the King and his god there was perfect accord. In September Wagner had addressed a long and fulsome poem of gratitude 'To my King', which Ludwig had immediately capped with another, 'To my Friend', in which he reaffirmed his faith in Wagner and his confidence in the ultimate triumph of their common cause. On the day after the concert in the Residenz Wagner wrote to the King, saying that he was now ready to devote himself to the great task of completing the *Ring*, whose composition had been interrupted seven years before at the end of the second act of *Siegfried*; he therefore requested an audience at which certain details – and naturally he had finance particularly in mind – could be settled. It was at this audience, which took place on the following day, that the contract mentioned in the previous chapter was agreed upon.

In the middle of October 1864 Wagner took possession of the house – 21 Briennerstrasse – which had been rented for him by the King and which Ludwig was in fact to buy outright for him a few months later; at that time both men still believed that Wagner would remain permanently in Munich. It was a palatial building, with a fine garden and a garden house, in the most expensive residential part of the town, and Wagner soon furnished it with those costly silks and satins, those rich carpets, which he saw, not as a luxury, but as a necessity for the creation of the atmosphere in which alone he could work; he could not even manage without a pair of peacocks. Sebastian Röckl tells us that on the first floor there was a large room in which stood Wagner's piano. From this room a door led into the so-called 'Grail' or satin room, whose walls were covered with fine yellow satin and finished with yellow valances of the same material. Everywhere was satin, silk tulle and lace. The white satin curtains were decorated with artificial roses; the frames of mirrors and pictures were puffed out with pink satin tied back with satin bows; there was even a rosette of satin in the centre of the ceiling.

Wagner's sybaritic way of life sometimes amused and sometimes shocked his visitors. Baron Völderndorff wrote ironically of his finding the Master 'in a violet mood. The window was covered with a heavy curtain of violet velvet. He was sitting in a violet armchair, on his head was a violet velvet cap which he raised ever so slightly when he got up on my entering.' Among those who were shocked were the ministers who from time to time had occasion to call on him on behalf of the King. All the costly materials in the house had been ordered by Wagner from Vienna, no doubt in the vain hope of keeping his extravagance a secret from the people of Munich; but in any case it was not possible to deceive the ministers, and Pfistermeister in particular rightly saw that he was inviting eventual trouble by such ostentation. He warned the composer, who replied that he was 'no Lola Montez'; before many months had passed, however, that was precisely what he had become to the Müncheners.

Besides the great task of completing the *Ring*, Wagner had to consider the training of suitable 'Wagnerian' singers and the erection of an opera house incorporating those innovations which he considered essential for the proper production of his works.

To create Wagnerian singers, the composer persuaded the King, as an interim measure, to invite to Munich an approved Leipzig singing teacher named Friedrich Schmitt and to allot to him one or two promising pupils to experiment with. But this was to be merely a beginning: he hoped in due course to found a singing school; indeed he hoped before long to have the whole musical life of the town under his thumb. The importation of Schmitt annoyed the local musicians, many of whom were more than adequate and some highly competent.

It was in November that the King finally made up his mind to build for Wagner in Munich an opera house with a sunken orchestra, an auditorium in the form of an amphitheatre, a new lighting system and those other revolutionary features with which visitors to Bayreuth are now familiar. Newman devotes a whole chapter[1] to the long and unhappy story of the Festival Theatre, which can here be told in outline only.

Towards the end of November Ludwig wrote to Wagner: 'I have decided to have a large stone theatre erected, so that the production of the *Ring* may be perfect. That incomparable work must be staged in a building that is worthy of it. . . .' For architect Wagner thought at once of an old Dresden friend, Gottfried Semper, at this time Professor of Architecture in Zurich, and a month later Semper arrived in Munich.

[1] Vol. III, Ch. xvii

At an audience with the King on 29 December he was definitely commissioned to carry out the work, which was to be completed by the summer of 1867, in time for the première of the *Ring*.

But immediately difficulties arose. The Cabinet, wrote Ernest Newman, were soon 'practising the delays and evasions that are the stock-in-trade of politicians all the world over'. Then Wagner sensibly suggested that it might be wiser first to build a temporary theatre in the Glaspalast (Munich's 'Crystal Palace') to test the practicability of his innovations. The King, however, with the impetuosity of youth, wanted to push ahead with the permanent theatre; lacking the capacity to visualize a building from plans and elevations, and remembering the toy bricks of his boyhood, he demanded models.

Meanwhile the months passed and still Semper could get no signed contract; the King's word, Wagner assured him, was enough, and it would not be wise to press him in the matter. The politicians were becoming apprehensive. Tendentious and inaccurate articles appeared in the newspapers; new excuses for delays were invented. Semper, summoned to Munich in September (1865) to consider possible sites for the permanent theatre, learned from Pfistermeister on his arrival that His Majesty was unwell and not able to see him; it was not difficult to guess that the King's indisposition was merely diplomatic. Wagner was of little help, being at the time much more concerned with extracting for his own use further large sums from the Royal Treasury.

In December 1865 Wagner, as the result of growing unpopularity, was driven from Munich, never to return except on short visits. Having shaken the dust of the town from off his feet, he not unnaturally began to lose interest in a theatre there; indeed it was really he himself, not the politicians, who finally killed the project. Ludwig, too, was gradually obliged to admit to himself that the theatre without the Master would have little meaning. In the absence of Wagner, Düfflipp, Pfistermeister's successor, was soon busy poisoning the King's mind against Semper. The sorry affair dragged on until the summer of 1868, when Semper finally took legal action to recover his costs; six months later his claim was satisfied. He had wasted four years of his life without a single brick or stone to show for it.

It was Semper who was throughout the victim of these intrigues; yet even Ludwig had by then been persuaded to believe that the architect was largely to blame. To Wagner the King wrote on 14 September 1868, 'I beg you to use your influence with Semper to calm him down; he remains as stubborn as ever. By his attitude he has forfeited a good deal of my regard.' Nor did time make Ludwig revise his opinion: five years later, when he sanctioned the award of the Order of Maximilian to Wagner and five other distinguished men, Semper's name was also put forward, but Ludwig refused to allow it to be considered.

We return to the autumn of 1864.

In November, while the King was busy with his plans to build Wagner his own theatre, he also found time to write to him on another matter which they both believed to be of the greatest importance: the education of the Munich public to treat the theatre as a serious cultural activity and not merely as light entertainment after the day's work:

> My aim is to bring the Munich public into a more thoughtful and lofty state of mind by the production of serious and important works such as those of Shakespeare, Calderon, Goethe, Schiller, Beethoven, Mozart, Gluck and Weber; to help it gradually to free itself from a taste for cheap and frivolous entertainment and so to prepare it for the marvels of your own works, facilitating an understanding of these by first putting before it the works of other great men: for everyone ought to be made conscious of the seriousness of art.

But, very naturally, Ludwig had no intention of waiting for a more enlightened public and a more adequate theatre before giving himself the supreme pleasure of hearing Wagner conduct one of his own operas, while Wagner too, with *Tristan* in mind, was eager to test the resources available to him in Munich; it was therefore decided that *The Flying Dutchman*, which had not yet been heard there, should be put into rehearsal. In order, no doubt, to humour local talent, the preliminary rehearsals were entrusted to a Munich conductor, Franz Lachner – a competent musician but one who was not in full sympathy with the work, complaining bitterly of 'the incessant wind that blew out at you wherever you happened to open the score'.

Ludwig suddenly announced that he did not intend to be present at the first performance, which he feared might lack polish; but Wagner, alarmed at the misinterpretation that might be put on his abstention, persuaded him to change his mind, and the King was in the royal box on the opening night, 4 December. After a first act rather coolly received by an audience already familiar with the maturer *Tannhäuser* and *Lohengrin*, the last curtain fell to enthusiastic applause. As for Ludwig, he was in ecstasy and four days later was also present at the second performance. Then, on 11 December, a royal command Wagner concert was given in the theatre in place of the advertised play – a last-minute change of programme which angered the regular subscribers, who pointedly absented themselves. The programme opened with the *Faust* Overture and continued with the *Tristan* Prelude and Liebestod, and excerpts from *Die Meistersinger, Die Walküre* and *Siegfried* – four operas never as yet staged, two being still unfinished.

Ludwig, who had been present at the final rehearsal on the previous day, wrote to Wagner before hearing the actual performance:

Beloved and only Friend!

Overwhelmed, inspired by the glorious evening of yesterday, I must follow my innermost promptings and tell you how indescribable is the happiness which you have brought me. I was transported into super-terrestrial spheres, I breathed immeasurable bliss. But how can I even begin to describe to you my ecstasy? Feeble and unspoken words are utterly inadequate. . . .

Wagner, who had had doubts as to whether the King might have been disappointed by the quality of the performance, had begun an apologetic letter to him when suddenly, while he still had pen in hand, the King's letter was brought to him. He let stand what he had already written then broke into a paean of praise and gratitude:

. . . Ah, heavens! Your letter has arrived this very moment.

And I so faint-hearted!

Even where my love for him, the Unique One, is concerned, it is he who must ever give me fresh courage! Without him I am as nothing! Even in loving him he was my first teacher. . . .

O my King! You are divine! . . .

And so on. Almost six hundred letters and telegrams which passed between King and composer have been published. Many of the letters are enormously long, and in bulk they are so cloyingly sentimental as to be almost as impossible to read as they are to translate into acceptable English.

For Wagner the New Year opened serenely; if there was a cloud on the horizon it was certainly no bigger than a man's hand and he may hardly have noticed it.

So far he had taken care to influence the King only in matters of art; whatever fears the politicians may have had that eventually he would meddle in politics, as yet they had no cause for complaint. They were, however, and not without reason, beginning to be seriously worried about the large sums of money that Wagner was wheedling out of the Royal Treasury; and the new Semper theatre project and the conservatoire for the creation of Wagnerian singers alarmed them further. Pfistermeister still seemed to Wagner an ally, though he was in fact already playing a double game. But the newly-appointed Minister-President and Minister of Foreign Affairs, Baron Ludwig von der Pfordten, was the composer's irreconcilable enemy: he loathed the man and all his works. Though a Bavarian, he had at one time been in the service of the King of Saxony and was well informed about Wagner's revolutionary indiscretions in Dresden in 1849. In that same year King Max had called von der Pfordten to Munich, where in due

24

course he had attempted to prevent *Tannhäuser* from being produced. Ludwig knew this, and his appointment of a declared enemy of Wagner's to such an important post can only be explained by the fact that at that time there seemed to be no other possible candidate. 'Pfi' and 'Pfo' (as Ludwig and Wagner called the two men) were soon actively working to separate the King from his Friend.

But more immediately dangerous to Wagner than the politicians, and often in league with them, were the gutter journalists into whose hands Wagner had played by his greed and extravagance, which were now common knowledge. It must be remembered that to the Bavarians Wagner appeared as a foreigner, as did also those musician friends of his – Peter Cornelius, Karl Klindworth, Heinrich Porges, Friedrich Schmitt, Ludwig Nohl and, in particular, the Prussian Hans von Bülow – whom he had persuaded the King to invite to Munich. Further, they were seen as foreigners snatching positions and salaries that should have come the way of good Bavarians; all this they should have realized, and stepped more warily. Bülow in particular, though he had had a musical triumph on Christmas Day when he made his first bow to a Munich audience, was often indiscreet, and Wagner was to owe some part of his unpopularity to Bülow's unwise behaviour.

But no one could possibly have foreseen, in those early weeks of 1865, that a rift was about to occur between Wagner and Ludwig. At the very end of January there was a little misunderstanding – a misunderstanding which Pfistermeister had soon cunningly manipulated to discredit Wagner in the King's eyes – over the payment for a portrait of the composer which Wagner had presented to the King; this was probably the principal cause of the trouble that flared up so suddenly on 6 February when Wagner, to his amazement, found himself turned away from the palace where he had arrived for a prearranged audience with Ludwig. 'I was told,' wrote the indignant composer later to the King, 'that the reason for this rejection was not that my King was ill but that he was deeply displeased with me.' There was also another little indiscretion on Wagner's part, which unluckily followed swiftly on the heels of the trouble over the picture. Wagner, in the course of a conversation with Pfistermeister, had in an unguarded moment referred to the King as *'mein Junge'* – 'my lad' – and it is said, though it has never actually been proved, that within the hour this *faux pas* had reached Ludwig's ears. Many of those who knew the King have placed on record the fact that, even at moments of the greatest affability, he might suddenly take deep offence at some very minor lapse of respect; it could hardly be expected that he would tolerate such impertinence, even from the Friend.

It was also too much to hope that news of Wagner's disgrace would not reach the long ears of the reporters, who at once began a vicious attack on the composer and his friends. 'What he demands in matters of everyday life and comfort,' wrote the *Allgemeine Zeitung* of Wagner, 'seems to be of so exquisitely sybaritic a nature that not even an oriental *grand seigneur* would object to lodging permanently with him . . . and eating at his table.' Then there were 'the thousands spent on rugs alone, all paid out of the purse of his generous benefactor'. But the main attack was yet to come. If Wagner and his friends, the article continued, 'persist in thrusting themselves between us Bavarians and our beloved King', then the sooner they leave Munich the better.

Wagner replied at some length and with much skill, maintaining, as Newman says, 'the right of the private man to run his private affairs according to his own notions', and thus distracting attention from the real issue, which was whether a particular private man had the right to run up huge debts by wild extravagance and then expect them to be settled out of public or semi-public funds. Bülow wrote also, attacking the anonymous 'infamous slanderer' and so doing further damage to the cause.

Meanwhile the King, a little penitent perhaps, had had an official denial published, to the effect that pressure of work had recently made it impossible for him to give much time to musical matters; it carried no conviction. In the weeks that followed, the King saw Wagner on one occasion only; but the interchange of affectionate letters continued. Wagner could not, however, hide from himself that there remained a certain constraint and that the old relationship had not been restored. In particular, he was hurt at the King's apparent reluctance to receive him. On 9 March he wrote sorrowfully and at great length to Ludwig: no longer, he said, could he bear to be kept at a distance from his 'glorious Friend and King'. Without Ludwig's full confidence and love he could not carry on. 'My King! I bring trouble upon you: so let me go, go to some distant land where jealousy and misunderstanding cannot follow me. . . .'

The King replied at once. 'Circumstances over which I have no control' – Wagner will have guessed that he was referring to the presence of his mother, a sworn enemy of the composer – 'make it absolutely imperative for me, indeed my sacred duty, not to speak with you, at least for the present.' But Wagner, who was in a very neurotic state, was still not satisfied; he had mentioned the possibility of his leaving Germany, and Ludwig had made no comment. He wrote again, now demanding 'just one clear word from my heavenly Friend, telling me what I must do':

Shall I go? Shall I stay?
Your will is my will.
If I go, then I shall go to a distant country and never return to

Germany. For my works I will do what I can, but I will completely sever the connection between the Man and the Thing.

If I stay, then my glorious Friend has given me strength to be patient, to bear every trial: for my trust is unshakable.

So the Friend must decide: a single word – and joyfully I accept my destiny.

But the decision must be made – and made this very day. My spiritual forces are near to breaking-point: I must know for certain by which decision I can bring peace of mind to my dear one.

Wagner well knew that there could be one answer only. In what was the briefest, yet possibly the most significant letter that Ludwig ever addressed to the composer, he wrote:

Dear Friend!

Stay, oh stay! Everything will be as glorious as it used to be. I am very busy.Till death,
your Ludwig

Joyfully Wagner seized his pen and replied, '*Ich lebe noch!*' – 'I still live!'

Chapter Four

TRISTAN

In January 1865 Wagner had drawn up for the benefit of the King a revised time-table for the future productions of his operas. The single item which remained as originally planned, indeed the only one in the revised list which was to be carried out more or less punctually, was the première of *Tristan* for the early summer of 1865.

Tristan had been composed by Wagner between 1857 and 1859, and already by January 1860 the first copies of the engraved score were in his hands. During the difficult years that followed before his rescue by Ludwig, he had been perpetually hopeful of getting the opera produced. Dresden, Paris, Karlsruhe, Vienna, Hanover and Leipzig were all sounded, but all in vain. Then in 1862 there came a change of heart, or rather an improvement in finance, in Vienna, and at last *Tristan* was accepted; after innumerable rehearsals, however, it had been abandoned as impossible. It was the most ardent desire of both King and composer that the opera should now be produced in Munich.

One of the causes of the failure in Vienna had been the inadequacy of the tenor who had been cast as Tristan. But Wagner had now discovered the almost ideal man for the part – Ludwig Schnorr von Carolsfeld, whose wife, Malvina, he also hoped to engage for his Isolde; it may be remembered that it was Schnorr whom Ludwig had heard as Lohengrin when he was Crown Prince. The Schnorrs, who were under contract to Dresden, came briefly to Munich at the end of February for discussions with Wagner and a single test-rehearsal, after which, through the good offices of the King who himself approached the King of Saxony, they were granted three months' leave of absence from the beginning of April.

Schnorr was twenty-nine years old – a big, burly man, full-bearded and very masculine, with a powerful *Heldentenor* (heroic tenor) voice; Wagner had a horror of what he called the 'eunuch' type of tenor. Intelligent and presentable tenors have always been rarities, and Wagner once cursed the fate that had driven him to allot his most intellectual roles to tenors. Newman wrote sarcastically of what he called the 'amphora *Heldentenor* ... who looks and behaves like an overgrown boy scout, and gives the spectator the impression of a man whose mental development was arrested at the age of twelve and has been in custody ever since'; 'amphora', he points out, is defined by classical dictionaries as 'a two-handled, big-bellied vessel, usually of clay, with a longish or shortish neck and a mouth proportioned to the size, sometimes resting firmly on a foot, but often ending in a blunt point. . . .'

In build Schnorr was, admittedly, an amphoric tenor, and Wagner, who had first heard him in Karlsruhe in 1862 as Lohengrin, had gone to the theatre with no high hopes. But within five minutes the great paunch was forgotten; only the great artist and the wonderful voice remained. For Schnorr was an exceptionally intelligent man, an ardent disciple of Wagner who had closely studied the texts and music of his operas; he amazed the composer by the complete understanding he showed of his intentions. He was also an accomplished actor. Personal acquaintance with the tenor had shown Wagner that here too was a singer entirely free from the usual naive conceit of that tribe. Malvina, nearly ten years older than her husband and far from sylph-like, was also a fine and dedicated artist.

After the rehearsal in February Schnorr wrote to his mother: 'Wagner's influence on me is immeasurable. Though I had in the main understood his intentions, the role has been modified by certain important new details which he pointed out to me today and for which I immediately thanked him. I can't tell you how happy I am.' The Schnorrs then went back to Dresden, but returned to Munich on 5 April. A few days later the rehearsals began.

Wagner, who was now fifty-two, did not feel equal to the strain of conducting *Tristan*; he therefore handed over the baton to the much younger Bülow, whom Ludwig had appointed *Vorspieler des Königs*[1] in the previous autumn. Bülow rehearsed sections of the orchestra each morning in the little Residenz Theatre,[2] while each evening Wagner trained the singers in his house; and it so chanced that it was on 10 April, the very day of the first rehearsals, that Cosima von Bülow gave birth to a daughter, Isolde, the child of Wagner.

Ludwig wanted *Tristan* to be given in the big Court Theatre, which seated two thousand; but both Wagner and Bülow at first favoured the much smaller and more intimate Residenz. Wagner wrote to the King on the subject on 20 April:

> *Lieber Erhabener* [Dear Exalted One]! Please, *please* let us stay in the cosy Residenz Theatre! You cannot imagine how happy we feel in it – as if we were already beyond the reach of the vulgar world. Music sounds wonderfully beautiful there, more beautiful than in any other theatre or hall that I know. The singers are delighted with the way their voices sound: everything is easier for them; even the

[1] The English equivalent would be 'Master of the King's Musick'.

[2] A gem of the Bavarian rococo and a victim of bombing in 1944. Much of the decoration was saved, and the theatre has now been brilliantly reconstructed, as the Cuvilliéstheater, in the Residenz.

most difficult things come off. . . . What takes place on the stage is all of a tender and an intimate nature, therefore every quiver of the face, every movement of the eyes, has to tell. Only in such conditions and in such a theatre would *Tristan* – *Tristan* of all works! – be possible. . . .

Ludwig of course yielded at once. But as the rehearsals proceeded, with the singers now using full voice and a full orchestra supporting them, Wagner was reluctantly obliged to admit that the King had been right after all: it would have to be the Court Theatre.

In the middle of April Wagner addressed an open letter to his friend Friedrich Uhl, the editor of the Vienna *Botschafter*, in which he extended an invitation to any 'friends of his art' to come to Munich for the first performance, which had been fixed for 15 May. Meanwhile rehearsals were going well, though Bülow, who had been very ill some months earlier and who never spared himself, was beginning to feel the strain and even on one occasion fainted. It was no doubt his overwrought condition which accounted for a disastrous incident which occurred at a rehearsal on 2 May. Bülow had wanted the orchestral area enlarged, but was told that this could only be done by sacrificing thirty stalls. 'What on earth does it matter,' he cried angrily, 'whether we have thirty *Schweinehunde* more or less in the place?'

The indiscreet remark, made in the darkened theatre and not meant for ears other than those of the theatre machinist, was unluckily overheard and duly reported in the *Neueste Nachrichten*. Bülow wrote to apologize; never, he assured its readers, had he intended any reflection on the 'cultured Munich public'; he was referring to the small band of anti-Wagnerians who were campaigning against the Master. In any case it was a private conversation which had unkindly been given such unwelcome publicity. The *Neueste Nachrichten* behaved generously and accepted his apology, but other papers were less forgiving; day after day, for a whole week, the *Neuer Bayerischer Kurier* hounded Bülow with a crescendo of abuse, and the *Volksblatt* was hardly less vindictive. Their intention was plainly to drive him out of the town and so wreck *Tristan*. Had it not been for Bülow, Wagner might have weathered the storm in Munich for longer than he did. Well might he have said, 'God preserve me from my friends; my enemies I can look after myself.'

As the great day approached, Wagnerians from all over Europe began to forgather in Munich. To Ludwig the suspense was becoming almost intolerable. On 10 May he wrote to Wagner:

My heart's rapture gives me no peace: I *must* write to you. Nearer and nearèr draws the happy day: *Tristan* will arise! . . .

We must break through the barriers of custom, shatter the laws of the base, egoistical world. The ideal must and shall come to life! We will march forward conscious of victory. My loved one, I shall never forsake you! Oh *Tristan, Tristan* will come to me! The dreams of my boyhood and youth will be realized! You should have nothing to do with the baseness of the world; I shall bear you high above all earthly cares! Complete happiness must be yours! . . .

My love for you and for your art grows ever greater, and this flame of love shall bring you happiness and salvation.

Oh, write to me; I yearn for it! – Until death

Your faithful

Ludwig

Next day came the final full rehearsal at which the King and some six hundred invited guests were present and which was therefore really the equivalent of a private performance. To mark the occasion, Ludwig granted a pardon to all those who had been involved in the revolution of 1849 – a gesture whose significance was obvious.

Before the Prelude, Wagner, who was deeply moved, came on the stage and in a short speech, which was described by a member of the audience as 'excellent, modest, simple and heartfelt', thanked the orchestra, who responded with spontaneous and warm applause. Then it was the turn of Bülow, who uttered a few fumbling words but at least said nothing embarrassing.

There were calls for the composer at the end of each act; but presumably Wagner did not wish to break the spell, for he refused to appear. As for the audience, they seem for the most part to have been completely worn out, both mentally and physically, by music and poetic diction so totally unfamiliar, by an experience whose utter novelty at that time it is hard for us today to realize. Frau von Kaulbach-Scotta, a violinist and the wife of the distinguished artist Wilhelm von Kaulbach, who had been given two seats by Cosima and who may be taken as typical of the intelligent but conservative opera-goer, wrote next day to her husband:

At last . . . the Prelude began, which was magnificently played and which did not go beyond our customary conception of what is music. . . . The whole of the second act consists of a forty-five-minute duet, without a single tune, of steadily mounting raging passion; I might almost call it completely barbaric – the passions of an antediluvian race: something impossible for our feeble nerves and ears to enjoy. The singing consists of nothing but screaming and shrieking; the singers storm, rage and roar, while the orchestra accompanies them with the most outrageous discords. Drums, trumpets and cymbals, together with other recently invented instruments, work

31

themselves up into an absolute frenzy.

The orchestra dealt with this difficult and exhausting work magnificently; in no other town would a performance of it have been possible. But the highest praise must go to Schnorr and his wife . . . to these two great artists alone is Wagner indebted for his success. After these three performances *Tristan and Isolde* will presumably have to retire into private life. . . .

Ludwig did not write to Wagner after the rehearsal; perhaps written words were inadequate to express what he felt. But on the morning of 15 May – '*Tristan* Day' – he sent him an ecstatic letter full of *Tristan* quotations:

> Day of rapture! *Tristan!* Oh, how I long for this evening! If only it were here! *When will the torch be extinguished; when will it be night in the house?*
>
> Today, today! Why praise and honour *me*? The deed is YOURS! YOU are the wonder of the world; what am I without *you*? Why, I implore you, why cannot you find peace, why are you ever in torment? . . . My love for you, I need not repeat it, will endure for ever! . . .

And so on, in the familiar vein.

But as things turned out, Wagner was to remember *Tristan* Day as one of the most disastrous in his whole life, for two blows, as unexpected as they were cruel, were to strike him within the space of a few hours.

The first was the arrival of the bailiffs. Five years earlier Wagner had been rescued during one of his innumerable financial crises by the loan of about 5,000 francs from a rich Frenchwoman, Mme Julie Schwabe. Hearing no doubt of Wagner's new opulence, Frau Salis-Schwabe (as she had now become) saw no reason why she too should not benefit from his good fortune; she therefore engaged a Munich lawyer, Dr von Schauss, to act for her. A polite approach from Schauss having been ignored by Wagner, the lawyer had a provisional distraint levied on his furniture; and it may or may not have been by chance that it was on the morning of 15 May that the bailiffs arrived at the Briennerstrasse house to demand immediate payment. Wagner had no ready money; yet the scandal that would be caused by the removal of his goods and chattels, at that of all moments and for every eye to see, was impossible to contemplate. From this, the first of the morning's disasters, he was saved by the prompt and generous action of the Treasury, to whom Wagner sent post-haste a messenger – presumably Cosima, who acted as his secretary – imploring them to spare him this 'calculated humiliation and may God reward you'.

But hardly had the bailiffs left with their money when Schnorr arrived with tears in his eyes: Malvina, as the result of taking a vapour bath, had suddenly lost her voice and the performance would have to be postponed. Wagner wrote at once to the King, telling him of this double calamity and adding that so dazed had he still been from the first blow when the second fell, that the latter had made no impression on him. 'I am fit for nothing more in the world,' he said gloomily. 'My life has been too long at the mercy of every vileness ... But I am inconsolable only in that I must make you – dear and glorious one – pass sad hours. ...'

It was late in the afternoon when news of the postponement was made public, and immediately wild rumours swept the town: some said that Wagner's vile music had wrecked Malvina's voice; others that Bülow, still unforgiven for his *Schweinehunde* indiscretion, feared a student demonstration and did not dare to show himself in the Theatre, or even that he had learned of a plot to assassinate him. Certainly the *Schweinehunde* still rankled: Frau von Kaulbach, writing to her husband, said, 'Not since the Lola affair have the Müncheners been so furious; they threaten to revenge themselves on the little man when he takes his place at the conductor's desk for the first performance of *Tristan*, to insult him in every possible way. But he has had a piece of luck, because Frau Schnorr has been taken ill ...' The enemies of Wagner and Bülow exulted in their discomfiture, and a section of the Bavarian press delightedly seized the opportunity to kick the men who were down.

Malvina's recovery took time; it was not until 6 June that the Schnorrs were able to return to Munich, and four days later the première of *Tristan* took place. 'The eagerly awaited day dawned at last,' wrote an Alsatian student who was present. 'The house was full to overflowing when the twenty-year-old King, looking radiantly beautiful, appeared alone and in civilian dress in the big, gilded royal box. ... Everything about him spoke of calm exultation, of the purest enthusiasm. His entry was greeted with a fanfare of trumpets and repeated cheers; but his eyes, sunk in his private dreams, seemed to be wholly unconscious of the crowd who applauded him.'

Old King Ludwig I had come to Munich to hear *Tristan*, and Duke Max in Bayern and Ludwig's uncle, Prince Leopold, were also present; but the King had chosen to sit alone: he dreaded the jarring intrusion of banal conversation. At the end of each act there was a certain amount of hissing, but the very large majority of the audience applauded; and when, after the final curtain, Wagner, dressed in a black morning coat and white trousers and looking very pale, appeared on the stage between the Tristan and Isolde to whom he owed so much, there was no mistaking that he had triumphed: the unproduceable opera had at last been produced!

Though it was now 11 o'clock, Ludwig could not allow this memorable day to end without a brief word of gratitude to the Friend. Back in the Residenz, he wrote:

> Unique One! Holy One!
> How glorious! – Perfect. So full of rapture! . . . *To drown . . . to sink down – unconscious – supreme joy.*
> Divine work!

Three days later came the second performance, at which the King was again present; but he stayed away from the third, on 19 June, perhaps because he could not face sharing this sublime experience with his very commonplace Uncle Otto, the King of Greece, who had just arrived in Munich. Then the Schnorrs, for whom neither Ludwig, Wagner nor Bülow could find words to express their admiration and gratitude, went to Tegernsee to rest. Schnorr had not been feeling well, complaining of the draughts which swept the stage from the wings; but he returned to Munich to make several more appearances before his leave of absence from Dresden, which Ludwig had managed to have extended, expired. There was a further performance of *Tristan* on 1 July – a performance which affected Ludwig so deeply that on his way back to Berg in his special train he suddenly pulled the alarm signal, wandered off into the blackness of the forest to calm his overwrought nerves, and then completed the journey in the locomotive. Schnorr also took the part of Erik in *The Flying Dutchman*; and on 12 July came a private Wagner concert in the Residenz at which he sang in excerpts from *Siegfried, Die Walküre, Das Rheingold* and *Die Meistersinger*. Then he and Malvina returned to Dresden.

Four days later Schnorr was to have sung in *Don Giovanni* in Dresden, and at the rehearsal on the previous day he had been in fine voice; but the next morning he was taken seriously ill with a general rheumatism, and on 21 July he died. His last words were, 'Farewell, Siegfried! Console my Richard!' When Wagner received a telegram saying that Schnorr was dead, he wired back, 'Which Schnorr?' The singer had several relations in Dresden, and it seemed to him inconceivable that his Tristan, who was not yet thirty, could have died.

Chapter Five

DECLINE AND FALL

Even before the première of *Tristan*, it had become alarmingly apparent to Pfistermeister and von der Pfordten that the realization of Ludwig's long-cherished ambition was bringing King and composer even more closely together than before the rift, and that this was highly dangerous.

To Pfi, Pfo wrote on 28 May 1865 that he was convinced that the King must dismiss Bülow and that, though existing contracts with Wagner would have to be honoured, 'personal relations between him and the King must be put an end to, if His Majesty's reputation is not to be damaged both at home and abroad.' Pfi transmitted this message to the King, who replied that he did not object to Bülow's leaving Munich for a while after the *Tristan* performances were over, but that he intended to keep Wagner there. He asked that it should be publicly announced that during the last four months he had received Wagner in audience once only.

Von der Pfordten, when told of this by Pfistermeister, commented sensibly that he was reminded of the old adage, *Qui s'excuse, s'accuse*. If Wagner, as man and as artist, was worthy of the King's favour, then why should they not meet? But *was* he? That was the real question. It seems, however, that it was the King who finally changed his mind and decided that this unwise announcement should not be made.

But Ludwig was well aware that his friendship with Wagner was making him unpopular; he therefore consulted Pfi and Pfo, who turned to Baron Sigmund von Pfeufer, the Munich Chief of Police, for guidance. Pfeufer, who said that he was not unduly alarmed, diagnosed three principal causes of public dissatisfaction with regard to Wagner and Bülow – a dissatisfaction which of course directly affected the popularity of the King. He defined his three groups of critics. First came those who mistrusted Wagner and Bülow for being foreigners, and Wagner for being a Protestant: this he considered ridiculous. Then there were those who were shocked by the money that the King was lavishing on his protégé: but (so far) it was technically *his* money – the King's 'salary', as it were, and his inherited personal fortune – that was being used for the purpose. He continued:

It is quite another matter, however, with the third group – those who count up the days and hours spent by His Majesty in seclusion and say, 'Our King keeps himself almost entirely to himself: he hardly ever sees anyone from the official, military, learned or artistic world. And the man who is to blame for this seclusion is Richard

Wagner, who has brought the King to feel at ease in no society but his, communes with him by the hour (if not orally, at all events by letter), pays homage to his kind of poetry and music and to none other, and shows no interest in the rest of the world.' This is the point of view that has the largest and most influential following in all sections of society – of the aristocracy and of the bourgeoisie. . . .

In short, if only the King can be persuaded to come out of his shell and go through the dreary and distasteful hoops of kingship, to come together with foreign royalty and receive ambassadors in audience (he had grown neglectful over this), and to show himself to his people more often – then he would be able to devote his earned leisure to this Friend, and no one would have cause to complain.

Presumably Pfeufer's advice was passed to the King in a diluted form; but it was advice that Ludwig found difficult to act upon. He longed to 'get away from it all': to be alone with his beloved Wagner in his beloved mountains. So whenever he could he escaped from Munich, and on 21 June we find him writing 'from the Alps' to the Friend he dared not take with him:

I write you this letter on a mountain in the high Alps, far from thronging crowds. I think of you all the time; always I see you in my mind's eye. You alone are the source of my happiness. . . .

The sun has set long since behind the chain of mountains; peace reigns in the deep valleys, the sound of the cow-bells and the song of a shepherd float up to me in my blissful solitude. . . .

How my soul longs for, thirsts after those works which your genius may yet create! Every bird-song in the woods reminds me of our fearless hero, the blessed, joyful Siegfried!

Though Wagner was still doing his best to steer clear of political involvement, his known influence with the King was often exposing him to approaches, and even to the offer of bribes, from various interested parties. Among these was Prince Max von Thurn und Taxis, father of the King's favourite aide-de-camp, Prince Paul von Thurn und Taxis, who was scheming to create a little kingdom for his son in the Westphalian Rhineland. Bavarian politicians, too, feared that the hour might come when their very survival could depend upon a timely good word, a favourable report, from the composer. Pfistermeister in particular was still playing the double game that for a while deceived Wagner; while outwardly approving and supporting the staging of *Tristan* (in gratitude to Wagner for his refusal to meddle in the Taxis affair), he was writing in his private diary of 'this damned *Tristan!*' and wishing that the devil would carry off all musicians to hell.

But it was the gradual realization of the big sums of money likely to be involved in the building of Semper's theatre and the founding of the conservatoire for singers, that finally convinced the politicians that there was only one possible solution to their problems: Wagner must go. As they gradually declared their hands, Wagner found himself driven to use his influence with the King to counter their intrigues and malevolence. He had come to realize that the philistine Pfistermeister, whom Ludwig had inherited from his father, King Max, was not, in spite of his earlier parade of sympathy, the right man to be the personal link between himself and Ludwig; he therefore suggested to the King that he should appoint a 'General Intendant of the Civil List' to take over Pfi's duties where the arts were concerned. He should be made the head of the theatre and the orchestra and be responsible for the allocation of funds to maintain them and to finance the new theatre and conservatoire. The name of Baron Moy was put forward; but for some reason or other – perhaps because of an unfortunate leakage to the Press – the plan came to nothing.

Even now Wagner might have triumphed over his enemies, had not his backlog of debts to creditors who could no longer be kept at bay with airy promises, and his insatiable appetite for more and more luxuries, driven him to make demands on the royal purse and the Treasury which finally became outrageous. In a letter to the King on 30 July he gave the first hint of his future intentions. After a long survey of his difficulties and tribulations, he wrote, 'I therefore find myself, as I have so often told the Friend, obliged to ask for a more basic, and in particular a more independent establishment of my own affairs, if I am to remain worthily by the side of my King, free and exempt from all cares'.

He had just accepted, with a great show of reluctance, a carriage and a Treasury grant of 1,200 gulden for its upkeep; but this of course was only the tip of the iceberg, whose real bulk was disclosed in a formal document attached to a long letter that he wrote to the King on 8 August. In this letter he assures Ludwig that he can carry out 'everything – more than the Nibelungs [i.e. the *Ring*], everything' – provided that this is 'made possible' for him. He continues, 'I have now weighed up what is essential for my earthly existence. If this is refused me then I am impotent. I am no longer capable of wanting anything in itself, for myself. If it is difficult for you, then refuse me: that is my fate. . . . But perhaps it is not so difficult after all. I repeat, I myself want nothing. I say it without the least bitterness, gently, earnestly, calmly.'

The King had just put his hunting-box at Hochkopf at Wagner's disposal to speed his recuperation after the strain of *Tristan* and the shock of Schnorr's death, and the composer concludes his letter in a lighter and breezier vein: 'And now, come wind and weather, off to the mountains! I pack my trunk; my faithful servant [Franz] and my trusty old dog [Pohl] go with me, and I am also taking an old Indian epic, the *Ramayana*. Siegfried in his various manifestations will breathe anew on the mountain-tops.'

In words which could not be bettered, and with the irony for which he was famous, Ernest Newman has summed up Wagner's new demands as they appeared to the composer: 'Once more, then, we observe, he was stoically facing a supreme renunciation. Without the least bitterness, gently, earnestly, calmly, this much-enduring man desired nothing at all – except a mere 200,000 gulden more of Bavarian money.'

This enormous sum was to be divided between an immediate cash payment of 40,000 gulden, principally intended – though this he does not admit – for the settlement of one or two trifling debts that until recently had escaped his memory, and the investment of 160,000 gulden from which he will receive 2,000 gulden interest quarterly. The Briennerstrasse house was also to be his, rent-free, for life, and he hopes that thus, and by exercising the strictest economy, he will somehow or other be able to muddle along. No doubt he hoped that by extracting a legally-binding contract he would secure his economic security against any eventuality such as the death or abdication of the King.

While Ludwig was studying this new ultimatum – this 'positively last territorial demand' – the sybaritic Wagner was far from enjoying 'roughing it' in the royal hunting-box; he was more than thankful to return, twelve days later, to Munich. Here Cosima, in her capacity of Wagner's secretary, received on 26 August a letter from Pfistermeister telling her that the King had agreed to much of what Wagner had hoped for: he was not, however, to receive the capital sum of 160,000 gulden, but the equivalent of the interest on it – 8,000 gulden a year; and with regard to the 40,000 gulden, Pfistermeister had worded his letter so ambiguously that it was impossible to be sure whether or not Wagner had absolute control over the capital. Naturally he assumed that he had; in due course he was to find out that, whatever Ludwig's original intention had been, the King had come to see it as available only for the interest it produced.

On 10 October Pfistermeister informed Cosima that the King was presenting Wagner with the Briennerstrasse property (the equivalent of a further 2,000 gulden a year in addition to his annual allowance of 8,000 gulden), but that he had no intention of letting the 40,000 gulden be used by him to pay off ancient creditors; in fact, he had no intention of continuing to pay Wagner's debts in the future. Wagner, already in a very neurotic state, was furious when he was told.

It is not possible further to follow in detail the events of that October.

Pfistermeister, finding his duties as speaking-tube (as he called it) between King and composer intolerable, asked to be relieved of them; to this the King agreed, and they were taken over by the second Cabinet Secretary, Johann Lutz. On the eighteenth of the month Ludwig, in spite of the strong protests of both Pfistermeister and Lutz, suddenly and inexplicably changed his mind and informed Wagner that the 40,000 gulden were his to use as he wished. Before the year was out he had disposed of half of them.

One of the best-known Wagner stories is that of the 40,000 gulden being paid by the bank in sacks of small coins, ostentatiously delivered at the Briennerstrasse under military escort in order to stir up public feeling against the composer. The facts seem to have been as follows. According to Wagner, Cosima, who went to the bank to collect the money, was informed that they had notes only for half the sum and that she would have to take the remainder in cash. She immediately ordered two cabs and herself helped to lift the heavy sacks into them. Cosima, however, told the King that to her 'indescribable astonishment' she was obliged to accept the *whole* sum in coin. It is impossible to discover whether or not the bank was actuated in its behaviour by malice.

Ludwig was not unaware of his growing unpopularity in certain quarters – an unpopularity that he needlessly aggravated by follies more of omission than of commission. He had, for example, alienated the sympathy of the Army by refusing a pressing invitation from the Commander-in-Chief to attend the autumn manoeuvres. ('If the King can ride for eight or ten hours in mist and darkness without endangering his health,' states a confidential police report of 22 September, 'then His Majesty is also able to devote a few days to his Army'.) He had inexcusably absented himself when his father's coffin had been transferred with great ceremony to the Theatinerkirche. He had also declined, with the excuse that he was suffering from an attack of rheumatism, an invitation from his grandfather, Ludwig I, to a family dinner party – something that he always hated; yet that very same evening (it was 18 October, the day that Wagner had been given his 40,000 gulden) he attended a performance at the Court Theatre of Schiller's *Wilhelm Tell*, in which a handsome young actor named Emil Rohde had taken the part of Melchthal. The ex-King was angry and saw trouble ahead: 'The follies of my grandson are very sad,' he is reported as saying. 'But it won't last long: the people will soon put an end to it.' He spoke from personal experience.

The day after *Wilhelm Tell* Ludwig suddenly decided to go for a fortnight to Switzerland. His destination was kept secret even from Wagner, who believed him to have gone to the Tyrol, and his first intention had been to take Rohde with him; but wisely he had had second thoughts. No doubt the tension in Munich made the King more than usually anxious to escape from the town, and it was because of Schiller that he chose Lucerne rather than Hohenschwangau. Travelling incognito and with a very small suite, he arrived at the Schweizer Hof where he was given the only three vacant rooms, which were on the fourth floor. When the manager discovered, to his embarrassment, that he had been entertaining royalty unawares, he begged the King to move into the state suite; but Ludwig said he was very happy to remain where he was. From Brunnen, at the far end of the Lake of Lucerne, where he stayed at the homely Gasthof Rössli, he visited the various sites of the Tell legend – the Tellsplatte, the Tell Chapel, and the Rütli where, on the night of 7 November 1307, thirty-three men had entered into that famous and solemn pact to drive the oppressors from their soil.

After his return to Bavaria the King received a cutting from the *Schwyzer Zeitung* in which reference was made to 'a foreign tourist ... quite a young man, tall, slim and of a noble appearance', who had been seen at Brunnen enthusiastically studying the Tell sites. The King himself replied with a letter of warmest greetings to his 'dear friends of the Uri canton, which I have loved ever since my childhood. The memory of my visit to the glorious heart of Switzerland and its honest and liberty-loving peoples, whom God bless, will become ever dearer to me.'

On 11 November Wagner arrived at Hohenschwangau to spend a week there as the guest of the King; it was the first time that the two had slept under the same roof. The weather was fine and mild almost as summer, as can sometimes happen even in mid-winter in the Bavarian highlands; and unclouded too was their happiness at being together. They passed that week in a dream-world of fantasy and medieval make-believe. From the turrets of the castle the oboists of the First Infantry regiment, brought specially from Munich, sounded at dawn an *aubade* of motifs from *Lohengrin*. Then King and composer, who could not meet till noon because Ludwig had State business to attend to, would write a short letter or a poem to one another. No love letters exchanged between man and woman could be more tender than those which now passed between the twenty-year-old Ludwig and the middle-aged composer. To Ludwig Wagner wrote on his first day at Hohenschwangau:

O my glorious, my heavenly Friend!
What bliss enfolds me! A wonderful dream has become a reality! How can I find words to describe to you the magic of this hour? I

am in the Gralsburg, in Parsifal's sublime and loving care. . . .
I am in your angelic arms! We are near to one another. . . .

Read in a divorce court, such a letter would carry but one interpretation
– but an interpretation which in this present context would be wholly
false.

Pfistermeister, now openly antagonistic to Wagner, had asked to be
excused attendance at Hohenschwangau while the composer was there;
his place was taken by Lutz, who kept the first Cabinet Secretary fully
informed and who seized the opportunity, but without success, to try
to bribe Wagner to further his own designs. Paul Taxis, with whom
Ludwig was now infatuated, was also in the castle and sometimes joined
the King and Wagner at table. When these days of bliss were drawing
towards their close, Ludwig gave Wagner a watch and other trinkets:
'When you open the dark-blue lid of the watch,' he wrote, 'you will
see a little picture (Lohengrin in the boat); for it was *Lohengrin* which
sowed in my heart the first seed of my enthusiasm and my glowing love
for you. . . . I also enclose a pair of swan cuff-links.'

Two or three days after Wagner's departure there was a firework
display at the castle, followed by 'the scene of the arrival of the Swan-
knight from Wagner's *Lohengrin* enacted on the Alpsee. A large
artificial swan drew across the lake a boat in which stood Lohengrin
(Prince Paul von Thurn und Taxis); the Swan-knight, the swan and
the boat were all splendidly flood-lit. While this was taking place, a
band played the relevant passages from *Lohengrin*. By command of
His Majesty the performance was repeated the following evening.' Later
in his life Ludwig would himself sometimes dress up as Lohengrin, and
after his death his Lohengrin costume was found among his effects.

It was hardly surprising that tongues in Munich were soon wagging.
To Frau von Leonrod, Ludwig wrote a few days later: 'I hear there
are still the most curious rumours about my relations with Wagner;
don't lend your ear to such gossip, I beg you. People must always have
something to talk about, and they exaggerate everything. . . .'

At the end of August Wagner had written, in the short space of three
days and at Ludwig's request, a long prose sketch for *Parsifal*. A copy,
on which Wagner had scribbled 'Is this how you want it?' was sent to
the King, who found it 'the purest and noblest religion'. A fortnight
later Wagner began the compilation of a journal in which he offered
Ludwig a survey of his views on a variety of subjects, including politics;
it was conceived as a kind of compendium of knowledge, for the King
to consult when its author was not at hand. Ludwig was so pleased
with it that he had a copy made for von der Pfordten and his colleagues,

who can only have seen in it yet further evidence that Wagner intended in the future to meddle increasingly in political matters.

Peter Cornelius, one of the shrewdest of Wagner's friends, observed with alarm the risk that the composer was running. To his fiancée he wrote in November:

> I have never yet told you that Wagner is getting himself politically involved with the King.... The King is said to have asked his opinion on German affairs, and since then Wagner has been setting forth his views for him in a series of letters.... When Bülow first told me this, a shudder ran through me: I saw the beginning of the end....

In Wagner's defence it must be admitted that he wished to interfere in politics only when the politicians were obstructing, or appeared to be obstructing, his schemes for the propagation of his concept of culture in Bavaria; he found it impossible to understand that they had other and, at all events to them, more important matters than music and the arts to attend to, and that in spite of being opposed to Wagner they might still be good at their jobs. So the issue appeared to him a simple one: Pfi and Pfo were in his way, therefore the King must be persuaded to get rid of them. Soon after his return from Hohenschwangau he wrote to Ludwig to tell him so.

The composer's desire to interfere did not stop here: he was confident that he knew the right man to form a new Cabinet. Max von Neumayr, who was not a personal friend of the composer's, had been Minister of the Interior until very recently, when after some rioting in the town he had felt it his duty to tender his resignation, which the King had accepted. To Wagner it seemed that he had been driven out of office by the malevolence of Pfi and Pfo, and any enemy of Wagner's enemies was Wagner's friend; he therefore recommended Ludwig to take his advice and replace von der Pfordten by Neumayr.

But Ludwig had no intention of letting Wagner choose his Minister-President for him; it was, indeed, said that whenever Wagner introduced politics into the conversation the King 'would gaze at the ceiling and whistle softly to himself'. Ludwig's reply, on 27 November, to Wagner's letter showed eminent good sense. He had already written several pages of the now all-too-familiar rapture when Wagner's letter was brought to him:

> I had go as far as this by midday when your letter of yesterday arrived....
>
> I have considered your advice very carefully. Rest assured, my dear one, that what I now write in answer is not the result of hasty and superficial consideration.... I had the best of reasons for letting

Neumayr go and for withdrawing the confidence I had long had in him ... so it would be wholly inconsistent for me now to entrust to this man – with whom (I repeat) I have *every reason to be dissatisfied* – the formation of a new Cabinet! There is no doubt that Pfisterme- ister is second-rate and stupid; I shall not keep him much longer in the Cabinet. But to dismiss him and other members of the Cabinet at this moment does not seem to me advisable; the time is not yet ripe. This I say most definitely; and believe me I have the best of reasons for saying it.

The article you sent me is scandalously written.... You will be astonished when I tell you that my Cabinet had nothing to do with it, however much it may appear that they had....

The article to which the King refers, and which had appeared in the *Volksbote* on the previous day, was in reply to another which had been published in the Nuremberg *Anzeiger* a fortnight before. The latter, entitled 'Plain Words to the King of Bavaria and his People on the subject of the Cabinet Secretariat', was a general attack on that institution as being 'unconstitutional', and dangerous in that it exercised too great an influence on the King; but there could be no doubt it was also a personal one on Pfistermeister and on the Treasurer of the Secretariat, Julius von Hofman – 'Mime' and 'Fafner' as Ludwig and Wagner called them. It was obviously written by, or at all events inspired by, Wagner.

The author of the *Volksbote* article did not fail to notice that the attack was really a personal one, and that though he did not for a moment wish to suggest that Herr Wagner himself had written it, 'under the circumstances there seems to be some reason to suppose that he may not have been wholly unaware of its contents.' So Pfistermeister and Hofman, he continued, were to be got rid of in order that a certain person could the more easily exploit the Royal Treasury to his own advantage. Then Wagner was again mentioned by name. In less than a year he had cost Bavaria 190,000 gulden, and then, only the other day, he had asked for a further 40,000 gulden! The reader could draw his own conclusions as to the real purpose of the author in writing to the *Anzeiger*.

Wagner, in the heat of his fury, replied in the Munich *Neueste Nachrichten* with an anonymous article[1] which by its folly and its intemperance sealed his fate. In it he viciously attacked certain people 'whom it is unnecessary to name since they are at the present moment the objects of universal and contemptuous indignation in Bavaria'. Moreover he dragged in the King's name again and again, using it

[1] It is given in full by Strobel (IV, 107–109). That it emanated from Wagner is proved by the existence, in the Wahnfried archives, of a draft in Cosima's hand.

freely to assure the readers of Ludwig's 'unshakable friendship' for the composer whom he had summoned to Munich. Then he added dishonesty to folly by writing, on the very same day, to the King, informing him that he, Wagner, had 'never been behind *any* newspaper article in any form'.

Four days later the King wrote to Wagner from Hohenschwangau shortly before returning to Munich: 'That article in the *Neueste Nachrichten* was very largely responsible for the unhappiness of my last few days here. It must certainly have been written by one of your friends; no doubt he meant to be of service to you, but sad to say he has harmed rather than helped you.' Ludwig must surely have guessed that Wagner himself was the author.

Punsch, the Bavarian equivalent of the English *Punch*, which at this time and later offered its readers a number of witty caricatures of the composer, now produced a parody of the famous 'Lord's Prayer of Lola Montez', which set all Munich laughing:

Morning Prayer of a Modest Man

O Lord! Give me health! Let me keep my little house, my little garden, and such money as is necessary for their upkeep; and send me in addition a few more hundred thousand gulden – not all at once, but for me to draw in small instalments. O Lord! bless all men, but especially a few who have such enormous tenor voices that I can use them for my own ends. I pray Thee to give strength to all the weak, to bring consolation to the sorrowful and recovery to the sick; Thou mayst, however, visit two or three men who are not in the least respected by the Bavarian people, with a little apoplectic or other fit, so that they may no longer stand in my way here on earth, but enter into eternal life. Amen.

In spite of everything, however, the Müncheners as a whole, whatever they may have felt about Wagner the man, still admired Wagner the composer of *Lohengrin, Tannhäuser* and the *Dutchman*; *Tristan* had not yet won popular acclaim. On 1 December, at the height of the newspaper storm, Wagner was loudly applauded when he chanced to be present at a concert which included the Sailors' Chorus from his *Flying Dutchman*; and an attempt by one of the Munich papers to organize an expression of public sympathy for Pfistermeister received little support.

But the real danger to Wagner came, not from the people of Munich as a whole, but from the King's family, the nobility, the Court officials, the politicians, and the heads of the Church, who 'descended on [the King] *en masse* on his return to Munich'. Wagner was still blissfully unaware of the mortal danger in which he stood; indeed the battle was in reality already lost, though it remained for von der Pfordten to write to the King, on 1 December, the letter which sealed Wagner's fate:

> Your Majesty now stands at a fateful parting of the ways; you have to choose between the love and respect of your faithful people and the 'friendship' of Richard Wagner. This man, who has the audacity to assert that members of the Cabinet who have proved their fidelity do not enjoy the smallest respect among the Bavarian people, is himself despised by every section of the community to which alone the Throne can look for support – despised not only for his democratic leanings (in which the democrats themselves do not believe) but for his ingratitude and treachery towards friends and benefactors, his overweening and vicious luxury and extravagance, and the shamelessness with which he exploits the undeserved favour of Your Majesty.
>
> This is the opinion not only of the nobility and the clergy, but of the respectable middle class and the workers also, who painfully earn their bread by the sweat of their brows while arrogant strangers luxuriate in the royal generosity and, by way of thanks for this, vilify and deride the Bavarian people and its condition.

Five days later Ludwig returned in the early morning to Munich, where he had discussions with his mother, his great-uncle Karl, and the Archbishop of Munich, and studied reports dealing with the temper of the people of Munich. At 2 o'clock he saw the devoted old family physician, Dr Gietl, who gave him the same advice on Wagner as had everyone else: that there were 'deep shadows' between him and his people, who feared that the composer would exert his influence on the King in matters other than musical. 'Yes,' the King replied, 'he interfered too much. Take my pulse; I feel utterly broken.' An hour later he made the fateful decision. Private feelings must be sacrificed to political expediency; Wagner must go.

That same evening Ludwig went to the theatre to hear the famous tragedienne, Janauschek, as Iphigenia. The audience, still ignorant of the decision he had taken, greeted him coldly, even with a few hisses. Meanwhile Lutz was joyfully carrying out the royal command to inform Wagner that the King requested him to leave the country for six months. For a moment Wagner was completely dazed. 'Then he pulled himself together and poured forth such torrents of abuse on Pfistermeister, whom he called the most abominable of intriguers, that Lutz said to him, "Control yourself! I am here in my official capacity".' The following day, 8 December, Ludwig told von der Pfordten of the step he had taken in order to 'show my dear people that its love and confidence come first with me. You will appreciate that this has been a difficult decision for me to make; but I have triumphed.' At the same time he wrote to Wagner:

45

My dear Friend,

Much as it grieves me, I must ask you to carry out the request that I made to you yesterday through my Secretary. Believe me, I had no choice. My love for you will endure for ever, and I beg you to keep for ever your friendship for me; I can say with a clear conscience that I am worthy of it. Sundered, who can part us?

I know that you feel with me, that you can plumb the whole depths of my grief. I could not act otherwise; rest assured of that. Never doubt the faithfulness of your best friend. It will certainly not be for ever.

Until death
your faithful Ludwig

Wagner asked the King that his departure from Munich should be kept as private as possible, and that it might be given out that he was going to Switzerland for the sake of his health. But no doubt von der Pfordten and Pfistermeister took good care to advertise their victory. An official notice in the papers stated simply that Wagner was leaving Bavaria for 'a few months', but to many people it must have seemed that the Augsburg *Allgemeine Zeitung* was right in interpreting this to mean 'for ever'.

Wagner, accompanied only by his servant Franz and his sick old dog Pohl, left Munich before dawn on the morning of 10 December 1865. Peter Cornelius, one of the four friends who went to see him off, wrote in his diary: 'We got to the station at 5 a.m. and had a long time to wait for Wagner; but at last the cab arrived. Wagner was like a ghost: he looked pale and worried, and there was an ashen sheen on his long, limp hair. We accompanied him to the train. . . . He spoke now and then to Cosima, and Heinrich [Porges] particularly overheard the words "Keep silent". Cosima was completely shattered. As the train disappeared behind the pillars, it was like the melting of a dream.'

Chapter Six

THE SEVEN WEEKS' WAR

Wagner had left Munich in anger and bitterness, determined never to live there again; but this was something that he did not at first tell the King, who was, he well knew, counting the moments until they could once more be united.

But in a letter to the King on 19 January, Wagner spoke plainly: 'You must not go on suffering, nor will I. You must now *act*, while I *create*. So, my dear one, listen carefully: *I will not return to Munich!* Tell this to the wretched people who deceived and betrayed you; but tell them also that you – are *King of Bavaria* and – intend to remain so.'

Yet even now Ludwig could not bring himself to believe that they might not soon be together again. If Wagner would not come to Munich, then he would go to Wagner. To the 'Freundin' (Cosima) he wrote in his anguish, 'I tell you, I cannot bear to live apart from him much longer. I suffer terribly! . . . this is no passing, youthful infatuation. . . .' If Wagner did not return to him in the spring, he said, then life would be impossible. 'If I can be of help to him, then I will go to him in distant lands (tell him that, I beg you). Yes, I will go to him, or – die! – Yes – die. . . .'

In February Wagner did offer to return to Munich – but on his own terms, which included the impossible demand that he should immediately be made a Bavarian citizen. Ludwig's ministers were unanimous in their refusal to consider this. If Wagner were granted letters of naturalization, then the government would fall; and the international situation was such – war with Prussia might break out at any moment – that the very survival of Bavaria as an independent state would be jeopardized by a political crisis. So, gradually, Ludwig came to realize the terrible truth: Wagner could not return to Munich; nor would it be possible for *him* to go to Wagner unless he abdicated, and Wagner had made it clear that he expected the King to stay at his post and rule.

Meanwhile Wagner, after searching in France and in Switzerland for a suitable house in which to work in peace, had rented for three months a villa near Geneva called *Les Artichauts*. But it soon became clear to him that it was far from ideal; in March, therefore, he moved to Triebschen, near Lucerne, where he was to spend the next six years – years that were to count among the happiest and most creative of his whole life. Soon he was hard and contentedly at work again on the *Meistersinger*, which he completed eighteen months later. At

Triebschen, too, he was to finish *Siegfried*, to compose *Götterdäm-merung* and the *Siegfried Idyll*, and to write some of his most important books on music (including his *Beethoven*) and his autobiography, *Mein Leben*, which he sent in instalments, copied by Cosima, to the King. The death in January of his wife, Minna, from whom he had been separated for nearly four years, had removed one of the two obstacles to his legalizing his position with Cosima, who soon joined him at Triebschen.

In March Wagner wrote to his friend Constantin Frantz a letter in which he sums up, clearly and concisely, his opinion of the King, his capabilities, and the problems which he will have to solve:

I consider young King Ludwig to be quite outstandingly talented; a single glance at his very remarkable features would tell you that. The great question now is how he is going to develop as a ruler. A quite incredibly foolish upbringing has made the boy utterly and invincibly reluctant to take any real interest in State affairs. He despises anyone he meets who has anything to do with them, and deals with these matters with disgust through the existing officials and the established routine. He loathes his family and the whole Court; he hates everything to do with armies and soldiers; he considers the aristocracy absurd and the mob despicable; he is clear-sighted and unprejudiced about the priesthood, but where religion is concerned he is serious and devout.

There is only one way to arouse his active sympathy and that is through me, through my works and my art which he sees as the only real world: everything else seems to him sham and ridiculous. Make contact with this one element and it is amazing what prodigious capabilities are aroused; here he sees and feels with astonishing assurance, and for the realization of my most far-reaching schemes shows a determination that at present is his whole being. . . .

As you may well imagine, his charming ignorance of real life – an ignorance that bears such promise – is bound to involve the young King in conflicts where circumstances make him behave with obvious weakness. As it is only through me that he can be influenced, so the only way to get rid of me was to make him believe that his love for me was putting *me* in grave danger. For my part I did everything possible to make him understand the importance of his royal duties, and there was only one way to bring this home to him: to make it a question of his love for me. . . .

It only remains to be seen how far his knowledge of the world will grow in strength and clearsightedness. I have given him my most uninhibited opinion of his ministers and Court officials. He accepts all I say, is full of hope and promises to deal with opponents and enemies; but it does not seem to me that he has as yet really seriously thought about what I told him, nor succeeded in forming a really accurate opinion of the state of affairs and of the men who control him.

In this last paragraph Wagner is of course lamenting that the King has not had the courage to act on his advice and sack Pfi and Pfo. To Wagner this seemed to show Ludwig's weakness; in fact it showed his wisdom in appreciating that to do so at such a time would bring disaster to Bavaria.

In 1864, when Prussia and Austria jointly attacked Denmark, Bismarck had said, 'I consider it right at the moment to have Austria with us. But whether the time for separation will arrive, and at whose insistence, remains to be seen.' By the spring of 1866 he had decided, against the wishes of the King of Prussia, to force a quarrel with Austria.

This policy of Prussian aggression threatened Bavaria's independence. Ludwig, though international affairs bored him, was well informed and felt deeply about the survival of an independent Bavaria; he therefore summoned the French Ambassador to discuss the possibility of an alliance with France. Napoleon III was only too willing, but the plan came to nothing when Ludwig realized that it would lead to the loss again to France of the Palatinate, which had been recovered from her in 1815. Bismarck heard and was delighted: 'I shall always look upon Ludwig II,' he said, 'as one of the most loyal and unprejudiced promoters of German interests.'

Though chivalry and the combat of medieval knights fascinated Ludwig, he was, as we have already said, totally and refreshingly unmilitary and hated everything to do with modern warfare. The Empress Elisabeth once saw him in full uniform, carrying his helmet in one hand and a very large open umbrella in the other; and when she laughed, he said angrily, 'I've no intention of spoiling my coiffure.' He described army officers as *'geschorene Igelköpfe'* – 'clipped hedgehog-heads'. And on one occasion, seeing a soldier on sentry duty in the Residenz who looked tired, he ordered a sofa to be brought for him. There is an oil-painting showing the King at a military review in the autumn of 1865. An exquisitely elegant young man is riding a fine white charger with obvious competence; yet it is all too clear that he is a fish out of water among these generals, who eye him with marked disapproval. One who was present recorded his opinion that the boy's hair needed cutting.

Incidentally it is not without interest to note that Ludwig, with all his horror of war, once expressed the hope that some day a murderous weapon might be invented which would mow down whole regiments in a few minutes and so shorten the agony. When Russia proposed the banning, by international agreement, of the explosive bullets invented by Pertinet, the King is reported to have said, '*Cui bono?* If battles are to be fought by machinery, let us all do our worst against each other until we are sick of carnage and then return to the time when nations settled their differences by single combat.' What would he have thought of the atom bomb?

What Ludwig now wanted, in this dangerous spring of 1866, was of course the neutrality of his country. Yet even in this moment of crisis he could not bring himself more than intermittently to take an active interest in the rapidly worsening international situation; again and again he sought refuge in the dream-world that for him had become the real world. Count Blome, the Austrian Ambassador, wrote: 'The young King idles away his time and sees virtually nobody except the pianist Bülow. He says, "I *won't* have a war," and troubles himself no further in the matter.' But was neutrality really still a possibility? Prussia had recently grabbed the Duchy of Lauenberg, and her policy of aggression was only too evident. Ludwig saw, as clearly as any of his ministers, that Bavaria's turn would come; to Prince Hohenlohe, who tried to assure him that 'Prussia's only ambition just now is supremacy in northern Germany,' he replied, '*Just now*, yes; but presently she will want more.'

If Bavaria were forced to take sides, then Ludwig favoured an alliance with Austria. His ministers informed him that in any case the Army must be ready, but at first he could not bring himself to order mobilization. On 9 May he announced that he would sooner abdicate in favour of his brother Otto than do so; yet the very next day he submitted to pressure and gave the order. Then he retired to Berg, maintaining that he was near enough to Munich if a sudden decision had to be taken. In ordinary times this might have been true, but now it was not. Moreover it was common knowledge that Ludwig, when he was at Berg, often disappeared for hours on end, and if he was not on the Roseninsel, a little island where he also had a villa, no one knew where to find him. Pfeufer, the Munich Chief of Police, reported to Pfistermeister that there was a lot of discontent in the city.

On the fifteenth Pfistermeister went to Berg, where he found the King in a highly neurotic state. He wrote at once to the Royal Physician, Dr Gietl: 'At noon today H.M. the King was in such an overwrought condition that he looked quite pale; he gave me messages for you which I cannot commit to paper. He talked of abdicating, on the grounds that his mind was not quite healthy, and going to live in Switzerland. . . .'

That same day Ludwig sent a long telegram to Wagner asking for guidance:

> I long more and more for the Dear One. The political horizon grows darker and darker. . . . I beg the Friend for an immediate answer to the following question: If it is the Dear One's wish and will, I will gladly resign the throne and its empty splendour and come to him, never again to part from him. . . . I say it yet again: to be separated from him and *alone* is more than I can bear; to be united with him and away from this mundane existence is the only thing that can save me from despair and death. . . .

Wagner replied urging him to come to no rash or hurried decision; a King without a throne, and therefore without a privy purse, did not at all suit his book, and there was also the awkward question of Cosima. But if by the autumn his resolve to abdicate was still unshaken, then Wagner would not attempt to stop him; much might happen in the next five or six months, and the composer was playing for time. Nor were von der Pfordten and Pfistermeister anxious for a change of ruler, which at that moment would have been even more disastrous for the country than a change of government.

But Ludwig was growing desperate for a sight of the Friend, to whom, in his unhappiness, he had recently written: 'I love no woman, no parents, no brother, no relations, no one fervently and from the depths of my heart – as I love you.' Separation from his idol had become impossible to bear any longer, and when Wagner declined to come to Berg, Ludwig decided that he would go to Triebschen and spend Wagner's birthday with him there.

It so happened that the opening of the *Landtag* (Diet) had been fixed for 22 May. Wagner begged the King to abandon all thoughts of coming to Triebschen, and to make the expected Speech from the Throne; and he added for good measure that he also hoped that he would show himself to his people as much as possible during the summer. But Ludwig had made up his mind. 'Faithful Friedrich', as he called his beloved young aide-de-camp Paul Taxis, was secretly despatched to Triebschen, and on the morning of 22 May Ludwig rode out as usual from the castle with his groom, Völk, took the train from Biessenhofen, and was in Triebschen by midday.

Of the ecstasy of Ludwig at that reunion no record survives to tell. Now, too, for the first time he met Cosima, still ostensibly no more than the composer's amanuensis, who had come with her family to live under the same roof with him at Triebschen; Bülow himself had not yet arrived. Their adoration of Wagner at first drew Ludwig and Cosima together, and it would seem that such was the innocence of the King that he failed to sense the nature of the bond between Cosima and Wagner. But later Ludwig was to write of the 'Freundin', 'She does not ring true; I prefer cow-bells [*Kuhglocken sind mir lieber*].'

Two days later Ludwig was back at Berg, fortified as always by even such brief contact with Wagner and resolved to take his advice and play the role of King. Then Ludwig I and his brother Karl drove over to Berg to 'lecture' him in the same vein and to implore him to make the Speech from the Throne at the opening of the *Landtag*, which had been postponed until 27 May. This he did; but it was badly received, and the 'confident hope' expressed by the Diet that the King would personally lead his armies into battle can hardly have been more than wishful thinking. That same afternoon Ludwig sent a telegram to Wagner: 'Icy reception! Press scandalous!'

'The King's journey to Switzerland,' Prince Hohenlohe[1] noted in his diary, 'has done him much harm with the people of Munich, who are said to have shouted abuse at him in the street. There was no cheering when he drove to church on the day of the opening of the Diet; they hardly even saluted him.' If, however, the King was unpopular, the villains of the piece were seen by all to be Wagner and Cosima, denounced by the *Neuer Bayerischer Kurier* as 'greedy, self-seeking, branded adventurers'; but no one except the Friend and the *Freundin* understood the deep spiritual tragedy of Ludwig's life.

The Press soon became even more vicious in its attack on the Triebschen ménage. On 31 May the *Volksbote* wrote of 'Madame Hans de Bülow' who not a year since had 'got away in the famous two cabs with 40,000 gulden from the Treasury for her "friend" (or what?). . . . Meanwhile the same Madame Hans . . . is with her "friend" (or what?) in Lucerne, where she was also to be found during the visit of an exalted person.' This was a direct challenge to Bülow, who wrote wildly to the editor of the paper demanding an apology or a duel and then rushed off to Switzerland to consult his wife and Wagner.

The result of his visit was a despicable joint conspiracy: Ludwig was to be persuaded to sign a *démenti*, drawn up by Wagner, to the effect that there was not a word of truth in the allegation that Cosima was Wagner's mistress. Cosima herself made a direct appeal to the King: 'My Royal Lord, I have three children, and it is my duty to hand down to them their father's honourable name untarnished. . . .' Of these three children one, it will be remembered, was Wagner's, and a fourth, also Wagner's, was already on the way. It was the meanest act of her whole life; even Wagner never sank lower.

Ludwig's loyalty to Wagner was still absolute; he signed the letter, and Bülow published it.

On 8 June Bavaria formally pledged her help to Austria and her allies

---

[1] Prince Chlodwig of Hohenlohe Schillingsfürst, soon to become Minister-President.

if they were attacked by Prussia, and on the refusal of Ludwig to lead his armies in person the command was given to his great-uncle Karl, a veteran of over seventy. A week later war was declared.

And where was Ludwig on that fateful day? An entry in Hohenlohe's diary for 16 June provides us with the answer: 'The King sees no one. He is living with Paul Taxis and his groom, Völk, on the Roseninsel, where he lets off fireworks. Even the members of the Upper House, who were to deliver the Address [from the Diet] to him, were not received – something quite without precedent in Bavarian history.' Julius Fröbel, who was in Bavaria at that time, wrote later in his autobiography: 'They said in Munich that von der Pfordten, when he went to Berg to speak with the King on a most urgent matter, was refused admission by the servants, who would not even announce his arrival. But the minister forced his way in and found the King and Prince Taxis, dressed as Barbarossa and Lohengrin, in a darkened room lit by an artificial moon. . . .' Frances Gerard, in her *The Romance of King Ludwig II*, gives a more colourful if less authentic account of this episode: 'One does not like, however, to hear of his enacting *Tristan* in the woods of Hohenschwangau dressed up in parti-coloured tights of apricot and canary colour while his troops were fighting for the Vaterland. It was in this costume that von der Pfordten found him when he came from Munich. . . .'

The people of Munich were justifiably critical of Ludwig's behaviour, Hohenlohe added: 'But others do not trouble their heads over the King's childish pranks because he lets the ministers and the Chambers govern without interference; he is, however, being very unwise because he will make himself extremely unpopular.' Ludwig may no longer have interfered in State affairs; but it must not be forgotten that by his inaccessibility he made the task of his ministers very difficult.

On 26 June Ludwig, acting on sensible advice from Triebschen, very reluctantly brought himself to visit his armies in the field. Paul Taxis, who accompanied him, reported to Wagner that 'the whole tour was a triumphant success'. Ludwig was indefatigable, one day spending twenty hours in the saddle. Uniform suited the unmilitary King, and a story is told of the impact he made on a young Hessian liaison officer named Fuchs at Army headquarters at Bamberg. Fuchs, who happened to be in the mess when Ludwig suddenly appeared in his blue and silver uniform and pleated cloak, was quite overwhelmed by this to him unknown Adonis. 'He was so beautiful, so divinely beautiful,' he told his grandson many years later, 'that my heart stopped beating. I was so deeply moved that a terrible thought seized me: this godlike youth is too beautiful for this world. I whispered to my Bavarian neighbour, who with all the Bavarian officers had risen when this glorious figure entered, "Who is he?" "Our young King," he answered.'

Fuchs recalled these memories in his old age, when they had no doubt been coloured by the passage of time. But the fact remains that Ludwig's strange beauty as a young man deeply affected men and women alike. Even the King's rather rash farewell speech at Bamberg before returning to his favourite and his toys on the Roseninsel, which closed with the words, 'I do not take leave of you, for my spirit will accompany you wherever you may be,' seems to have been taken in good part.

Ludwig was delighted with the quite unexpected success of his tour; apparently it was only in the streets of Munich that people still murmured against him. But now that he was back on the Roseninsel he did not want to hear anything more about the War. Paul Taxis was with him. There were brief moments of happiness, interrupted by lovers' tiffs followed by little scribbled notes of reconciliation to 'My most beloved Angel' (Taxis) or 'Most precious Ludwig'. The Commander-in-Chief wrote angrily to his brother (Ludwig I) saying that when he despatched an adjutant to the King with important news, the latter showed no interest whatever and did not even cross-question him. 'You'll see what will happen,' the Commander-in-Chief added prophetically; 'it will end in his being deposed.'

Meanwhile the war was going even worse than Hohenlohe had feared. 'The Bavarian Army is not properly prepared,' he had written. 'Prince Karl is too old to be Commander-in-Chief. The officers lack self-confidence. I do not think we can hope for much in the way of laurels. . . .' The Duke of Hesse, who was supposed to join forces with the Bavarians, was so intimidated by the Prussians that he decided instead to defend Frankfurt (which did not need defending); the Saxons surrendered and the Elector was taken prisoner; King George of Hanover, who had declared that 'as a Christian, a monarch, and a Guelph' he would resist Prussia, was hopelessly beaten. The decisive battle of the Seven Weeks' War, as it came to be called, was the overwhelming defeat by Moltke on 3 July of the Austrians at Königgrätz (Sadowa). There was panic in Munich, where preparations were made to evacuate the town. But this did not prove necessary: a week later, the Bavarians – who even their enemies admitted had been 'fighting like lions' – were routed by von Falkenstein at Kissingen and shortly afterwards laid down their arms.

In these dark closing days of the war Ludwig must surely often have recalled the opening words of Sachs' 'Wahn Monologue' in the *Meistersinger*, the opera upon which Wagner was working at that very moment in peaceful Triebschen: '*Wahn! Wahn! Überall Wahn!*'[1] Vainly

[1] *Wahn* is impossible to translate. 'Disillusionment (everywhere)' comes closest to the meaning here.

the old cobbler searches the ancient chronicles in an attempt to discover why mankind is for ever engaged in futile and bloody strife. Wagner was finding deep satisfaction in creative work and in the companionship of Cosima; but Ludwig, even with Paul at his side, was not happy. To Cosima he wrote, on 21 July, a letter in which he poured out his troubles and repeated his resolve to abdicate and join the Friends at Triebschen. He opens it with an unconvincing protestation that really he is not in the least wretched, nor is his proposal made in a transient fit of gloom:

Dear *Freundin*,

I implore you not to be alarmed by the contents of this letter. It is not, as you might imagine, written in a mood of doubt and deep depression. No, I mean what I say; and yet I am cheerful. . . .

I am compelled to tell you that it is *absolutely impossible* for me to have to remain any longer apart from him who is everything to me. I cannot bear it any more. Fate has intended us for each other; only for him am I on earth. With every day that passes, I see and feel this more clearly. . . . Oh, dear *Freundin*! I assure you that no one understands me here, nor ever will. I am losing all hope. . . . Things cannot go on like this. No, no! without him I have no will to live. . . . We must be united for ever. The world does not understand us; and what concern of ours is the world? Dearest *Freundin*, I beg you to prepare the beloved one for my resolution to lay down my crown. He must have pity on me; he must not ask me to endure these hellish torments any longer. My true, my God-given vocation is this: to abide with him as his faithful and loving Friend, nevermore to leave him. , . . Then shall I be able to do more than is now possible for me as King; then shall we have the power to live and work for generations yet unborn.

My brother is now of age, and I will hand over the government to him. I will come with my faithful Friedrich and remain whither I am called, where I belong. . . . Write quickly, I beg you, with the joyful news that the Unique One, the Adored One, understands that there are greater crowns and nobler kingdoms than these unhappy ones on earth; that he approves my plan, appreciates my love for him. . . . Oh my *Freundin*! then and then alone will I begin to live; rescue me from this sham existence. . . .

Do not call my design extravagant or fantastic; by heaven it is not! Some day men will understand the power of this love, and that it was foreordained. . . . It is not the difficult political situation that has driven me to come to this decision; that would be cowardice: it is the recognition that my true destiny can never be accomplished in the political field. Here, in conditions such as these, I can be nothing to my Dear One; that is obvious to me. My place is with him; Fate summons me to his side!

First Cosima, then Wagner, replied to this pathetic *cri de coeur* with soothing words and an urgent plea to the King to do nothing rash. With his mind very full of the *Meistersinger*, Wagner suggests that Nuremberg might be made to replace hostile Munich as the artistic, perhaps even the political, capital of Bavaria, with the Bayreuth Residenz as a subsidiary royal palace. On 26 July Ludwig telegraphed to Triebschen: 'Marvellously fortified, I feel brave as a hero. I will hold on.'

Now came Bismarck's peace terms. Prussia, by her victory, had destroyed Austria's power, and she herself had become the dominant German state. It might have been the end of Bavaria's independence, at all events of Ludwig's rule. But Bismarck, who always had a soft spot for Ludwig and who had admired the skill with which he had handled the capitulation of the Bavarian armies, saw that Bavaria might one day be of use to him; he therefore treated the young King like a naughty schoolboy who deserved a punishment short of expulsion. Bavaria was obliged to concede some territory – not too much – and to pay the relatively small indemnity of thirty millions; but slipped unobtrusively into the peace terms was a secret clause of mutual aid, the significance of which was not fully appreciated at the time.

In fact it seemed to the King that 'Onkel' Wilhelm – for the King of Prussia was his mother's cousin – was being extraordinarily generous under the circumstances. Ludwig had been ready enough to abdicate in order to go and live with Wagner in Switzerland, but Wagner had prevented him from taking this drastic step. However, had Prussia decided to absorb Bavaria, had Bavaria ceased to be a sovereign state, then there can be little doubt that Ludwig would have passed on his crown to Otto. 'Never,' he told Wagner, 'will I become a *Schattenkönig ohne Macht* – an impotent shadow-king!'

But Wilhelm had made one demand that was very disturbing: he wanted the Burg, Nuremberg's ancient castle, to become his property. On 29 August Ludwig wrote to his uncle making a proposal that Wilhelm accepted: that they should own it jointly. 'When from the towers of the castle which belonged to our common ancestors shall float the banners of Hohenzollern and Wittelsbach,' he wrote, 'may this be seen to be a symbol that Prussia and Bavaria are joint guardians of the future of Germany, to which the providence of your gracious Majesty has given new life.'

Encouraged by the success of his visit to Bamberg at the beginning of the War, Ludwig, on the advice of his ministers and with the approval of Wagner, decided in the later autumn to make a month's tour of Franconia, which had borne the brunt of the fighting. His people had now decided that Pfi and Pfo were the criminals who had led the country into war, Prince Karl the incompetent Commander-in-Chief who had lost it, and their King the hero who had won for them so unexpectedly favourable a peace; they were already prepared to give him a sympathetic reception. But when they saw him their enthusiasm knew no bounds; they were completely captivated by his youthful charm and romantic beauty. Never had this King, who not long before had been talking of abdication, been so popular; and he reacted graciously to the warmth of his welcome.

On 10 November he arrived at Bayreuth, driving in state through cheering crowds and brilliantly illuminated streets to the Residenz where he addressed the citizens from the balcony of the palace. At Bamberg he was the guest of his uncle Otto, the ex-King of Greece. Here there were banquets, a ball in the Concordia and a Court ball, a torchlight procession of the militia and a review of the garrison troops, various audiences, and a visit to the wounded in hospital. At Bad Kissingen he went out in a heavy snowstorm to the field where his armies had fought with great bravery their last and hopeless battle of the war. Passing through Aschaffenburg and Darmstadt he reached Würzburg, where he was so moved by his visit to the war cemetery that he asked that the theatre performance arranged for that evening might be cancelled; he felt in no mood for frivolous entertainment.

But of all the towns he visited it was Nuremberg that excited him most, and he summoned his brother Otto to join him there; indeed it so caught his fancy that for a moment he considered the possibility of taking Wagner's advice and making it his capital, a suggestion which horrified the citizens of Munich. The local newspaper reported: 'We doubt whether a sovereign ever found himself in such mixed company as did our young monarch at the Citizens' Ball; yet he seemed thoroughly to enjoy himself. For four hours he danced uninterruptedly with partners of all ages and all walks of life, and talked freely with all the gentlemen who were presented to him.'

It was Ludwig's first and proved to be his only visit to Nuremberg, and he stayed there longer than in any other town, 'doing the sights' like any tourist and attending a performance of *Il Trovatore*. To Wagner he wrote on 6 December:

It is evening. The bustling festivities of the day are long over; their glitter is hidden, stars of rapture shine! I am sitting in my cosy Gothic chamber in the noble, venerable Burg; I feel almost like our Master Sachs on the morning of St John's Day, after the clamour and turmoil of the past hours in the streets. In no town do I feel so at home as I do here. The people are intelligent and truly noble, so agreeably different from the Munich mob! Recently I made a pilgrimage on foot to the place where the house of our Sachs once stood. . . . Oh, how this place draws me to you! How my heart longs in friendship for intimate hours in the company of the dearest upon earth! . . .

He also wrote to Cosima, mentioning that Otto had joined him in Nuremberg. Cosima took this to mean that the two brothers got on well together, and in her reply expressed her pleasure; but a letter from Ludwig soon disillusioned her:

While we were corresponding recently when I was in Nuremberg, you said that you imagined that my brother was an understanding and companionable friend to me. Oh no, my dear *Freundin*! He is a thoroughly commonplace person, completely without feeling for anything noble or beautiful. He often hunts all day, spends a lot of his time with my dull and superficial cousins, and of an evening is much in the Aktientheater, where what he likes best is the ballet.

Before the year was out, the growing unpopularity of Pfi and Pfo made it possible for Ludwig to get rid of both of them. Von der Pfordten was put into a position where he had no choice but to resign. The King inquired of him whether he had any personal objection to Wagner's being recalled to Munich. The Minister-President saw that the game was up; feeling that he might as well be hanged for a sheep as for a lamb, he gave petulant expression to the pent-up anger of many months: 'I consider Richard Wagner,' he said, 'the most evil man under the sun, a man who would ruin the young King in body and soul. Therefore I can only stay if His Majesty promises to sever all connection with him.' It was more than enough to seal von der Pfordten's fate.

Wagner was of course delighted when he heard; but to Bülow the fall of Pfistermeister was even more welcome, and his joy knew no bounds when he learned that 'this most abominable beast' had been 'hounded out'. Pfistermeister was succeeded by Max von Neumayr and von der Pfordten by Prince Hohenlohe.

Chapter Seven

ACTRESSES AND SINGERS

One evening in May 1866, at the very time when the political situation was at its most critical and when Ludwig's yearning for Wagner was leading him to pay his rash visit to Triebschen, the King attended a performance of Schiller's *Maria Stuart* in which the title role was played by a Hungarian actress named Lila von Bulyowsky.

Mary Queen of Scots had always been one of Ludwig's great heroines, second only perhaps to Marie Antoinette among the goddesses in his Valhalla. Lila was an attractive twenty-eight-year-old brunette with a rich contralto voice; and just as Ludwig had fallen in love with the composer of *Lohengrin* and *Tannhäuser*, so now he fell in love with the interpreter of Maria Stuart. The story of this strange romance – if such it can be called – is related in full by Gottfried von Böhm, author of the standard biography of Ludwig, who knew Lila well and received it from her at first hand.

The King's apparent lack of interest in women had begun to cause gossip in Munich; therefore news of this attachment, which did not long remain a secret, was greeted on all sides with approval: an actress-mistress was in the best traditions of royalty. It was believed that this sensible, mature woman was just what the shy boy needed to break down his reserve and so prepare him for marriage to a suitable princess. Ludwig ordered the Court painter Franz Heigel to make two portraits of her as Maria Stuart; and letters to her, addressed to 'the beloved Friend', signed 'Mortimer' or 'Romeo' and full of quotations from Schiller and Shakespeare, poured from the royal pen. *Maria Stuart* was given again, and after the performance Ludwig ordered the church of the Holy Trinity to be specially opened for him so that he could say prayers for the repose of the soul of the Queen.

There followed visits with Lila to the Roseninsel, and midnight walks through the park during which the affairs of the theatre, rather than those of the heart, were discussed. On one occasion it had been raining heavily earlier in the evening, and Lila saw with disgust that her long dress, which etiquette did not permit her to hitch up in the presence of the King, was being ruined. Then Ludwig picked some flowers and handed them to her; now it was to be the turn of her gloves! But (wrote Böhm), 'The King understood and said, "Give them back to me; I will send them to you in a different form"'. No suggestion could have delighted Frau von Bulyowsky more; she dreamed of diamonds and pearls. Fräulein Sendelbeck was present when the flowers arrived "in a different form": they had been pressed, and framed in velvet! The actress was furious. "Look at that rubbish!" she cried. "And no one has asked me how much money this outing has cost me!" '

The emotional climax of their relationship came during her three-day visit to Hohenschwangau. After the King had shown her the principal rooms of the Castle he led her to his bedroom:

> It appears [wrote Böhm] that it was decorated with erotic pictures, by which Frau von Bulyowsky, who was no prude, was deeply shocked.[1] 'I have a protection against them,' said the King, taking from a small altar a painting of Lila von Bulyowsky as Maria Stuart. They both sat down on the edge of the bed and began to recite *Egmont*. When they reached the scene of the kiss ... Lila became coy, and they drew apart without anything further taking place. I don't remember whether it was at this moment, or earlier, or later, that he told her he had never slept with a woman, and that often during the night he thought of her and smothered his pillow with kisses. After this confession he let his head fall and almost swooned on her breast. She made no answer, but laid the head gently to one side.

It was after this episode that the Queen Mother sent for Lila and told her that so long as she, Lila, remained in Munich the King would never marry; she asked the actress to leave the city when her contract expired, and to this she agreed.

So Lila (according to her own account of what took place) was no Lola. 'I didn't like the idea of seducing a young man,' she told Böhm. But supposing she had acted otherwise: supposing she *had* seduced him. If Lila's story is true, then it shows Ludwig to have been bisexual rather than purely homosexual; and it would certainly seem that his engagement to Sophie in Bayern, which will be discussed in the following chapter, was the result of an experience almost indistinguishable from that of 'falling in love'. Is it not possible that Lila, had she seduced him, would have shown him that such an experience was not as alarming as he had feared? Might he not then have married his princess after all and, though bringing her little happiness, have maintained a façade to satisfy the world? Had Ludwig chosen for wife a woman with sufficient strength of character and sufficient hold over him to make him attend to the affairs of State, then the tragedy of Lake Starnberg twenty years later might never have happened.

But how accurate was the story that Lila told Böhm many years later? Böhm was inclined to accept it, though he admitted that quite different accounts were also current. It was said that Lila, after her visit to Hohenschwangau, had cried, 'He is as cold-blooded as a fish!'

---

[1] There is gross exaggeration here, for they can have been none other than the relatively innocuous Rinaldo and Armida murals, which may be seen to this day.

and Ludwig subsequently maintained that she was a 'flirt' who had pursued him round the bedroom and forced him to take refuge in a corner. Was it the case of a woman reluctant to seduce an innocent boy, or a boy who had no desire to be seduced? Naturally Lila would have preferred the world to believe it had been the former.

The strange relationship between the King and the actress continued intermittently for six years, and was not wholly interrupted even during the months of the King's engagement in 1867. But there were many stormy scenes, some of which were doubtless the result of mischief-making by people jealous of her success, and we find the King writing on 27 November 1867 to one of his ministers that 'this impudent beast of a Bulyowsky can go to the devil'. As she had promised, and with Ludwig's full approval, Lila left Munich when her contract expired. 'But,' wrote the King, 'I wish her to leave Munich for a short time only, not for good. I am perfectly ready to treat her as before, provided that she does not again forget the respect due to a King. Try to put her into a good humour and calm her down, because women who have been scorned in love are like hyenas.' The words 'scorned in love' are certainly significant. A year later he wrote, 'Frau von Bulyowsky is a miserable woman and I never want to see her again. She is permanently in disgrace. . . .'

The King saw her for the last time in 1872. As he said goodbye to her, he laid all the blame for the troubles that had arisen between them on his mother, stamping his foot and crying, 'It was all the fault of the *dumme Gans* – that silly goose.'

Though other actresses and singers were on occasions summoned to private audiences with the King, few stayed the course for any length of time; it was only too easy to put a foot wrong and so fall from grace.

The usual setting for these rendezvous was the Winter Garden which the King had had made on the roof of the Residenz. Palm-houses were fashionable in Europe in the nineteenth century, and Ludwig would undoubtedly have taken careful note of the fine example to be seen at the Paris Exhibition of 1867; but that in Munich was unique. It has been described in detail by the Spanish Infanta, Maria de la Paz, the wife of Ludwig's cousin Prince Ludwig Ferdinand, who seems for a time to have enjoyed the King's favour. (She was, however, expected strictly to conform to Court etiquette; reproved on one occasion by Ludwig for not curtseying low enough to him, she bravely excused her ignorance of the correct procedure on the grounds that she had really hardly known any other kings except her father and her brother.) The Infanta wrote:

With a smile the King drew the curtain aside. I was dumbfounded, for I saw an enormous garden, lit in the Venetian manner, with palms, a lake, bridges, pavilions and castellated buildings. 'Come,' said the King, and I followed him fascinated, as Dante followed Virgil to Paradise. A parrot swinging on a golden hoop cried 'Good evening!' to me, while a stately peacock strutted past. Crossing by a primitive wooden bridge over an illuminated lake we saw before us, between two chestnut trees, an Indian town. . . . Then we came to a tent made of blue silk covered with roses, within which was a stool supported by two carved elephants and in front of it a lion's skin.

The King conducted us further along a narrow path to the lake, in which was reflected an artiticial moon that magically illuminated the flowers and water-plants. . . . Next we came to an Indian hut, from whose roof native fans and weapons were hanging. Automatically I stopped, but the King urged me forward. Suddenly I felt as if I had been transported by magic to the Alhambra: a little Moorish room, in the centre of which was a fountain surrounded by flowers, carried me to my homeland. Against the walls were two splendid divans, and in an adjoining circular pavilion behind a Moorish arch supper had been laid. The King invited me to take the centre seat at the table and gently rang a little hand-bell. . . . Suddenly a rainbow appeared. 'Heavens!' I involuntarily cried. 'This must be a dream!' 'You must also see my [Herren]chiemsee castle,' said the King. So I was not dreaming after all. . . .

After this highly coloured description such photographs as survive of the Winter Garden, whose construction was begun in 1867, come as something of an anti-climax. But these were of course taken in crude daylight; the cunning artificial lighting may well have made it appear romantic by night. Curiously enough, the Infanta makes no mention of one of the main features of the Winter Garden: the vast back-cloth of the Himalaya, painted by Christian Jank, scenic artist of the Court Theatre, which covered the whole of one end wall. Nor does she mention that the royal parrot had learned very successfully to imitate the King's loud and nervous laugh: so successfully, indeed, that a servant or a gardener was often misled into believing that Ludwig had arrived unexpectedly.

Ludwig was constantly modifying his Garden and adding to its livestock and bric-à-brac; by the Constitution he was obliged to spend twenty-one nights each year in his capital, and while there he found in this artificial paradise his one escape into his dream-world. In February 1871 we hear of him ordering Effner, the Royal Gardener, to procure bananas and date-palms, which are 'absolutely essential'; and in the same month followed a further command, 'Get me at once a pair of gazelles and make inquiries about a young elephant'. The Winter Garden was demolished in 1897.

Among those women of the theatre world who were invited to the Winter Garden was the soprano Josefine Scheffzky, who was later to take the part of Sieglinde in the first complete performance of the *Ring* at Bayreuth. She charmed the King by her voice but not by her appearance, and her ungainly Wagnerian bulk had always to be carefully concealed in the shrubbery (but even the nightingale hides in the bushes when it sings). Scheffzky played her cards badly, giving the King unsolicited criticism of his entourage, and to her operatic colleagues an exaggerated account of her adventures in the palace. Then she committed an even greater folly. It was a recognized practice for favoured ladies to make the King expensive gifts in return for those he himself made to them; they were then expected to send in the bill to the Chancery. Scheffzky gave the King a fine Persian rug, but the bill was 'doctored' to show a figure five times the true amount. The fraud was detected. Ludwig ordered that she should be denounced on the stage in front of the whole company, and then dismissed.

Either the Scheffzky or some other singer is said to have fallen 'accidentally' into the shallow artificial lake in the Winter Garden, in the confident hope that the King would himself come to her rescue. But she misjudged her man; Ludwig merely rang the bell for a servant and gave orders for her to be fished out, dried, and removed permanently from the royal presence. Sailer reproduces a contemporary illustration, presumably from a Munich newspaper, showing the lady attitudinizing in eighteen inches of water, the Monarch occupied with his own thoughts, and in the background an attendant arriving in answer to his summons.

Lilli Lehmann, who knew Josefine Scheffzky and who was a shrewd critic, wrote that she was 'a big strong woman with a powerful voice, but possessed of neither the poetry nor the intelligence to express in the very least what, as a matter of fact, she did not even feel, not to mention the inadequacy of her technique.'

Another singer who charmed the King for a time was Mathilde Mallinger, creator of the role of Eva – a woman exceptional for being slender and pretty in an age of corpulent and unattractive primadonnas; Ludwig commissioned a bust of her. But perhaps the most rewarding of his friendships with women of the stage was that with the actress Marie Dahn-Hausmann, whom he had first seen as Thekla in Schiller's *Wallenstein* when he was still a boy. Ludwig I had known her family well and had often spent evenings in their company. His grandson found her enormously sympathetic and 'made her his Frau von Stein'.[1]

[1] Charlotte von Stein, Goethe's friend and his senior by seven years, with whom he formed a *Seelenbund* (union of souls).

In 1875 he invited Marie Dahn, who was by this time a grandmother, to Herrenchiemsee, which he had just acquired; and in a letter written to her a year later he spoke of 'our souls, which have I feel this in common that we both have a hatred of what is mean or unjust – and this gives me great pleasure.' He felt that he could talk and write freely to her; and in a postscript to the same letter, he added, at 2 a.m.:

You seemed yesterday to think that I was in general unhappy. That is not so. On the whole I am happy and contented – that is, when I am in the country and among the mountains that I love. I only feel unhappy and miserable, often deeply melancholy, lonely and isolated, in the hateful town. I cannot breathe in tombs; my breath is freedom. As the alpine rose withers and dies in the stifling atmosphere of a hothouse, so can I live only in the sunshine and the balm of the breezes. To remain here [in Munich] for any length of time would kill me.

Marie was fifteen years Ludwig's senior, and it was, perhaps, only with women older than himself that he could hope to feel at ease. His one attempt to marry, when he chose for his bride a girl younger than himself, was to end in disaster.

Chapter Eight

SOPHIE

One day, probably some time in the year 1866, the Minister of Justice, von Bomhard, was received in audience by the King. The conversation had turned to a recent engagement when Ludwig suddenly said, 'Do you think I ought to get married soon?' Bomhard gave the appropriate answers: he hoped there would not be too long a delay, yet of course His Majesty must look around, take his time. Perhaps some *Protestant* princess? (he himself was a staunch Protestant). The King listened attentively, then firmly brought the discussion to a close: 'No – I simply haven't the time to get married. Otto can see to that.' He meant, of course, that the perpetuation of the dynasty could be left to his brother.

Ever since his accession Ludwig had been pursued by artful women and scheming mothers. He was constantly receiving love letters which, it is said, he read with a wry smile and then threw into his waste-paper basket. 'Almost unbelievable efforts were made,' wrote Rosalie Braun-Artaria in her *Memoirs*, 'to come upon him "by chance". Mothers from the best families wandered up and down the corridors of the Residenz until a sentry appeared and brusquely ejected them. . . . The minds of countless women and girls were haunted by a single thought: If I could only meet him alone – just once!' But except for the King's interest in singers and actresses, and his almost brother-and-sister relationship with his cousin Elisabeth of Austria, there was at first little evidence that he was interested in women.

In the autumn of 1866, however, it did not escape the notice of the Queen Mother and of the Duchess Ludovica in Bayern that the King, when he was at Schloss Berg, spent a good deal of his time in the company of his cousin, Sophie in Bayern, the Empress of Austria's youngest sister. Sophie, not yet twenty, was an attractive girl with a slim figure, good features, and abundant ash-blond hair which she wore in plaits; but she was far from being as beautiful as Elisabeth. In Ludwig's eyes, however, she had one great merit in addition to that of being Elisabeth's sister: she was a Wagner enthusiast. The King was always finding his way to Possenhofen, where far into the night she would sing for him the arias of Elsa, Elisabeth and Senta; and these sessions were followed by the exchange of letters, signed 'Elsa' and 'Heinrich', in which the Master and his works were endlessly discussed. Sophie had a small voice and was not really particularly musical; but she made up by her enthusiasm for what was lacking in her performance.

Ludovica, herself a King's daughter, had made impressive matches for her own daughters. Elisabeth was an Empress, and Marie that gallant Queen of Naples, who at the age of only nineteen had stood up to Garibaldi at Gaeta before losing her throne. And now another King for a son-in-law? But Elisabeth was unhappy, and Marie crownless and bored in exile with a dull and feeble husband; would the marriage, if she could bring it about, of Sophie with this handsome but strange great-nephew of hers bring her youngest daughter happiness?

Ludovica was ambitious for Sophie. But she was also watchful of her honour, and by the middle of January 1867 she had decided that the time had come for Ludwig to declare himself; she therefore sent one of her sons, Karl Theodor ('Gackl'), to the King to ask him his intentions. Ludwig replied firmly that he was fond of Sophie but that he was not yet considering matrimony. Then, said Ludovica when she was told, all these midnight meetings, all this letter-writing and music-making, must cease. In a last letter Ludwig told Sophie how sad he was to lose a 'friend'; but when he learned through a third party that she was very much in love with him and that she was miserable at not seeing him, he had a message conveyed to her, possibly through his brother Otto, that on further consideration he thought that he *might* perhaps soon be capable of entertaining feelings for her more intimate than those of mere friendship. So, presumably with the approval of Ludovica, the old relationship was resumed.

A few days later both Sophie and Ludwig were present at a ball where it was observed that she was frequently his partner. Next morning, before it was light, Ludwig ran to his mother's bedroom and in a state of wild excitement told her that he had decided to marry Sophie. The carriage was immediately ordered, and by 8 o'clock, after a brief and formal discussion between the two mothers, the King had heard from Sophie's own lips that she accepted him. That same evening Ludwig attended the première of a new comedy at the Court Theatre. When the curtain fell on the first act he rose and went with the Queen Mother to fetch Sophie from the Duke's box and lead her to the royal box. Sophie entered on the King's arm, bowed to the audience, and then took her place between mother and son. Thus the astonished people of Munich first learned of the engagement of their King; but possibly no one present was more surprised at his engagement than the King himself.

In February there was a Court ball in honour of the King and his bride. 'They made a delightful pair,' noted Robert von Mohl, the Baden Ambassador. 'The King, a very tall, slender young man with burning dark eyes, looked extremely handsome in his uniform of the *chevaux-legers*; she, tall and slim also, was charming in her white and blue ball dress.' Yet Mohl could not escape the feeling that all was not well: somehow or other the young couple did not look happy, and he thought there was a certain frigidity in the bride's expression.

Bomhard, however, considered it was the King who looked ill at ease. This was the general opinion of those who were close enough to judge, and it was soon the gossip of the Court that Ludwig had offered to marry her only after he had been told that she was pining of love for him. When, as soon happened, the King was informed of the innumerable receptions, deputations and festivities that were being prepared in his honour, he was heard to mutter, 'What, *already*? I didn't realize there was all this hurry.' Bomhard added, 'When, shortly after his engagement, I attended an audience at which His Majesty presented me with a photograph of himself with his bride on his arm, I felt, from the whole appearance of it, that this was no portrait of a lovesick bridegroom.'

Triebschen had of course immediately been informed of the engagement by telegram: 'To dear Sachs Walther joyfully gives the news that he has found his true Evchen [little Eve], that Siegfried has found his Brünnhilde.' A fortnight later Ludwig wrote to Wagner, 'I will be true to Sophie until death. But even in death will I remain true to you, the lord of my life. Sophie knows this, knows that with your death my earthly pilgrimage is over.'

Wagner and Cosima were delighted. So too was susceptible old King Ludwig I, who at once addressed a sonnet to his grandson and his bride in which he compared them to Venus and Adonis. But in Munich the news of the engagement met with a rather mixed reception. Some people had hoped that the King would marry the Tsar's daughter as soon as she was of age, and so strengthen the bonds between Bavaria and Russia; others saw danger in the marriage of cousins in a family where there was known to be mental instability, while Protestants for their part regretted that he was to marry a Roman Catholic. But the bride and bridegroom made such a handsome couple that soon the match was generally approved.

The King, whatever his inner misgivings may have been, did for the moment all that was expected of a royal bridegroom and showered his bride with magnificent gifts; but the so-called 'wedding coach', said to have cost a million gulden and now preserved in the Marstall Museum at Nymphenberg, was not in fact constructed until three or four years later. The suite of rooms in the Residenz overlooking the English Garden was extravagantly refurnished and redecorated, the walls being covered with rich brocades bearing Lohengrin motifs. Medals of the royal pair were struck, and all the shops were full of photographs. The Müncheners might grudge money being lavished on a Lola or a Lolus, but nothing was too good for the Queen elect. Outwardly all was well.

Then, during a ball given by Prince Hohenlohe in honour of the King and his bride, there occurred an unfortunate little episode which gave the first open hint of possible trouble ahead. At 10 o'clock, when the festivities had barely begun, Ludwig turned to Bomhard and asked him the time; would he, he added, still be able to reach the Theatre for the last act of the Schiller play which was being given that evening? Bomhard was acutely embarrassed:

> I told the King that everyone was looking at him; what would people think of me, I asked, if they saw me take out my watch in his presence? The King said he would stand in front of me. He did so, and I managed unobserved to show him my watch and tell him that he would be able to see a part of the play; but would his bride approve if he left so soon? He thanked me, and soon afterwards everyone was saying, 'The King has left!' The astonished guests maintained that he went away without taking leave of his bride, but I do not know whether or not this was true. After such happenings I was forced to admit to myself that the King was not in love with his bride.

Sophie was annoyed, but not as yet alarmed: Ludwig had always been unconventional and unpredictable. There were his visits to Possenhofen, at midnight and without warning, which roused the whole household and caused a lot of inconvenience to everybody. These meetings, at which a lady-in-waiting had always to be present, concealed behind a screen or pot of palms, had been gradually becoming an embarrassment to them both. The King kissed his bride on the forehead only, and often could find nothing to say for half-an-hour beyond, 'You have such pretty eyes!' Sophie would work interminably at her dull embroidery and wonder how it was all going to end, and Ludwig, however eagerly he might have anticipated his visit, soon grew bored; he was beginning to discover that Sophie was, after all, really quite commonplace and even to doubt whether her interest in Wagner was as sincere as she pretended.

She must have told him of her fears, for one day he wrote to her – though in terms that can hardly have allayed them:

> My dear Elsa,
>   My warmest thanks for your dear letter of yesterday. I can completely reassure you about the doubts you expressed at the end of your note. Of all living women you are the dearest to me; of all my relations, Wilhelm [his cousin Prince Wilhelm of Hesse]. Of my subjects Künsberg [an aide-de-camp] is one of the dearest. But the god of my life is, as you already know, R. Wagner. . . .

Very different is the letter which he wrote to Wagner at the beginning of March when he heard that the composer was coming to Munich:

My only beloved Friend! My saviour! My god!

I rejoice in heavenly rapture, I am in ecstasy! Yesterday, when I read to Sophie your godlike letter announcing your coming, her cheeks glowed deep red, so heartily did she share my joy. Ah, *now* I am happy, now no longer abandoned disconsolate in the wilderness, for I know that my Only One draws near. Stay, oh stay! adored one for whom alone I live, with whom I die.

Your own
Ludwig

Which of these two could be considered the love letter?

Wagner arrived in March, and since the composer was not *persona grata* at Possenhofen Ludwig arranged for him to meet Sophie clandestinely at the house of her eldest brother, Ludwig, who had married an actress. Wagner approved of the bride and expressed the hope that the marriage would take place as soon as possible; for his own convenience (which he always placed first) he was very anxious to see the King settled. He also took the opportunity to call upon Hohenlohe to inform him that it was *he*, Wagner, who had long since spoken highly of him to the King and who now recommended him as the most suitable man to replace von der Pfordten; he added that it was *he* who had prevented the King from abdicating. Wagner then gave Hohenlohe some gratuitous advice on the political situation, to which the seasoned diplomat listened with politeness; reading between the lines of Hohenlohe's diary it is not, however, difficult to guess his true opinion of Wagner the amateur politician.

But the principal reason for Wagner's visit was to discuss with Bülow a 'model' performance of *Lohengrin* in June, upon which the King had set his heart. There had been trouble over a Lohengrin, Niemann having refused to sing unless the usual cuts, to which he had grown accustomed, were made. Wagner now proposed Josef Tichatschek, the sixty-year-old creator of the role of Tannhäuser, who had always had 'more voice than brains' and who by this time had more *embonpoint* than either. Ludwig grudgingly agreed. But when he came to attend the dress rehearsal he was horrified by what Ernest Newman has described as the 'sagging face painted and plastered into a simulacrum of youth' and the 'ancient body maintaining its uncertain equilibrium in the boat only by clinging to a pole let into the deck for that charitable purpose'. Ludwig's illusions were shattered and, taking the law into his own kingly hands, he defied the Master and commanded that Tichatschek be replaced by a young tenor named Heinrich Vogl. He also demanded a new Ortrud.

Wagner, who had been staying at Starnberg, returned to Triebschen in a very nasty temper, leaving to Bülow the difficult task of coaching the two new singers in the limited time available. The performance took place on 16 June. The King was very well satisfied with it and wrote a personal letter to Vogl; but it took time, and all Wagner's and Cosima's diplomacy, to re-establish good relations between the King and the Master.

In 1867 Paris was staging an International Exhibition, the largest ever held. Ludwig may have felt that it was politically expedient for him to visit it, and indeed he may not have been altogether sorry for the excuse of a brief respite from Sophie before the irrevocable step had been taken. Moreover, through his considerable knowledge of seventeenth- and eighteenth-century French literature he had already begun to fall in love with the absolute monarchy of the Bourbons. Yet though he longed to see the monuments of the *Grand Siècle* he did not like the idea of modern Paris – the stronghold of 'materialism, low sensuality and godless frivolity' as he called it when writing to Wagner. But Wagner urged him to go: Paris, he said, was the centre of the civilized world and the city which had taught him so much; moreover the visit would enlarge the King's outlook. So in July Ludwig, travelling as the Count von Berg, set out for Paris.

Napoleon III, with thoughts of possible Prussian aggression in mind, received with calculated politeness this monarch of an ancient dynasty, who for his part disguised his true feelings for the very parvenu Emperor. But Ludwig prided himself that his visit had been politically useful; to his grandfather he wrote on his return, 'Thank heaven there seems to be a general movement towards peace. Perhaps it will be possible to create a reasonable situation in Europe without bringing on the dreaded catastrophes.'

In Paris Ludwig proved an indefatigable sightseer, spending many hours in the Exhibition and making innumerable purchases among which were, of course, many presents for Sophie. Time was found for several visits to the Opera, for some yachting on the Seine, and for excursions to the Versailles of the Roi Soleil and to Pierrefonds – a medieval castle, newly restored by Viollet-le-Duc. Ludwig saw Napoleon and his Empress again a month later, when they were passing through Munich on their way to Salzburg. Sophie was formally presented to them; but Eugénie, laying ceremony aside, took the girl in her arms and embraced her warmly.

At first an August wedding had been suggested; then the date had been postponed to 12 October, the day on which both Ludwig I and Max had been married. It was of course an appropriate choice; but was this the real reason for the postponement? There was further speculation when, on 3 August, the King and his bride were seen to occupy different boxes at a semi-private performance of *Tannhäuser*. Ludwig and Sophie again sat apart at a rehearsal in September, causing Liszt, who was present, to observe, '*Les ardeurs matrimoniales de Sa Majêstê semblent fort tempérées.*[1] Some people believe that the wedding will be postponed indefinitely.'

Wagner had hoped to send the King, for his birthday on 25 August, the manuscript of *Die Meistersinger*; but it was not ready in time and he had nothing to offer but a six-line poem which he telegraphed from Triebschen to Ludwig at Hohenschwangau. The King replied two days later with a letter in which he made no attempt to hide his growing misery and perplexity: 'Oh, if only I could be carried on a magic carpet to you and the *Freundin* at dear, peaceful Triebschen – even if only for an hour or two; what would I not give to be able to do that!' He was dreading the pomp and ceremony of the wedding festivities in Munich, he said, and wished that the marriage could take place privately. 'Forgive me for telling you about these little worries,' he added.

But Wagner and Cosima understood that the little worries were in reality one big and terrible worry: not the pomp of the marriage ceremony, but the marriage itself. Yet Wagner let a month go by before he could bring himself to tell Ludwig that he had guessed his secret. He wrote tenderly, lovingly: 'Open your heart to me. I still live for you alone, and I well know that no counsel can help you as much as that which stems from my sympathy and love for you. Tell me, my dearest friend, my adored lord and protector, what oppresses you. An inner voice gives me the answer, but I can only reply to it if it comes to me from you. . . .' The King did not reply.

On one of his visits to Possenhofen – which, incidentally, were growing steadily less frequent – Ludwig brought with him the Queen's crown for Sophie to try on. The King seemed to find the fitting and adjusting, which took a long time, a source of amusement; he either failed to notice, or chose to ignore, that Sophie was nervous and unhappy. As soon as he had left, the wretched girl broke down and fell sobbing into the arms of her mother's lady-in-waiting, Nathalie Sternbach, crying, 'He does not love me! He is only playing with me!'

Ludwig too, as the fateful day drew ever nearer, was growing desperate, saying to the Court Secretary, Lorenz von Düfflipp, that he would rather drown himself in the Alpsee than marry. He was seen peering at himself in the looking-glass and muttering, 'I almost think I am going out of my mind'; and it was rumoured that he had asked the Royal Physician to give him a certificate stating that he was unfit

[1] 'His Majesty does not seem to be a very ardent suitor.'

71

to marry. Was it at this moment that Ludwig became aware of his homosexuality – a condition not at that time discussed openly as it is today, and from the knowledge of which his secluded upbringing would in any case have shielded him?

At last Sophie, acting no doubt on the advice of her parents, wrote to her fiancé offering him his freedom. But, strangely enough, Ludwig still hesitated to take this decisive step; instead he suggested a further postponement until December. Meanwhile the two mothers – the Queen Mother and the Duchess Ludovica – had been conferring over what should be done; but it was Duke Max who, on 3 October, finally brought the issue to a head by sending the King an ultimatum. The document is lost, but the substance of it can be gauged from a letter which the Duchess addressed to the Queen Mother:

> The repeated postponement of the wedding has created an unhappy atmosphere among us, and has led to such unpleasant gossip that Max felt he had to write to the King to say that, for the sake of Sophie's good name, he must respectfully ask the King either to fix a definite date towards the end of November, or to withdraw the request for Sophie's hand that he made us more than eight months ago. By this he does not in any way want to force him into this union, for it has never been our wish to press our daughter upon him.

Ludwig was indignant when he received Max's letter; it was no way, he told Düfflipp, for a subject to address his King. To this Düfflipp very sensibly replied that the Duke had written as a father, not as a subject. But now at last Ludwig brought himself to a decision: he could not marry Sophie. It is said that he told her this in a brief note in which he laid the whole blame on her father: 'Beloved Elsa! Your cruel father tears us apart', and that he then hurled the bust of his bride, which stood on his writing-table, out of the window. It is possible that he wrote this letter, though it does not appear to have survived and a long letter of 7 October exists which makes no such charge; as for the destruction of the bust – this may well be one of the many wild rumours which circulated in Munich as soon as the news, which came as little of a surprise, was made public. Among the most odious of these rumours was a base slander that Sophie had been having an affair with the Court photographer.

Some months later Ludwig wrote Cosima a letter in which he stated, briefly and clearly, the whole sad story:

> I had known her [Sophie] since I was a boy, loved her always as a fond relation, deeply and truly as one loves a sister, trusted her, given her my friendship – but not love! You may imagine how

dreadful it was for me, as the day of the wedding drew nearer and nearer, to be obliged to recognize that this union could bring happiness to neither of us. Yet how difficult it was for me to make the break!

And in another as yet unpublished letter the King told Cosima that it was from a performance of *Lohengrin* that he 'drew the strength to burst asunder the burdensome fetters' that confined him.

But it is an entry in the King's diary for 10 October, the day the public learned that the engagement was at an end, that reveals to us the fullness of the sense of relief that Ludwig felt: 'Sophie is finished with [*abgeschrieben* – written off]. The gloomy picture vanishes. I longed for freedom, I thirsted for freedom, to wake from this horrible nightmare.' And to Wagner he wrote some days later that he felt as if he had recovered from a dangerous illness.

But Duke Max and his family were of course both indignant and humiliated, and even the Empress Elisabeth found it impossible to forgive her cousin's conduct. To her mother she wrote:

> You may well imagine how angry I am about the King; and so is the Emperor. There are no words for such behaviour. I can't understand how he can show his face in Munich after all that has happened. I am glad that Sophie has taken it as she has: God knows she could never have been happy with such a man. . . .

In fact, Ludwig had no desire whatever to show his face in Munich. The mountains called him and he left at once for Hohenschwangau from where, on 21 November, he sent a long letter to Wagner:

> I write these lines in my cosy Gothic bow-window, by the light of my lonely lamp, while outside the blizzard rages. It is so peaceful here, this silence so stimulating, whereas in the clamour of the world I feel absolutely miserable: all that wearing oneself out to no purpose, as happens at audiences, balls and festivities of every kind, I simply cannot endure. . . .
>
> Thank God I am alone here at last. My mother, who was such a burden to me last summer, is far away . . . so too is my former bride, who would have made me wretched and unspeakably unhappy. Before me there stands the bust of the one Friend whom I shall love until death, who is with me everywhere, who gives me courage and power of endurance, through whom and for whom I would be ready to suffer and to die. Oh, if only the opportunity were given me to be allowed to die for you!

The following year Sophie married Prince Ferdinand d'Orléans, duc d'Alençon, a grandson of King Louis-Philippe. Thirty years later she died heroically in a fire at a charity bazaar in Paris, refusing to leave the burning building until all the girls who were working at her stall had been rescued. So little remained of her charred body that only her dentist could identify her.

Chapter Nine

MEISTERSINGER, RHEINGOLD
AND WALKÜRE

The breaking-off of his engagement marked a turning-point in Ludwig's life.

In the two preceding years he had made a genuine attempt to follow Wagner's advice to conduct himself like a true king. His visit to his armies in the field in the summer of 1866, and still more his triumphal tour of Franconia later in the year, had proved to him that, except in Munich where Wagner was still unforgiven and unforgotten, he had only to show himself to his people to be welcomed enthusiastically. He had made an effort to take an interest in the dreary affairs of State. And finally he had attempted to do what was expected of every monarch: to marry and so ensure the continuity of the dynasty.

But nowhere except in Wagner and in his own dream-world could he find any happiness or peace of mind. The brave face he had worn during his provincial tour had been only a clever smiling mask to hide his inner misery. With his country defeated, his Friend no longer at his side, and his plans for marriage shattered, he began that gradual withdrawal from the world which was to lead to the building of his fantastic castles and to eccentricity so close to the borders of insanity that the world, though it was probably mistaken, may well be excused for considering him to be mad.

Much of the King's time during the next three or four years was spent at Berg in conditions of simplicity which fell little short of squalor and which were in marked contrast to the luxury and ceremony that obtained in the Residenz. Robert von Mohl, who several years later was summoned to an audience at Berg, has described his experiences. He arrived there to find no porter or servant at the gates, merely a policeman who had not been warned of his coming. At last Mohl discovered an adjutant who too had received no orders and who therefore deposited him in an icy anteroom alongside two shivering ministers also awaiting audiences. In an attempt to get warm – it was late October – the three of them decided to walk in the grounds until they were summoned.

Mohl relates that the rooms on the first floor, which he was able to examine before being taken to the King's study on the second floor, were

> very simple, either with no ornaments or else with very miscellaneous objects. The furniture was worn. In the corridors and vestibules a variety of domestic servants, lackeys, kitchen boys and housemaids,

all shabbily dressed, were wandering about. The whole place reeked of photographic chemicals [the King had recently taken up photography]. In brief, the mixture of the royal, the secluded monastic, and the chaotic bachelor ways of life was very odd indeed. In these conditions the young ruler lived for at least three-quarters of the year, completely on his own and seeing no one except his Cabinet Secretary, occupied in reading books and documents dealing with the age of Louis XIV. Late in the evening he usually went riding until long past midnight with one of the grooms, or, again unaccompanied, sailed up and down the lake in his little steam-launch [the *Tristan*].

In the opening months of 1868 relations between the King and Wagner became seriously strained; from 30 November 1867 to 9 March 1868 not a single letter passed between them. Much of the trouble arose from a series of articles which Wagner had been contributing to a new government newspaper, the *Süddeutsche Presse*, on 'German Art and German Politics'; though these were published anonymously, everyone recognized that Wagner was the author.

The earlier articles, in which Wagner had sung the praises of Ludwig I and Max and stressed the importance of the encouragement given by the present monarch to the theatre, had very naturally pleased the King. But by the time Wagner had reached the twelfth instalment he had wandered dangerously into criticism of Church and State and attacks on France and French culture, expressing opinions quite unsuited to publication in a Government newspaper. After the appearance, on 17 December 1867, of the fourteenth instalment, Ludwig sent an official to the office of the *Süddeutsche Presse* ordering that the publication of these 'suicidal' articles should cease. To make matters worse, Cosima's appeal to Ludwig and Wagner's to Hohenlohe failed to get the order rescinded.

There was also a more serious trouble that throughout 1867 had been gradually coming to a head. Malvina Schnorr, since the death of her husband, had been in a highly neurotic state and, driven by jealousy of Cosima, had been informing the world in general and Ludwig in particular that Wagner and Cosima had been living together as man and wife. In that last letter before the interruption in their correspondence – Wagner's letter of 30 November to the King, to which the latter did not reply – the composer had savagely attacked Malvina and once again sworn his innocence, inviting the King to imagine the effect of the scandal on poor Bülow, 'morbidly sensitive and already sufficiently harassed as he is, and not less on his wife, who in complete innocence showed nothing but kindness to this worthless woman!'

But Düfflipp, the Court Secretary, was, like almost everyone in Munich, convinced that Wagner had all along been lying, and told the

King that he had been tricked. On 13 December Ludwig wrote to Düfflipp from Hohenschwangau: 'If this sorry rumour should prove to be true – which I have never been able to bring myself to believe – if it is really a case of adultery: then alas!' But already Ludwig must have known in his heart that it could hardly be otherwise than true.

In the end it was the King who broke the three-months' silence. Saddened and disillusioned though he was, the time came when the estrangement from Wagner was intolerable. On 9 March he wrote: 'I can no longer endure being without news of you! If you want me soon to be whole and well again, I implore you to hesitate no more, dearest of men, and let me have a long letter without delay.' Wagner replied at once:

> Why this to me? Why do you reawaken the old hopeful chords of my soul, that should by now have died in silence?
> 'Once upon a time' – that is the sad song that now alone can resound within me. . . .

And cunningly he went on to tell the King that it was *he*, Ludwig, who was responsible for all that had gone wrong between them, for all that was destroying his whole life. He had tried to guide the young King, but Ludwig had failed him: had failed to follow his advice and heed his warnings.

Poor Ludwig was penitent, but he felt that Wagner had not really understood the difficulties that he had had to contend with. Once the world had seemed rosy to him, and men noble; then he had come to know how vile it was, how vile they were. But he would pull himself together: 'I am strengthened,' he wrote. 'I will forget and forgive the dreadful things men did to me. I will throw myself bravely into life, earnestly do my duty, for I clearly recognize my great task. . . . I will tear, tear fiercely, at the Friend's heart until the barrier that separates us has been broken down. . . .'

For a time the personal relations between the King and Wagner were less strained; with Wagner the musician there had never been a real break. Yet when the composer came to Munich on 17 March, only a day after Ludwig's penitent letter, the King, who was in the Residenz at the time, did not send for him. A month later Wagner was again in Munich for a gala performance of *Lohengrin* given in honour of Crown Prince Friedrich of Prussia. On this occasion the King, who could not bear the Crown Prince, pleaded sickness and took to his bed. Wagner asked if he might visit him, but the proposal was politely refused; perhaps Ludwig felt that a meeting with the Friend at that moment would be too great an emotional strain, or possibly he feared that the old magic of the composer would lead him into some course of action that he would later regret.

Ludwig did, however, invite Wagner to pass the composer's fifty-fifth birthday (22 May) with him on the Roseninsel, but the experiment of meeting was not repeated. It seems that it was Wagner who found the atmosphere too highly charged; at all events it was he who a few days later pleaded that for everybody's sake he should be left in peace to get on with his work – the rehearsing of the *Meistersinger*.

The *Meistersinger*, which had been occupying much of Wagner's time and energy since the autumn of 1866, had been completed a year later, and the composer had presented the full score to the King as a Christmas gift. This had been rendered possible by the labours of a young musician, Hans Richter, who had been living at Triebschen where he had made a copy of most of the score to pass on to the engravers; of this clever and eager youth, dog-like in his devotion to Wagner, we shall hear more in the future.

Wagner had hoped that the opera would be ready for performance in the spring of 1868; once, too, he had hoped that it would receive its première in Nuremberg; in the event, however, this was to take place in Munich and not until the summer. The *Meistersinger* was the most important work that Wagner had yet created; it was also a paean in praise of German art which happily coincided with the growing national consciousness, and he never doubted its success with the public. Ludwig had at first viewed it in the light of an interruption to the completion of the *Ring*, once promised for 1867 but not in fact to be heard in its entirety until 1876. Further, for one who dreamed always of gods and heroes, of Valhalla and Versailles, there was less romantic appeal in a chorus of tradesmen than in one of Valkyries. But acquaintance with the music must soon have convinced him that any fears that he may have had were groundless.

For cast there was Nachbaur as Walther and the attractive Mathilde Mallinger as Eva; Franz Betz of Berlin was to take the part of Sachs, Hölzel that of Beckmesser; Schlosser of Augsburg was the David and Sophie Diez the Magdalena: it was probably as fine a team as could have been assembled in all Germany at the time, and two of the principals – the Eva and the Magdalena – were local singers. Once again Bülow, faithful still to the music of the man who had stolen his wife from him, was the conductor; but the strain of his domestic situation not unnaturally made him neurotic and depressed, and at rehearsals Wagner was often very conscious of his hostility. To both men it had by now become clear that the pretence could not be kept up much longer.

The dress rehearsal, which was attended by five or six hundred people including the King, took place on 19 June, and at the close of it Wagner thanked his team from the stage for their devoted cooperation. Though two or three members of the orchestra, and in particular the boorish but indispensable horn-player Franz Strauss, father of the composer Richard Strauss, made trouble (this 'charming specimen of German beer-culture' did much, said Bülow, on this and other occasions to poison the pleasure of his successes), there can have been few people present who did not realize that with Wagner 'a new day had dawned for German art'. Writing immediately after the end of the rehearsal, Ludwig told his 'dear Sachs' that he had expected much but had never dared to dream that it could be so wonderful. He had been so moved that he could not bring himself to break the spell by clapping. And he signed himself 'Walther'.

Then, two days later, came the première at which Ludwig was again present, as were also many distinguished musicians who had come from all over Europe to attend. Wagner, as etiquette prescribed, presented himself to the King, who made him sit beside him in the royal box: 'Horace by the side of Augustus', people were soon saying. The audience called for the composer at the fall of the first curtain, but Wagner did not respond; at the end of the second and third acts, however, he obeyed Ludwig's command to acknowledge the tumultuous applause by bowing from the box. No doubt the King had withdrawn; but that a commoner should behave thus was considered deeply shocking by the Munich aristocracy, and according to a Press report the general public was 'struck dumb. People looked up at the splendid ceiling of the great theatre to see whether so unprecedented a demonstration of favour might not bring it crashing down. Wagner, the heretic, the exile, who scarcely two years earlier had been unable to find protection in the favour of the same King from the hostility of the populace, both high- and low-born, of our art metropolis – this man has been rehabilitated in an astonishing way. . . .'

Ludwig was even more enthusiastic after the première than he had been after the dress rehearsal, writing again at once to his Sachs and addressing the envelope 'To the immortal German Master, Richard Wagner'. 'Fate,' he said, 'called Us to a great task. We came into the world to testify to the truth. . . . I owe everything, everything – to you. Hail German art! In this sign will We conquer!' Wagner replied in words full of gratitude to his 'saviour and redeemer' at whose feet, he said, he threw himself speechless. He promised that *Siegfried* would soon be finished; he promised, too, to meddle no more in government affairs in Munich. He would live in future away from the world, giving all his energies to creative work.

Wagner went back to Triebschen on 24 June and did not return to Munich for any of the five further performances of the *Meistersinger* later in June and in July. In spite of the success of his opera, he had now determined never again to take part in the production of any of his works in Munich. The decision was made because his relations with Cosima were rapidly reaching a point where the truth could no longer be withheld from the King. This would inevitably cause a breach between himself and Ludwig; neither of them, however, could then have foreseen that it was to be eight years before they would meet again.

In August Ludwig was at Bad Kissingen, where he once more met the Tsar and his family. Later the Tsarina visited Munich and was the King's guest at a night festival on the Roseninsel – a party which, for the splendour of its fireworks and illuminations, was long remembered in the neighbourhood.

On 10 July Ludwig had written to Cosima informing her that the 'calumnies' about herself and Wagner were circulating afresh in Munich. Cosima of course sent the letter to Wagner, who wrote to the King once again vehemently denying the story; but it must have been plain to Wagner that the King no longer gave any credence to his protestations of innocence. Ludwig now *knew* that Wagner had all along been lying to him. Between 14 September 1868, when the King wrote to the composer to thank him – belatedly – for the birthday gift of a dedication copy of the printed score of the *Meistersinger*, and 10 February 1869, all Wagner's letters went unanswered.

It may at first sight appear strange that Bülow, long aware that he had lost Cosima for ever, did not sue for divorce. But he hesitated to take this step because he was happy in his work in Munich and saw that the scandal might well cost him his job. Moreover there was a further difficulty in that Cosima was a Roman Catholic. As for Wagner, he had tried to postpone the crisis because he had needed Bülow in Munich for the production of his operas; when he saw that bluff was no longer of any avail, that any moment now the storm might break, he realized that Munich would soon be lost to him for ever.

Cosima had left Munich a few days after she had received the King's letter and was supposed to have joined her sister in France; in fact she was with Wagner in Triebschen and subsequently in Italy, and in order to keep this from the King Wagner found himself caught in a complicated web of petty lies. She was soon to become pregnant with a third child by Wagner – this time a boy, Siegfried, born on 6 June 1869. At the beginning of November 1868 Wagner went to Munich and asked for an audience with the King; but this was refused. There is documentary evidence that his intention had been to make a clean breast of his troubles to Ludwig – something that he felt he could do more persuasively by word of mouth; and it is more than probable that the King guessed his intention and did not wish to expose himself to such a risk.

Wagner had finished *Das Rheingold*, the first opera of the *Ring* drama, in the spring of 1854; Ludwig now demanded that it should be brought to performance in Munich. Wagner was not on principle opposed to the operas of the tetralogy being staged independently before the completion of the whole cycle, but with the Cosima situation still unresolved he had grave doubts as to the wisdom of *Rheingold* being given its première in Munich. Indeed he even for a moment considered the possibility of abandoning Ludwig and throwing in his musical lot with Bismarck and the Prussians; but Cosima dissuaded him from this act of treachery. So in the summer of 1869 preparations began for a performance of *Rheingold* at the Court Theatre at the end of August.

In June Bülow, worn out by the physical and emotional strain of the past months, had tendered his resignation as *Kapellmeister*. The King had responded by giving him three months' leave of absence in the hope that when he had recovered his health he would reconsider the position; but in any event Bülow would not be available to conduct *Rheingold*. To replace him there seemed to be only one possible man – Wagner's brilliant young amanuensis and protégé, Hans Richter.

The composer did not propose coming to Munich for the rehearsals, but he had every intention of controlling the production from Triebschen. To Triebschen therefore there came from time to time throughout the summer the conductor and the singers; Christian Jank with his designs for the stage sets; and the machinists, who had to solve such awkward problems as the metamorphoses of Alberich into a serpent and a toad, a practicable rainbow bridge from the mountain top to Valhalla, and Loge's fire. Worst of all was the swimming of the Rhine-maidens – that 'aquarium of whores' as the *Bayerische Vaterland* was to dub them in its review of the première; after one of them had become sea-sick at a rehearsal, permission was given for them to sing in future from the wings, their places on the trolleys being taken by three ballerinas who were 'good sailors'.

Meanwhile in Munich workmen were busy reconstructing the stage and lowering the orchestra pit in accordance with Wagner's instructions, and Richter was rehearsing his orchestra. Richter's position in the Theatre was not an easy one. Bülow, because of his musical reputation and his seniority, had been accorded by the King and by the adminis-trator of the Theatre, Karl von Perfall, privileges and a degree of independence that no young and untried newcomer could reasonably expect to receive. Richter resented interference and thought of resigning, but Wagner urged him to hold on and to fight for his rights, or what Wagner considered to be the rights of anyone chosen by him; the composer had, in fact, a plan up his sleeve by means of which he hoped to force the authorities at pistol-point to agree to even his most outrageous demands.

The final rehearsal took place on 27 August in the presence of the King and various distinguished musicians. Musically the performance was satisfactory enough, but the stage effects left (as they often still do) a good deal to be desired, and the opera was not well received. Richter wired to Wagner that the première, fixed for 29 August, must at all costs be postponed, and Wagner at once relayed the information to the King. On the evening of 28 August Richter told Perfall that he would not conduct the following day; the stage effects were inadequate, and a public performance under such conditions would only do Wagner and his cause a disservice. After a discussion at which Düfflipp was present, Richter informed Perfall that he took his orders from no one but Wagner. Perfall therefore did the only possible thing: he suspended Richter on the spot.

To Wagner, the inspirer of this villainous plot, the outcome of the situation did not seem in doubt: the King demanded his performance; he would therefore insist upon Richter being reinstated on his own terms, and the resignation of Perfall, rather than that of Richter, would follow. Apparently it never occurred to him that his bluff might be called. But for once Wagner completely misjudged Ludwig. The King was furious. On 30 August he wrote in royal anger to Düfflipp, warmly approving the line that he and Perfall had taken and calling for full revenge on the conspirators:

The behaviour of Wagner and the theatre rabble is absolutely criminal and impudent: it is an open revolt against My orders, and this I will not tolerate. Under no circumstances is Richter to conduct, and he is to be dismissed forthwith. The theatre people will obey My orders, not Wagner's whims. In many of the papers it is stated that it was *I* who cancelled the performance. I saw this coming. It is easy enough to spread false rumours, and it is My will that they give the true story and do everything in their power to make the performance possible; for if these dreadful intrigues of Wagner's succeed, then the whole crowd will get steadily more brazen and more shameless and finally completely beyond control. Therefore this evil must be torn out by the roots; Richter must go, and Betz (the Wotan who was in league with Wagner] and the others brought to heel. Never before have I met with such impertinence. I repeat how satisfied I am with the way you are handling the situation....

Vivat Düfflipp! *Pereat* the theatre rabble!

With kindest regards and all best wishes to yourself, but with curses on that vulgar and impudent pack....

Ludwig followed up his letter to Düfflipp next day with a telegram to him – a telegram whose contents must inevitably have become public property: 'I command that the performance take place on Sunday [5 September]. . . . If W[agner] dares to disobey further, his allowance is to be stopped permanently and never again are any of his operas to be staged in Munich.' So far as the Sunday performance was concerned, without Richter this was clearly an impossibility. Wagner, still unable to appreciate the measure of his defeat, appealed to the King to relent and allow his protégé to conduct; he received no answer. He hurried to Munich, only to find that the King had vanished to one of his mountain retreats. But, angry though Ludwig was, he can hardly have seriously considered taking on Wagner the whole revenge that he threatened.

The full story of this unsuccessful *Putsch*, which damaged not only Wagner's personal relations with the King but also his public image in Munich, belongs more to Wagner's biography than to Ludwig's; it can be read in all its sordid details in Newman's masterly life of the composer. Three or four conductors (including Saint-Saëns) were invited to take over from Richter, but either loyalty to Wagner or a reluctance to risk their reputations on so hazardous an undertaking made them refuse. In the end it was Franz Wüllner, a conscientious if not very inspiring conductor associated for the past five years with the Munich Theatre, who a month later, and in spite of threatening letters from Wagner – 'Hands off my score!' the composer wrote, 'that's my advice to you; if not, then to hell with you!' – finally brought *Rheingold* to performance. But Richter, made wiser perhaps by his youthful follies, was later to make his name immortal by conducting the first cycle of the *Ring* at Bayreuth.

Though the Bayreuth-slanted biographers of Wagner prefer to maintain that the Munich premières of *Rheingold* and *Die Walküre* were disastrous failures, this is quite untrue. Even the problems of the scenic effects in *Rheingold*, over which Richter and Wagner had raised such an outcry, were soon solved and can never therefore have been as serious as they found it expedient to pretend; indeed they were solved more successfully than in Bayreuth in 1876. Nor was the Press unfavourable to the music: it was the man who caught the lash.

Where Ludwig was concerned, Wagner guessed that he had merely to wait until the King could bear the estrangement no longer. He was right: on 22 October Ludwig broke the silence with a letter to the 'dearest and best of friends' which gave the composer the opening that he wanted. Wagner well understood how eagerly the King would be waiting to know whether the extended hand of friendship would once again be clasped; he therefore let a whole week pass before replying. Then, writing more in sorrow than in anger, he gently but firmly put

Ludwig in the wrong for all that had happened between them, and so invited him to a complete capitulation.

Only the first part of Ludwig's reply to this has survived, and since both his and Wagner's letters are always dated at the end, the date here is missing. Probably the letter was written about a fortnight later, by which time Ludwig had come to realize that the Friend would not speak again until he had surrendered unconditionally:

> I cannot remain silent any longer. Oh, the foolish chatter of myopic and malevolent persons who could believe that we had parted from one another! . . . I hate lies. I will make no excuses, but admit frankly that it was *my* fault and that I am penitent. . . . Your ideals are my ideals; to serve you is my mission in life. Nobody can hurt me, but when *you* are angry with me it kills me. Oh, write to me and forgive your Friend who realizes that he is to blame! No, no! We will never part! . . . I should become the victim of utter despair; I should not be far from thoughts of suicide. . . . What is the dazzling possession of a crown in comparison with a friendly letter from you? . . . Yes, Parcival knows his duty, believe me, and purified will come through any trial. . . .

Encouraged by this victory, Wagner wrote Ludwig a very long letter. The performance of *Rheingold* in the ordinary theatre repertory was still rankling with him, and he begged the King to wait until the whole *Ring* was finished and could be produced under ideal conditions. And rudely he wrote:

> Do you want my work as *I* want it done,
> Or don't you?

Ludwig did not reply.

In the New Year further difficulties arose between King and composer. Ludwig was determined to have a performance of the *Walküre* and, without informing Wagner, ordered it to be produced in the Court Theatre that summer. Since the score was legally his property and indeed actually in his possession, Wagner could not prevent this; he therefore informed the King that provided he were given dictatorial powers and *carte blanche* he would co-operate to produce a model performance of the opera – but not until 1871. The absolute control of the Theatre that he demanded was, as a result of his past behaviour, clearly no longer possible; nor was Ludwig prepared to wait until 1871. Düfflipp, writing on behalf of the King, attempted to persuade Bülow to come to the rescue, but he was recuperating in Italy and firmly declined either to face the physical strain or to expose himself once again to the hostility of the Press or the malice of the people of Munich.

In the event it was Wüllner who, on 26 June, conducted the very successful première of the *Walküre*. The cast was composed of local talent, and the Ride of the Valkyries was executed by some of the King's grooms, wearing masks and mounted on horses from the royal stables. Among those present were Joachim, Brahms, Saint-Saëns and Liszt; Wagner, after a vain last-minute appeal to the King to keep the performance private, stayed away and also attempted to dissuade his friends from attending. Nor was the King present; he had decided to wait until the second performance in order that he might hear *Rheingold* (which was being repeated that summer) and the *Walküre* in the proper sequence.

Chapter Ten

THE FRANCO-PRUSSIAN WAR

A great deal else besides the première of the *Walküre* had been happening, in that summer of 1870, which vitally affected the lives of Ludwig and Wagner.

On 18 July a Berlin court dissolved the marriage of Hans and Cosima von Bülow on the grounds of Cosima's desertion, and five weeks later she and Wagner were married in the Protestant church at Lucerne. The day for the wedding, 25 August, had been carefully chosen: it was Ludwig's birthday, and the King sent them a gracious and forgiving telegram.

The same day that Cosima gained her freedom, the Vatican Council, summoned by Pope Pius IX, defined Papal Infallibility. This dogma was bitterly opposed by many Bavarian churchmen, especially by Ignaz von Döllinger, the great Bavarian theologian and historian, who had for a time been one of Ludwig's tutors. The King, who was extremely well informed on Church matters, strongly supported Döllinger and thus aroused the hostility of the so-called Bavarian Ultramontane party, principally Jesuits, who were loyal to the Pope; indeed the Ultramontanes even began an intrigue which aimed at forcing the King to abdicate. In the event it was Ludwig who triumphed, and a year later the Jesuits were expelled from Bavaria; but for a time the King's future was in doubt, and Wagner began to fear for the continuation of his allowance. His thoughts turned again to the eventual production of the *Ring* elsewhere than in Munich and in a theatre under his own control. It was now that the idea of Bayreuth, which had already been at the back of his mind, took definite shape.

But by far the most important event of the summer of 1870 was the outbreak of the Franco-Prussian war. There is no need to discuss here the circumstances immediately responsible for it, or indeed the details of the campaigns. Prussia had long been preparing for war, and Bismarck cunningly manipulated the situation so that her enemy was made the technical aggressor: on 19 July France declared war on Prussia, and Bavaria and the other German kingdoms and smaller principalities sided with Prussia. The issue was never in doubt. On 1 September the French were disastrously defeated at Sedan and next day the Emperor capitulated, bringing the Second Empire to an inglorious end. On 28 January 1871, after a terrible siege of 131 days, starving Paris opened its gates to the enemy. In six months the French armies, proudly confident of being ready for war 'down to the last gaiter-button', had been defeated, and France humiliated.

Early in July 1870, when the international situation had begun to look dangerous, Ludwig left Munich for the mountains. It was announced that he had gone to a remote shooting-box where he was not to be disturbed unless it was absolutely necessary; in fact he went no further than Linderhof, where, on the fourteenth of the month, he was informed that Düfflipp had suddenly arrived and requested an immediate audience.

The King was at first reluctant to believe that war was really imminent. He felt little inclined to comply with the Court Secretary's urgent request that he should make himself more readily accessible by returning at once to Munich or at all events to Berg; indeed his impulse was to fly still further into the solitude of the mountains. Knowing the influence that could be brought to bear on the King through his head groom, Richard Hornig, and his *chef de cuisine*, Zanders, Düfflipp enlisted their support before returning in a mood of the deepest depression to Munich. While waiting for his train at Murnau station the Court Secretary suddenly heard the sound of galloping horses: the King had relented and was hurrying to Berg.

Eisenhart, the Cabinet Secretary, was waiting at Berg, where from 11 o'clock that night until 3 the following morning he conferred with the King; throughout the whole audience the unfortunate Secretary was left standing, while Ludwig strode up and down the room or from time to time reclined briefly on a *chaise longue*. 'Is there *no* way, *no* possibility of avoiding war?' asked the King again and again. Eisenhart assured him that there was not, and that though there was strong feeling among the peasants against Prussia, Bavaria was bound by treaty to support her. In an hour or two, he said, Graf Berchem would be bringing from the Minister-President, Graf Bray-Steinburg (who had succeeded Hohenlohe earlier in the year), the resolution of the Cabinet. Ludwig then went to bed, ordering that he was to be woken as soon as Berchem arrived.

Berchem appeared at 5 a.m. with the Cabinet's request for the King's decision about the honouring of the treaty. Eisenhart went at once to Ludwig, whom he found 'lying on his "bed of Heaven" with its blue silk hangings', and read the document to him. The King had already made up his mind. He did not for a moment contemplate joining forces with the French; the France he loved was the old France of the Bourbons, not the land of the upstart Napoleon. Nor was neutrality possible, because in the event of a Prussian victory a Bavaria which had remained neutral would inevitably be robbed of her independence, while if France were to win, then Bavaria would be the next victim. Bavaria could not keep out of the war; and that being so, there was everything to be gained by prompt and generous action. '*Bis dat qui cito dat*' – 'he gives twice who gives quickly' – he cried, and ordered the mobilization of the Army. Only Ludwig could have issued such an order in the language of the country his army was being mobilized to attack: '*J'ordonne la mobilisation*,' he wrote, '*informez-en le Ministre de la Guerre*.'

The pacific King seemed suddenly strangely elated. 'I have the feeling,' he said that evening to one of his aides-de-camp, 'that I have done a good deed.'

After an initial stubborn refusal, Ludwig agreed to return to Munich; he was now perpetually changing his mind and his opinions. On his arrival a great crowd soon gathered outside the Residenz, calling for the King, who showed himself again and again at the window. The cheering continued undiminished. 'Shall I go to the window once more?' he asked one of his ministers who was present and who saw with astonishment that the King seemed positively to be enjoying himself. He crowned the day by attending, in the evening, a performance of the *Walküre*.

Ten days later the Prussian Crown Prince Friedrich, now appointed Commander-in-Chief of the Southern Armies, also arrived in Munich. Ludwig had always disliked his patronizing, blond-bearded cousin, the husband of Queen Victoria's eldest daughter and the father of 'the Kaiser' of the First World War; that evening, at one of those family dinner-parties that the King so much hated, the atmosphere was strained. 'I was afraid the young man might do something silly,' the Crown Prince said later, 'but he got through it all very properly.' Dinner was followed by a gala performance of Schiller's *Wallensteins Lager* (preceded by a patriotic prelude written and declaimed by Ernst von Possart), and once again Ludwig behaved very correctly, warmly embracing his guest and leading him to the front of the box to acknowledge the tumultuous applause of the audience.

Late that night Ludwig wrote a long letter to the Crown Prince in which he expressed his confidence that the King of Prussia, after the war was over, would respect Bavarian independence. The letter was handed to Friedrich next morning as he was getting into his carriage to leave with Prince Leopold and Prince Otto for the front; 'the hand-writing is uncouth and graceless,' he noted, 'and the lines slope.' He also jotted down in his diary his impression of his host:

> I find him strikingly changed. He has completely lost his good looks, and his front teeth are missing.[1] He is pale, and he has a nervous, restless way of talking, never waiting for his question to be answered but while the answer is being given asking further questions about

[1] The result, it is said, of his passion for sweets.

something quite different. He seems to be heart and soul with us and unselfishly to support the great national movement.

But to the King the war soon became a bore, and nobody could persuade him to visit his troops in the field. Whenever he could he escaped for a few days to Berg or to breathe the clean mountain air of Hohenschwangau or Linderhof. He was in a neurotic condition; one day at Hohenschwangau, as he sat in the bay of his study looking out at the incomparable view of water and mountains spread before him, he wrote in his diary: 'The cold waters of the Alpsee beckon to me.' It is related that on 7 August, just as he was about to go for his afternoon drive, Eisenhart arrived (at the Residenz?) in a state of great excitement and waving a telegram. It was the first instalment of important news (the battle of Wörth), and more was expected shortly: 'A telegram of the greatest importance about a big and it seems a victorious battle,' he cried to the King. 'The rest of it, with the outcome, has not yet arrived. Your Majesty must postpone his outing for a while.' '*Must?*' said Ludwig. 'A King never "must" anything. . . .' And he climbed into his carriage and was driven away. In order to annoy Eisenhart he stayed out for an hour longer than usual.

Ludwig happened to be in Munich on 1 September, the day of the great German victory of Sedan; he had come there, much against his inclination of course, to receive some Russian royalties who were passing through. The Queen Mother eagerly showed herself to cheering crowds from a window of the Residenz, but Ludwig announced one of his now famous headaches and would not appear. Nor would he remain in Munich until the third, when the victory was to be officially celebrated; noise, he said – any kind of noise, even cheering – made his head ache. (Yet he could apparently survive the loudest Wagner unscathed!) When asked for his orders about the decoration of the streets, and whether the so-called German flag might be flown from government buildings, he replied that there was as yet no Germany and he did not wish to see the flag of a mere 'geographical concept'; there were to be the blue and white Bavarian flags, or none at all. In the event there was such a downpour on the day that it mattered very little what flags were flying.

But by that time Ludwig was back in the mountains. His mood had changed: though he still favoured a united Germany, he had begun to appreciate that a German victory under Prussian leadership must inevitably result in some diminution of his country's independence. There were moments when he felt strongly anti-Prussian, indeed little short of pro-French; on one occasion he refused to receive his mother on the grounds that he was in no frame of mind to see 'a Prussian Princess'. Yet so capricious was he that after the capitulation of Metz on 27 October he spontaneously despatched a congratulatory telegram to the King of Prussia.

The German armies had reached Versailles and the moment was approaching when the Iron Chancellor had to carry out the most difficult of all his self-imposed tasks. Although Prussia was the largest and most powerful of the German states, theoretically she stood on an equal footing with her neighbours; it was Bismark's intention, not only that Prussia should be recognized as the dominant partner of a German Federation, but that the Hohenzollerns should reign over this Federation as hereditary emperors. To achieve this he had decided that Ludwig, as ruler of the kingdom next in importance after Prussia, must be persuaded to invite the King of Prussia to become Emperor. Already in September an emissary, Rudolf von Delbrück, had been despatched to Bavaria to pave the way. Ludwig had received him courteously and had at once embarked upon a detailed discussion of Papal Infallibility, a theme from which all Delbrück's skill had failed to deflect him.

The Versailles Conference opened on 20 October. Bavaria was represented at it by Bray the Minister-President, Lutz the Minister of Justice, and von Pranckh the Minister for War, with Otto replacing Ludwig who stubbornly refused to leave Bavaria; Prince Luitpold, Ludwig's uncle, who was to act as Regent after his death, was also present. This time the King pleaded trouble with his teeth; toothaches and headaches now alternated as excuses for avoiding the fulfilment of disagreeable duties.

Otto was beginning to show marked signs of the mental instability which was soon to reduce him to complete insanity; he now suffered periodically from melancholia, panic fears and fits of weeping. He had been briefly with the armies in France, but proving quite unfit to face the rigours of a campaign had been recalled 'to undertake more important duties'. The Prussian Crown Prince found him 'pale and ill; he sat before me shivering as with a fever while I explained to him that it was necessary for the Army and the diplomats to work together. I could not discover whether he grasped these matters, or even whether he was really listening.' In the absence of Ludwig there was inevitably a good deal of coming and going between Versailles and whatever castle the King had chosen to retreat to at any particular moment, and on 5 November Otto returned to Bavaria to report to his brother. Latterly Ludwig's thoughts had once again been turning to the possibility of his abdicating in favour of Otto; but when he looked at him he knew at once that this way of escape was no longer open to him. To his old governess, Frau von Leonrod, he wrote not long afterwards, 'It is really painful to see Otto in such a pitiful state, and he seems to grow worse every day.... He behaves like a madman, makes terrible faces, barks like a dog and sometimes says the most indecent things; and then again he is perfectly normal for a while. . . .'

At the Conference Bavaria, in return for her quick response to Bismarck's call, was offered special privileges in the new Federation which would give her the illusion of independence. She was to preserve her own railway and postal systems, a limited diplomatic status in her dealings with foreign countries, and a degree of military, legal and financial autonomy. These terms were accepted by the Bavarian delegates on 23 November. Having thus propitiated the Bavarians, Bismarck now turned to the delicate question of Ludwig's invitation to the King of Prussia to become German Emperor.

Telegrams passed between Bray and Ludwig, who was far from agreeable to this proposal. He had already suggested that a Prussian and a Bavarian monarch might rule either jointly or alternately over the Federation; now there was talk of a Prussian becoming *Emperor* of the united Germany. He decided to send a private emissary, his equerry and Master of the Horse, Count Holnstein, to Versailles to see Bismarck. The two men had met before, and the Chancellor, well aware of the intimacy that existed between the King and his equerry, treated Holnstein with marked condescension and civility. Here was his chance to win over the King. Two days later Holnstein was on his way back to Hohenschwangau, bearing with him the draft of a letter to the King of Prussia which Bismarck hoped Ludwig could be persuaded to copy and sign. Rumour later had it that Holnstein also brought the promise of a substantial annual grant of money to the King, a grant from which he himself would receive a percentage in return for his good offices; such a grant was in fact agreed on, but probably at a later date.

Graf Holnstein arrived at Hohenschwangau on the morning of 30 November. Hardly had the King been informed of this when he took to his bed, pleading a sudden and severe attack of toothache and refusing to see anyone. Holnstein waited with growing impatience from 10 o'clock until a quarter to four without being summoned, then asked that it should be explained to the King that he was the bearer of an important document from Bismarck, that he was obliged to leave for Versailles punctually at 6 o'clock and that it was imperative for him to take back an answer.

Ludwig did not usually respond favourably to such tactics; but Holnstein was a privileged person, and he was now conducted to the royal bedside. He found the King with his head swathed in bandages, in a room reeking of chloroform. Ludwig carefully studied Bismarck's letter and the draft of the letter to the King of Prussia; then there followed a long discussion. Holnstein stood there, watch in hand, as the minutes passed; finally he plucked up his courage to remind the

King that he would soon have to leave. Then Ludwig yielded. He rose from his bed and went to his writing table. But now he could not find suitable paper, so the letter, he said, could not after all be written. Holnstein in desperation asked permission to ring the bell for a servant; but mysteriously the right paper was suddenly to hand and Ludwig wrote the all-important letter, the famous *Kaiserbrief*, to his Uncle Wilhelm, inviting him to assume the title of Emperor. In it he did not exactly follow the original draft, and of his own accord stressed the importance of a united Germany.

Holnstein hurried to Versailles with the precious document, which was duly approved by the Bavarian delegates and handed to Bismarck by Prince Luitpold. On 18 January King Wilhelm of Prussia was proclaimed Emperor in the Galerie des Glaces. He had never been eager to assume the new honour; but Bismarck had persuaded him of the necessity of accepting it, and as Baron von Roggenbach, the Baden Envoy, wrote, there was never likely to be another King of Bavaria who would offer the Imperial Crown to someone because he had toothache. Otto, who had all along opposed Bismarck's conspiracy, was present at the ceremony and wrote a surprisingly sane letter to his brother:

Alas! Ludwig, I cannot describe to you how unhappy and wretched I felt during the ceremony, how every fibre of my being revolted at what I saw. Everything was so cold, so brilliant, so ostentatious and showy, so empty and unfeeling. I felt so oppressed, so stale in that great hall.

Then France surrendered. Peace was signed at Frankfurt on 10 May, and on 16 July came the ceremonial entry into Munich of the victorious Bavarian Army. A week before this, Ludwig had written to his brother:

Just imagine, Otto: as a political necessity, and driven to it on every hand, I have had to invite the Crown Prince to the Victory Parade. I am absolutely in despair about it. It really isn't surprising that since last year (campaigns, conclusions of treaties, etc., etc.) I should have come to hate ruling, to hate people. And yet to be king, to govern, is the finest and noblest thing on earth. Alas that I was born at a time when every pleasure in life is taken from me!

The great day dawned and the King rode out with his detested cousin to the parade ground near Nymphenburg, where the Crown Prince reviewed the troops and distributed Iron Crosses on behalf of the Emperor. Then came the victory march of the Army, with the Crown Prince at its head, through cheering crowds and down the broad, beflagged Ludwigstrasse to the Odeonsplatz in the centre of Munich where Ludwig, who had returned independently to the town, was waiting with his mother and other members of the royal family. In the evening there was a gala performance at the Opera, and once again the unhappy, unmilitary King was obliged publicly to embrace his cousin and pretend that he was enjoying playing second fiddle to the hero of the hour.

Next day came a family luncheon on the flowery Roseninsel, for Ludwig an even more hateful occasion. It ended in an unpleasantness between the two cousins – a silly little misunderstanding about an Uhlan uniform which Ludwig invited his guest to wear – and the King began to sulk and withdraw into his shell. After the return of the party to Munich he suddenly announced that he had no intention of attending the State banquet that evening in the Glaspalast, to which nine hundred distinguished guests had been invited. 'I need rest,' he told Eisenhart, and nothing the latter could say would make him change his mind. Ludwig's absence aroused very unfavourable comment; no one believed that he was really ill: he had cried 'wolf' too often on occasions such as this.

At dawn the next morning the King, without a word of farewell to his guest, slipped out of the Residenz and headed post-haste for the mountains. He was almost at the end of his tether; only solitude could heal him.

Meanwhile all had been going very well with Wagner and Cosima in peaceful Triebschen. They were living there in the usual style, with eight servants, a horse and carriage, a spacious and well-stocked garden, and various luxuries such as an aviary of golden pheasants. On Christmas Day 1870, which was Cosima's thirty-third birthday, came the famous first performance of the *Triebschen* (later called *Siegfried) Idyll*. Early that morning a small orchestra from Lucerne assembled on the stairs of the villa and under Wagner's direction played this exquisite piece of music as a surprise Christmas and birthday gift for his new wife. Among those present was the young and at that time ardent Wagnerian, Friedrich Nietzsche.

But the war brought out the worst in Wagner, who like Cosima was now fanatically pro-Prussian and anti-French. The *Kaisermarsch*, with its jingoist choral finale, was a relatively harmless expression of his chauvinistic fervour; but for the crudity of *Eine Kapitulation* – described by Newman as 'a tasteless, witless farce, the loutish Teutonic humours of which are ungraced by a single touch of literary finesse' – no possible excuse can be found. In it Wagner jeers spitefully at the misery of the starving, beleaguered Parisians. His attempt to have it set to Offenbach-style music by Richter and to stage it mercifully failed. The text was not in fact printed until 1873, when its cold-blooded publication in peace-time did incalculable harm to Wagner's reputation in France.

But during the war Wagner was also, and more profitably, at work on the *Ring*. The full score of *Siegfried* was completed by February 1871, and in June he started the second act of the *Götterdämmerung*; but in his fear that Ludwig might try to have *Siegfried* produced in Munich, as legally he was fully entitled to do, the composer had been a good deal less than truthful when writing to him about its progress. He intended, by delaying tactics and such deception as might be necessary, to keep the last two operas of the *Ring* for Bayreuth, where he was now firmly resolved to stage the première of the complete cycle.

In a long letter on 1 March Wagner told the King in vague terms of his determination to produce his *Ring* elsewhere than in Munich, and within a few weeks Ludwig had learned what a good many other people already knew – that Wagner had decided upon Bayreuth. At this time the composer was still thinking of using the existing Court Theatre; but a visit to Bayreuth soon convinced him that this little rococo building, charming though it was, could not possibly be adapted to meet his very special requirements, and on 12 May he publicly announced his intention of building his own theatre.

The King had no longer any illusions left about Wagner: the Friend had finally decided to abandon his great benefactor. But gradually, over the past two years, Ludwig had found himself in a position to develop, in a practical form, a latent interest which no doubt helped to alleviate the pain of his desertion.

He had begun to build.

Chapter Eleven

THE KING AND HIS CASTLES

Building, no less than hunting, is the sport – one might almost say the occupational disease – of kings.

It may be remembered that Ludwig, as a child, had spent many agreeable hours with his toy bricks. What he then created were castles in the air; but now that he was King, and more particularly when on the death of his grandfather in 1868 he became entitled to a larger share of the Civil List,[1] he was in a position to bring them down to earth, to make them a reality. Though it had by this time become clear that the Semper Theatre would never materialize, Ludwig had found huge enjoyment in watching the plans for it develop and in playing with the models which Semper so obligingly provided for him; moreover, in the preparation of apartments in the Residenz, first for himself and then for his bride, and in the creation of his Winter Garden, he had tasted the scarcely inferior pleasures of interior decoration and garden planning. His grandfather had built the new Munich, his father had made the broad Maximilianstrasse and restored Hohenschwangau and Berg; now it was to be *his* turn. But whereas most kings, from the Pharaohs onwards, have built in order to leave monuments that would outlast them, Ludwig was to build for the sheer satisfaction of giving substance to his dreams; he can hardly at first have understood that he had found the answer to his long search for a mode of self-expression other than through Wagner, nor as yet have had any premonition that reckless indulgence in his new hobby, with those long periods of absence from the capital and consequent neglect of State duties that its pursuit necessitated, were to play a considerable part in his eventual downfall.

In the spring of 1867 Ludwig had visited the famous Wartburg, near Eisenach in Thuringia, in whose minstrels' hall Wagner had set the singing contest in *Tannhäuser*, and his excursions from Paris that same summer to Pierrefonds and Versailles had further deeply stirred his imagination. The Wartburg and Pierrefonds had appealed to the deeprooted medieval in him; the former was now to be the inspiration for the castle that later became known as Neuschwanstein, while Versailles and its Trianons had further kindled a passion for the Bourbons which found expression in the palaces of Linderhof and Herrenchiemsee. The building of Neuschwanstein was begun in 1869, of Linderhof in 1870 and Herrenchiemsee in 1878; Linderhof was virtually complete by

[1] In effect, more income.

1879, but the other two castles still remained unfinished at the time of Ludwig's death in 1886.

It may be mentioned here that the total sum expended on the three castles was about thirty-one million marks: approximately the amount of the indemnity paid to Prussia after the Seven Weeks' War, and paid without a murmur because her treatment of Bavaria was considered generous. To the cost of the indemnity must be added the cession of territory, the military expenses of the campaign and the many dead and wounded; while from the cost of the castles should be offset the millions of marks subsequently paid by tourists from all over the world who visit them. The personal debt that Ludwig had incurred by the end of 1883 – the sum which was so to shock his ministers – amounted to no more than seven and a half million marks.

The first evidence we have of Ludwig's intention to build a pastiche medieval castle in the Swan Country – a castle that was to be as it were a shrine to Lohengrin, Tannhäuser, Parsifal and the knights of the age of German chivalry (and also, it must be confessed, to provide a refuge from his unloved mother who was all too often at Hohenschwangau) – is to be found in a letter he addressed to Wagner on 13 May 1868:

> I propose to rebuild the ancient castle ruins of [Vorder]hohenschwangau, near the Pöllat Falls, in the genuine style of the old German knights' castles, and I must tell you how excited I am at the idea of living there in three years' time. There will be a number of guest-rooms, comfortably and conveniently furnished and commanding wonderful views over the majestic Säuling, the mountains of the Tyrol and the distant plain. You will know who the guest is whom I want to invite and entertain there. The spot is one of the loveliest that can be found, inviolable and inaccessible, a worthy temple for the godlike Friend through whom alone can flower the salvation and true blessedness of the world.
>
> There will also be reminiscences of Tannhäuser (minstrels' hall with a view of the castle beyond) and of Lohengrin (castle courtyard, outside passage-way and approach to the chapel); this castle will be in every respect more beautiful and more comfortable than the lower-lying Hohenschwangau, which is yearly profaned by my mother's 'prose'. The outraged gods will take their revenge and sojourn with us on the steep summit, fanned by celestial breezes.

In the immediate neighbourhood of Hohenschwangau there had formerly stood four castles. Out of the substantial remains of the original Schwanstein Max had made the castle that he renamed Hohenschwangau; but of the other three, little was left beyond fragments of walls of an ancient *Palas* (keep) or the base of a ruined watch-tower. The most spectacularly situated of these castles had been Vorderhohenschwangau, which dominated a craggy peak near Hinterhohenschwangau about a mile from Hohenschwangau; it was here that Ludwig had decided to build, or, as he preferred to call it, to '*re*build'.

The planning of the castle was entrusted to a Court architect named Eduard Riedel, who had been employed by King Max for the restoration of Schloss Berg; but in the event the design was to owe much to the personal suggestions of Ludwig, who kept a sharp eye at every stage on every detail, and to Christian Jank, scenic designer at the Court Theatre, who provided highly romantic theatrical sketches of fairytale buildings which would have delighted Pol de Limbourg.

Riedel's first design, which concerned only what is now the upper part of the castle, was for a three-storeyed, late-Gothic building reflecting the architecture of Nuremberg. His second design, of July 1868, covered approximately the whole area of the present castle; there were now to be five storeys, and most of the Gothic had been replaced by Romanesque. Jank's sketch, made a year later, shows a building not very different from that finally erected, though it was much modified in detail and simplified as work proceeded.

In 1868 the ruins of the old watch-tower, which could not be incorporated in the new castle, were removed, and more than twenty feet of the rocky summit of the mountain blasted away in order to provide a level platform on which to build. Water was brought up from the valley and a road constructed; and in February 1869 building began on the gate house, in whose red sandstone façade many people will find a discordant note of colour. On 5 September of the same year came the laying of the foundation-stone of the main block – a large slab of Untersberg marble enclosing a plan, some coins, and a miniature of the King, who was of course present at the ceremony. The foundation deed runs: 'We, King Ludwig II by God's grace King of Bavaria, etc., hereby declare that We have decided to build a new castle for Ourselves and Our Court on the spot where once the castles of Vorder- and Hinterhohenschwangau raised their battlements. . . .'

The Franco-Prussian War of 1870 was not apparently allowed to interfere with the building programme. By 1871 the gate house had been roofed, and the following year the foundations of the *Palas* were laid. In 1874 Riedel retired and was succeeded by Georg Dollmann – son-in-law of Ludwig I's principal architect, Leo von Klenze. By 1881 all the *Palas* was finished in the rough, and soon afterwards work was started on the *Ritterhaus* (house of the knights). Then, two years before the King's death, Julius Hofmann succeeded Dollmann.

Pictures will serve, far better than words, to convey an idea of the appearance of the castle both externally and internally. Seen from afar,

Neuschwanstein looks like a tiny pendant such as might have come from the hands of a medieval craftsman working in ivory; it seems absurdly small. In fact the castle is not really a very large complex of buildings, the area that it covers being far less than that of Westminster Abbey, or indeed of the Wartburg which in part inspired it. Its great charm comes from its superb position above the rushing Pöllat and the fir-covered slopes, from its ivory whiteness, and from its romantic silhouette. It is one of the most fascinating toys in the world.

Within, the architectural styles employed are for the most part based on the Romanesque and the Byzantine, but the King's bedroom and oratory, the first rooms to be completed, were carried out (after designs by Julius Hofmann) in the most ornate late Gothic. The bed, of carved walnut, is surmounted by 'a perfect forest of tiny Gothic spires' which give it the appearance of a canopied tomb; the *boiseries* of this room alone are said to have kept seventeen skilled wood-carvers occupied for four and a half years. There is dark woodwork everywhere throughout the living quarters, and the general effect is ponderous and Teutonic; on every wall are paintings or mock-tapestries illustrating the sagas on which the Wagner operas were based. The craftsmanship of the furniture and the panelling, for the designs of which Hofmann was largely responsible at a time when he was still working under Dollmann, is of the highest quality.

In all the details of furnishing and decoration Ludwig showed the same watchful interest that he had taken in the niceties of the architectural design of the building. His criticism was practical and historical rather than aesthetic; for example, we find him sending instructions to August von Heckel about a painting of Lohengrin: 'His Majesty wishes that in the new sketch the ship be placed further from the shore, that Lohengrin's neck be less tilted, that the chain from the ship to the swan be of gold and not of roses, and finally that the style of the castle shall be kept medieval.'

The paintings in the King's study illustrate the Tannhäuser legend, and the erotic element in the story has not been shirked. From this room there is access to an artificial grotto, which was clearly conceived as the Grotto of Venus; it contained a cascade and a functional artificial moon, but could be further illuminated by electric lights coloured to suit the Monarch's mood. Beyond the grotto came a small conservatory or 'winter garden' with a Moorish fountain left over from a projected but never executed Moorish room. Here were exotic creepers and jasmins, tubs containing orange trees, and (according to one writer) 'humming-birds flying freely everywhere'.

The two most important rooms at Neuschwanstein are the minstrels' hall (*Sängersaal* or *Festsaal*) and the throne room, the former being, of course, the real *raison d'être* of the castle. The throne room, for whose design Ludwig was himself largely responsible, extends through two floors at the western end of the building and is modelled on a Byzantine basilica. Its walls are arcaded on two levels; the floor is a mosaic of plants and animals, and the roof a blue, star-studded sky; blue, porphyry and gold are the predominant colours. The walls behind and above the arcades are painted with historical and religious subjects, and in the centre of the hall there hangs a magnificent candelabrum. At one end of the building white marble steps ascend to an apse where the throne should have stood – a throne that was never made and which would not in any case have served any practical purpose in a room where audiences were never held; indeed the apse, with its roof painted with a Christ in glory and its walls lined with the figures of the six Holy Kings, seems to call for an altar rather than a throne.

The minstrels' hall, as finally carried out, is far removed from its prototype in the Wartburg. As in the throne room the mood is religious rather than secular, the murals illustrating scenes from *Parsifal* and the legend of the Grail. Yet though the themes are solemn the room is far from gloomy; the glittering gold standard and hanging candelabra, and the arabesques on the walls, give it in fact a gaiety such as one finds in a Moorish palace. There is a minstrels' gallery where no minstrels were ever to play, and from the windows of both this room and the throne-room are magnificent views over forests, mountains and lakes.

Such was Neuschwanstein; and though Ludwig did not live to see the very last touches put to the building he may well as he looked at it have apostrophized, as did Wotan (in *Das Rheingold*) when he gazed up at the splendid Valhalla that had been built for him:

> *Vollendet das ewige Werk!*
> *Auf Bergesgipfel die Götterburg;*
> *Prächtig prahlt der prangende Bau!*

'Completed is the immortal work! There on the mountain top stands the citadel of the gods; gloriously gleams the glittering building!' Wotan continues: 'In a dream I conceived it; my will called it into being. Strong and fair it stands, a fortress proud and peerless!'

At Linderhof, in the green Graswang valley some fifteen miles to the east of Neuschwanstein, stood a little hunting-box – a very humble affair faced with weather-boarding – which Ludwig had known and loved since the days when he and his father had made use of it on their hunting expeditions in the Ammergau hills. The place owed its name to an ancient lime tree (*Linde*), though it was doubtful whether the big lime which was still to be seen near the hunting-box was in fact the original tree. In 1869, at the very moment when the King was embarking

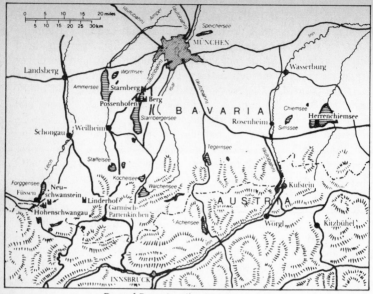

Part of Bavaria, showing the position
of Ludwig's castles

upon the building of Neuschwanstein, his thoughts turned also to Linderhof and another castle: or rather, this time, a palace – for *Schloss* carries both meanings.

Sketches exist of a mock Versailles (1868–9) and a Byzantine palace (1869–70), both inscribed 'Linderhof'. The former project, to which Ludwig gave the curious secret name of 'Meicost Ettal' – an anagram of Louis XIV's proud boast: '*L'état c'est moi*' – was to be realized later in Herrenchiemsee, the latter never. But already by the end of 1868 the King had a simpler and more practical scheme in his head. Writing to Düfflipp in November, he spoke of a pavilion like the Grand Trianon at Versailles: a modest building with a small Renaissance garden, a 'unique jewel' for which plans were to be put in hand at once. To Baronin von Leonrod he wrote, 'Oh! it is essential to create such paradises, such poetical sanctuaries where one can forget for a while the dreadful age in which we live'.

In 1870 one extra bedroom was added to the existing building, and the present palace begun as an extension to the hunting-box. Work on the latter was carried out in two stages, the northern part being erected between 1870 and 1872 and much of the remainder during the following three or four years. At first the whole exterior was faced with weather-boarding; but in 1874 this was replaced by ashlar, and at the same time the hunting-box was dismantled and set up again further to the

The King, Queen, Ludwig and young Prince Otto at Hohenschwangau,
lithograph by E. Correns, 1850

Ludwig in uniform

Oil-painting of Richard Wagner
by F. von Lenbach, 1874

Schnorr von Carolsfeld as Tristan

Ludwig sleighing at night from Neuschwanstein to Linderhof, by R. Wenig, 1880

Sophie and Ludwig

Neuschwanstein

Linderhof

Hunding's Hut

Ludwig and Kainz

Portrait of Ludwig by G. Schachinger, completed 1887

west. Work continued in various parts of the palace until 1879, after which no further changes were made beyond an extension to the King's bedroom.

Linderhof is, as Ludwig intended, a Trianon by comparison with the Versailles he was later to build on the Chiemsee. Externally it is a compact and very white building, designed by Dollmann in an ornate and stylistically impure baroque which combines features borrowed from various periods and countries. Heinrich Kreisel suggests that 'Marly, the little garden chalet near Versailles, was perhaps able to provide a type for Linderhof, but it was not the model.' In fact there is no resemblance to the former château at Marly, and indeed Linderhof externally, except in a few details, bears no resemblance to French seventeenth- or eighteenth-century architecture; the pediment is much closer to German baroque – the garden front at Würzburg, for example. French influence may, however, be seen in the banded columns, in the four herms which support the balcony above the entrance (*cf.* Puget's herms at Toulon, themselves derived from Italian models), and in the curved form of the roof (a French device but used also in many German baroque buildings).

Though the exterior of the palace seems ornate, by comparison with the interior it may be considered a model of restraint. For within is a riot of rococo: of the flash of mirrors and the glitter of gold; of rich tapestries, gay but indifferent paintings, and lush velvets; of cut-glass candelabra; of lapis, malachite and porcelain. 'It will probably,' says Baedeker (1929) guardedly, 'impress the modern visitor as artificial and exotic.'

The most dazzling of the rooms are the mirror room and the King's bedroom. The latter was enlarged and enriched, shortly before Ludwig's death, after designs by Eugen Drollinger based on those of Cuvilliés for the bedroom in the '*Reiche Zimmer*' of the Residenz. In the oval dining room there is a *Tischlein deck' dich* ('little table, serve dinner') – a table which could be lowered through the floor and then raised again recharged with dishes, thus allowing the shy King to eat without the distasteful presence of servants. Four small rooms – the yellow, mauve, rose and blue cabinets – separate the bigger rooms, and since all are *en suite* the colour schemes have been chosen to attract and surprise the visitor as he passes from one to the next.

Franz Seitz and Christian Jank, both of whom were employed at the Court Theatre, made many sketches for the interior decoration under the direction of Dollmann. Since Linderhof was a palace in praise of Ludwig's beloved Bourbons (who figured in many of the paintings and sculptures), it was only to be expected that French rococo should be a strong influence; but with the richness and elegance of Bavarian and Franconian rococo ready to hand, those too played their part. Under Dollmann worked a team of artists and craftsmen who were obliged, as were all who worked for Ludwig, to submit the most detailed drawings of everything for the approval of the King. Ludwig studied these minutely and criticized them savagely if they fell in any way short of what he had stipulated or envisaged; typical of many is the following letter which he ordered to be sent in October 1872 to Düfflipp to protest that his instructions had not been exactly carried out:

His Majesty the King is very angry because His Majesty has been deceived over the completion of the work.

It shows great lack of taste on Herr Dollmann's part to have made the deities above the doors and on the ceilings, as well as the Bavaria in the study, white; His Majesty is amazed and indignant and orders that they be gilded immediately.

An equal lack of taste is evident in the study, where the gold decoration has been applied to a green and not a white ground; there are no words to describe such bad taste.

The deities above the doors, who are holding escutcheons, are not stylistically correct, and they must be better modelled; for this, Herr Dollmann's lack of supervision is to blame.

The Bavaria is also abominable because it is not as shown in the first sketch and as on the ceiling of the red drawing-room in Munich; here the arms are outstretched.

His Majesty strictly ordered that in the former dining-room the Venus and Cupid was to go above the chimney-piece and the Venus and Bacchus over the window; exactly the opposite has been done. His Majesty is most of all annoyed about this, because it is now too late to interchange them.

His Majesty does not approve of the figures on the ceiling of this room having feet in relief; the deities too should not have been modelled, but simply painted on the ceiling.

The arms of the writing-table chair should be more curved, as the style demands, if this is still possible. . . .

The artist Herr Zimmermann had promised that he would begin the new picture at once and that he would have it ready in six weeks; now he says it will take him three months. Your Excellency must relieve him of this work and give it to someone who can make just as good and thorough a job of it in six weeks.

Linderhof owes a large part of its charm to the beauty of its natural setting and to the fine and ingeniously planned French formal gardens, designed by Karl von Effner, which merge almost imperceptibly into the green hillside. In the centre of the parterre in front of the palace is a large pool with a fountain whose jet rises to a height of nearly a hundred feet – higher, that is, than any at Versailles though far from the equal of the famous fountain at La Granja in Spain. There is sculpture everywhere; there are hedges of pleached hornbeam, pyramids of box, cascades, pavilions, a temple, carpet-bedding, lawns; and beyond the formal gardens nature has been allowed to take over. In addition, the park contains several buildings of interest. There is, as we have already said, the Königshäuschen (as the original hunting-box is called); and there is also a small seventeenth-century Chapel of St Anne, built by the Abbot of Ettal. The most visited of the buildings today are, however, the grotto and the Moorish kiosk.

The kiosk, which is made of cast iron and walled with zinc plaques stamped in relief, was bought by the King in 1876 from the owner of Schloss Zbirow, in Bohemia; it probably came originally from Paris, where the Moorish style was then the rage. It was erected, in a modified form, at Linderhof the following year and provided with a spectacular peacock throne made for the King in Paris by Le Blanc-Granger. In 1878 Ludwig also bought in Paris a small 'Moorish house', which is now in private possession in Oberammergau.

But undoubtedly the chief attraction in the park is the artificial grotto, constructed in 1876-7 a few hundred yards above the palace on the slopes of the hillside. Inspired by the Blue Grotto at Capri, and Max's very small grotto at Hohenschwangau which Ludwig had known since his childhood, this large and expensive 'folly' was furnished liberally with stalactites of cast iron coated with cement. It is entered by an 'open sesame' rock giving access to a long corridor leading to the main chamber, which contains a lake fed by a waterfall and a stage hung with a drop-scene representing the first act of *Tannhäuser*. The room was heated by means of a hypocaust, and electric light, the first full-scale installation in Bavaria, can be controlled to change the colours of the set at will – for instance to blue for Capri, or to red to represent the Grotto of Venus in the Hörselberg, where Tannhäuser dallied with the goddess of Love. On the lake, which could be ruffled by artificial waves, Ludwig kept two swans, and a cockle-boat, designed by Seitz, in which he used to be rowed by a servant. It is alleged that an attempt was once made to stage the first act of *Tannhäuser* in the grotto, but that the roar of the cascade and the freakish acoustics of the chamber rendered the singers inaudible and reduced the orchestra to a babel of sound; the story may well, however, be apocryphal.

Louise von Kobell says that by means of a mechanical device each of five different lighting effects could be made to play for ten minutes in turn, the programme concluding with the appearance of a rainbow over the Tannhäuser painting. The result, she agreed, was fantastic; 'but those who peeped behind the scenes found it sadly prosaic: a weary electrician, seven furnaces stoked by workmen to produce and maintain a constant temperature of *exactly* 16° Réaumur [20°C.],[1] and in addition the huge sums of money gradually swallowed up by the cost of the Blue Grotto. But the King had no desire to be told about the mechanics of it: "I don't want to know how it works," he said, "I just want to see the effects".'

There were other projects at Linderhof which never materialized. One was to replace St Anne's Chapel by a baroque chapel for which Dollmann prepared sketches and plans. Much more interesting and important would have been the theatre, intended for private performances for the King, which was originally to have been attached to the palace and then to have been placed where the Temple of Venus now stands. Several architects, including Dollmann and Ferdinand Knab, submitted designs, that by a young architect named Julius Lange being based upon Cuvilliés' Residenz Theatre in Munich.

In the neighbourhood of Linderhof was Hunding's Hut, a log cabin constructed in 1876 by Dollmann in imitation of Jank's set for the première of *Die Walküre*. Built round a big ash tree, it was furnished with bear-skins, weapons and trophies of the chase; it was burned down by rangers in 1945. Nearby was also a hermitage, constructed of logs to represent Gurnemanz's hermitage in the third act of *Parsifal*; it dates from 1877, but it was badly built and recently fell to pieces. Not far from Ammerwald, on Austrian soil, there was begun in the last year of the King's reign the Hubertus Pavilion, a new version of the Amalienburg in the park at Nymphenburg, another gem of the Bavarian rococo; it was never taken further than the rough brickwork, and after the King's death was pulled down.

One of the earliest of Ludwig's essays in the Oriental manner was the reconstruction, about 1870, of a little hunting-box which Max had built on an alp below the 6,000-foot Schachen, a peak of the Wetterstein range south of Garmisch-Partenkirchen. Externally it is a fairly simple wooden structure with a balcony – a house that at first glance seems almost Bavarian, but which also has its counterpart on the shores of the Bosphorus; Dollmann was probably the architect. The interior, after designs by Georg Schneider, is richly decorated in the Turkish style and furnished with divans and a central fountain; photographs of the recently built palaces of Beylerbey and Yildiz on the Bosphorus served as models. The hunting-box, with its superb view of the Zugspitze, Germany's highest mountain, may still be visited from Garmisch-Partenkirchen by the young and energetic.

About fifty miles to the south-east of Munich lies Bavaria's largest lake, the Chiemsee. It is a lake of the plains, spacious and placid, fringed with reeds, wide open to the sky but bordered on the south by the

[1] Not 15°, not 17°. This was achieved by 'fixing' the thermometer!

mountains. On it are three islands: the substantial Herreninsel with an ancient castle that once served as a college of Augustinian canons; the little Fraueninsel whose abbey of Benedictine nuns, founded in A.D. 782, is now a convent school for girls; and near the Fraueninsel a tiny and uninhabited scrap of land, the Krautinsel, which according to legend afforded a place of rendezvous for amorous monks and nuns. In 1873 Ludwig purchased the Herreninsel and decided to build on it the 'Versailles' that had once been considered for the Linderhof site. The following year he went to Paris to renew his acquaintance with the palace of the Sun King.

It was not until May 1878 that the foundation-stone was laid and the building begun of the last and greatest of Ludwig's three principal castles. Meanwhile Dollmann's original design had been considerably enlarged and a dozen times modified at the command of the King, for whom a suite of rooms had been fitted up in 1874 in the old castle so that he could stay the night on the island if he wished. What Ludwig envisaged was a monument in praise of absolute monarchy, a temple, as it were, in honour of his beloved Bourbons, and most especially of Louis XIV; the state rooms, which included a fairly close copy of the *Galerie des Glaces* and a *chambre de parade* that was finally far to surpass in exuberance its counterpart at Versailles, were never intended to be lived in. (The furnishing of the state bedroom is almost unbelievably lush: each curtain weighs a hundredweight, and thirty or forty women spent seven years making the covering for the bed.) For the King's own use, and not fitted up until after the state apartments – that is to say, not until after 1883 – was a suite of rooms corresponding to the apartments of Louis XV at Versailles; Hofmann, who had succeeded Dollmann in 1884 and who had already been working under him, was largely responsible for these, with the assistance of Franz Paul Stulberger and his collaborators. Of Hofmann, Kreisl writes:

> He was a very skilful decorator with great experience and a lively imagination, a brilliant draughtsman, a quick, resourceful worker, not a 'civil servant' but a human being and, in emergencies, enough of a diplomat to achieve the impossible. He was very versatile and at home in every style. He seems to have been an indefatigable worker. Men who worked under him described him as a wiry, bearded man, sitting at his drawing-board wrapped in a cloud of smoke, drawing ornament after ornament at a speed that seemed almost supernatural.

The casual visitor to Herrenchiemsee may very naturally form the conclusion that it is no more than an imitation Versailles. Certainly it is the most eclectic of Ludwig's three great castles; one has only to look at the garden façade or the *Galerie des Glaces* at Herrenchiemsee to see how closely Le Vau, Mansart and Lebrun have been followed. The staircase is an almost exact facsimile of Le Vau and Lebrun's *Escalier des Ambassadeurs*, destroyed in 1752 but known from engravings. But there is throughout much in the detail of the decoration which must be considered as German, rather than French, neo-rococo. Here, as at Linderhof and Neuschwanstein, enormous stimulus was given to the arts and crafts workshops in Munich.

To feel the full magic of Herrenchiemsee it is necessary to attend one of the evening concerts, given there from time to time in the summer months, when the palace is floodlit and the rooms illuminated by more than four thousand candles; then, if one can bring oneself to forget the presence of the other visitors, one can almost believe oneself back in the Court of the Grand Monarque. And it was thus that Ludwig, who came in the end to live only by night, will have known it, in all the splendour of its glittering candlelight reflected in a hundred mirrors – known it, and loved it.

No Versailles could be considered complete without its gardens, and here again the general pattern, though not all the details, follows that of the prototype, but in a simplified form. There are a Fountain of Apollo and a Latona Fountain, a canal, garden sculpture, boscage. But whereas the Palace of Versailles is today confronted by a fair-sized town, that of Herrenchiemsee is isolated, girdled by water, and set against the superb background of the Bavarian mountains. Therein lies much of its charm.

Ludwig occupied Herrenchiemsee Palace on one occasion only: for ten nights in the autumn of 1885. At the time of his death only the central block and a part of one of the wings (since taken down) had been built, and already the cost – more than sixteen million marks – was greater than that of Neuschwanstein and Linderhof together. My palaces, the King once said, are holy places; they should not be seen by the mob, because that would 'desecrate and defile' them. How fortunate that he can never have guessed that the time would come when they would provide each year recreation and enjoyment for hundreds of thousands of chattering, footsore tourists from all over the world, milling through the turnstiles to gape at these 'follies' of the 'mad' King.

Two vast projects, neither of which was to be realized, date from the closing years of the King's life: a castle on the Falkenstein, to the west of Neuschwanstein, and a Chinese palace on the shores of the Plansee, on Austrian soil to the south.

The ruins of the medieval Castle of Falkenstein, largely destroyed in the seventeenth century, stand a thousand feet higher than Neuschwanstein and on an even more spectacular crag. It was in 1883 that

Ludwig first conceived the idea of crowning the mountain with a mock-Gothic castle. Jank's fantastic sketch was made in that year, and Dollmann was ordered to produce plans and elevations; but knowing that the royal coffers were by then almost empty, he (or more probably one of his assistants) designed something far more modest and economical, which the King scornfully rejected.

So the work was entrusted to Max Schultze, Prince Thurn und Taxis's architect in Regensburg, who was much flattered by the royal commission and little aware that there was small chance of any building ever materializing. Schultze designed a kind of robber knights' castle, a picturesque and simplified version of Jank's sketch, and at the same time (1884) a road was constructed and water piped to the summit of the rock.

But Schultze soon discovered that being Ludwig's architect was no bed of roses. The King was, as always, much concerned with the designs for his bedroom, which had constantly to be changed and enlarged; Gothic was replaced by secular Byzantine, and finally he settled for a kind of Byzantine church with apses and an altar. In 1885 the wretched architect could bear it no longer and resigned. From then on, Hofmann (who had just succeeded Dollmann as Court Architect) and another architect named Eugen Drollinger kept the King supplied with designs which, since both men knew that nothing would ever be built, could safely be made as fanciful, costly and impracticable as he wished. Drollinger was actually at work on a fourth scheme for the bedroom, which was now to have stained glass windows and a mosaic dome, when news reached him that the King was dead.

The Chinese palace was yet another project for which, in January 1886, Hofmann produced designs in the knowledge that he could give his fantasy full rein. It was to be based on the Winter Palace in Pekin and was envisaged by Ludwig as the setting for elaborate Chinese ceremonial for which he and his courtiers would wear Chinese dress.

Such were the castles, palaces and pleasure pavilions that Ludwig built or hoped to build. For the last eighteen years of his life they afforded him a happiness that he was never to find, except fleetingly, in a human relationship: an outlet for his creative urge, a substitute for living, and a way of escape from the harshness of a real world which grew ever more distasteful to him.

Chapter Twelve

KING OF THE ALPS

It is not easy to say at what precise moment it began to be whispered in Munich that the King's mind might be seriously deranged.

Very soon after his accession it had become apparent that Ludwig was eccentric, capricious and morbidly shy, and it could not be denied that his worship of Wagner was extravagant. Then with the dismissal of Wagner and in due course the announcement of his engagement came the hope that he had taken himself in hand, that all would be well; but with the breakdown of that engagement tongues certainly began to wag. In the early seventies Ludwig, though he sought every excuse to escape from the capital, still showed himself from time to time to his people on such annual public occasions as the Corpus Christi procession; he always found a certain pleasure in stately ceremonial.

Chivalry particularly appealed to him. He was Grand Master of the Order of St George, the Bavarian equivalent of the English Order of the Garter, and a painting attributed to Friedrich Eibner (c. 1875) shows the King giving the accolade in the Court chapel of the Residenz and clearly enjoying the occasion. The sculptress Elisabeth Ney – one of the few women with whom the King found himself at ease – made a clay model of the King in his Grand Master's robes, which was later copied in marble by a Berlin sculptor; and there is also a well-known posthumous portrait of the King in his robes, by Schachinger (1887). The ceremonies of the Order included a banquet at which Ludwig, when he chose to be present, was to be seen in his sunniest mood. He attended for the last time on St George's Day 1880.

After the middle seventies the King, even during his compulsory annual sojourn in the capital, had become virtually invisible to his loyal subjects; a military review in August 1875, at which he received a great ovation, was probably his last public appearance there. He would not even take part in the festivities in 1880 to celebrate the seven-hundredth anniversary of Wittelsbach rule in Bavaria. 'Everyone tried to force me to be present,' he said, 'but I wouldn't go. What could possibly happen if I didn't? There wouldn't be a revolution.' Ludwig von Bürkel, at that time Court Secretary, describes the effort that he made to persuade the King to change his mind:

I pressed him, telling him how his people loved him and what a reception Munich would give him after all these years. 'I can't! I can't!' he cried, beating his brow. 'It's dreadful! I can't any longer stand being stared at by thousands of people. I can't stand having to smile and to bow a thousand times, having to ask questions of people who are nothing to me and listen to answers that bore me. No! no! I can't come out of my shell not ever again!' Then, softly and sadly, he added, 'Sometimes when I am tired of reading and everything is silent as the grave, I feel the irresistible need to hear a human voice. So I summon a lackey or a postillion and get him to tell me about his home and his family.' And it tore my heart-strings when he concluded by saying, 'If I didn't, I would lose the power of speech.'

Ludwig's brother Otto, though he had been seriously disturbed mentally for several years past, was also present at the review in 1875; but not long afterwards he was pronounced incurably insane. He had been living at Nymphenburg under mild restraint since 1871, and his recent but happily rare appearances in public had sometimes proved an embarrassment. During High Mass in the Frauenkirche on Corpus Christi Day 1875 he had caused a public scandal by bursting into the church 'dressed in a shooting jacket and wide-awake', throwing himself on the altar steps at the feet of the Archbishop and loudly confessing his sins. Thereafter it became necessary to keep a closer watch on him, and finally, when all hopes of a recovery had been abandoned, he was deprived of his liberty.

Otto's fate affected Ludwig deeply – not so much on personal grounds, for the two had never been close, but because he could no longer conceal from himself the possibility that before long he might follow in his brother's footsteps; there can be no doubt that his increased withdrawal from the world from 1876 onwards was the direct result of Otto's condition. At first the King paid fairly regular visits to Fürstenried, the castle on the outskirts of Munich in which Otto was confined; he had forbidden the use of any kind of force, and he was the only person who could calm him in his mad outbreaks. But soon the strain of these visits became intolerable to the King and they had to be discontinued.

Otto was, in name only, King of Bavaria from 1886 until 1913, when his first cousin, Ludwig (III), brashly assumed the crown. Otto died in 1916 and two years later Ludwig was dethroned, bringing to an end, after more than seven hundred years, the rule of the Wittelsbachs in Bavaria.

One of the first eccentricities of the King to arouse comment was his habit of turning night into day; his beloved Louis XIV was the Sun King, and Ludwig might well be dubbed the Moon King. Already in 1865 we find him instructing Pfistermeister to install an artificial moon and rainbow in his bedroom at Hohenschwangau, where the ceiling was painted with orange trees against a blue sky and a little fountain played to create the illusion that he was sleeping à la belle étoile; and at a later date we read of his ordering Bürkel to arrange for the repair of the moon, 'which is shining much less brightly than it used to'.

And how did the King spend his wakeful nights? In February 1868 Graf Trauttmansdorff, writing to a friend in Vienna, records one singular nocturnal activity which was at that time taking place in the Court riding school:

> The King likes to imagine that he is riding to some particular place. He calculates the distances according to the circumference of the riding school, and then, night after night, rides round and round from 8 o'clock in the evening until 2 or 3 o'clock in the morning, followed by a groom and changing horses when necessary. After several hours he dismounts and has a picnic supper brought to him on the spot, then remounts and rides on until he calculates that he has reached his goal.... The groom who recently rode with him 'from Munich to Innsbruck' received in reward a gold watch and chain.

Trauttmansdorff adds that this strange behaviour was giving rise to a good deal of malevolent gossip in the town, but that he himself saw in it no more than the expression of the King's very lively imagination.

When Ludwig was in the country his night riding had no longer to be bounded by the four walls of a riding school, and soon the stories of his midnight excursions in the valleys of the Bavarian Alps and into the Tyrol became legendary. Even in the depths of winter the peasants, snug in their warm beds, might hear the bells of his gilded rococo sleigh and the muffled tread of galloping horses – for the King had an almost twentieth-century passion for speed – rushing past beneath their windows. And sometimes, when caught in a sudden blizzard, he would seek refuge in a woodman's hut. The family would hurriedly dress, logs would be piled on the stove and beer brought, while the King chatted easily with his host; he was never shy or silent in the company of simple people. Then, the storm abating, he would wrap himself up again in his huge fur coat, pick up the broad-brimmed hat with its sparkling diamond clasp and vanish once more into the night. And a few days later some inappropriate gift, such as a great bunch of lilies from the hot-houses at Nymphenburg, would be delivered in gratitude for hospitality received – tangible proof that the royal visit had after all been a reality and not a dream.

A charming account of a nocturnal jaunt made within a few months of Ludwig's death is given by a young trooper named Thomas Osterauer, who was sometimes his companion on these occasions. At 2 o'clock one morning they found themselves in a small village in the Tyrol. Noticing a skittle-alley next to the village inn, the King alighted and said that he would like to try the game. Osterauer describes what then ensued:

I set up the skittles and rolled the ball to him. The King had had three or four shots when I suddenly heard the sound of swearing, and the innkeeper appeared on the scene; he was dressed in his pants and carried a hefty stick, and he was making a fearful shindy. The King sprang out of the alley and ran off across country while I leaped forward, ball in hand. When the inn-keeper found himself face to face with me – I was in full uniform, which we had to wear on Sundays and holidays – he opened his eyes and mouth wide, dropped the stick, turned on his heels and ran into the house, bolting the door after him. I went in pursuit of the King, who imagined that the inn-keeper was at my heels; but after I had called to him a number of times he calmed down. . . . Two days later came a letter from the inn-keeper, begging for forgiveness.

Excursions were of course also made by day. The writer Ludwig Thoma, whose father was the King's head ranger in the Vorderriss, recalls in his autobiography his boyish impressions of the visits of the King to the little royal hunting-lodge. Often there was only very short notice of his intention: an hour or two beforehand an outrider would appear, and then there was feverish activity to get everything ready in time. The pebble-strewn drive was swept, flowers were gathered and garlands made. Now for the children came the excitement of the arrival of the kitchen and provision waggons, with chefs and lackeys bustling about their duties and shouting orders that broke the habitual silence of the mountain solitude.

Soon the Thoma family and the other rangers and their wives, all in their Sunday best, were assembled and waiting. Then suddenly the gates were flung open by outriders and the royal carriage entered the drive at a spanking pace. The King greeted everyone and took off his 'Scotch cap trimmed with ribbons' (i.e. glengarry), while Frau Thoma presented him with a bouquet of hastily gathered garden flowers or wild *Alpenrosen*. Then Thoma approached the carriage and exchanged a few words with the King, who alighted and entered the hunting-lodge with his suite.

What chiefly made such occasions memorable to young Thoma and the other children was the lavish distribution of cakes and ices which the kindly cooks never forgot; in fact, for many years to come Ludwig Thoma thought of kingly power and splendour solely in terms of the delicacies he associated with them.

As the years passed, the King took a steadily decreasing interest in government and parliamentary affairs. But papers still had to be signed, and it may well be imagined what difficulty his ministers had in tracking the Monarch down when, as often happened in summer, he migrated as the fancy took him from hunting-lodge to hunting-lodge. 'I wouldn't be my own Cabinet Secretary for anything in the world,' he once said. Occasionally a member of the Cabinet, after repeated requests for an audience, might eventually find himself summoned at the shortest notice to some remote retreat in the mountains, and Louise von Kobell relates how her husband August von Eisenhart, when Cabinet Secretary, was instructed to wait upon the King at a ranger's cottage at Altlach, on the Walchensee:

> The ranger . . . had brought a table and chairs out on to the meadow, spread a red woollen cloth over the table and on it placed an enormous bunch of flowers, and banished the dachshunds to the kennels. . . . The King and his equipage arrived, then Eisenhart with his portfolio, and the session took place in the open.
>
> The setting was unconventional. Further off on the meadow the grooms had encamped and drawn up the vehicles in a row. The King, wearing travelling clothes and a glengarry, seated himself at the table. Behind him, stiff as ramrods, stood two lackeys, while in front of him, standing also, was the head of his Cabinet in a black morning coat, his opera hat under his arm, loudly declaiming the proposals and suggestions of the various ministers. Now and again there intruded the sound of a cow-bell or the barking of the dogs, angry at being shut up.
>
> As soon as the King had come to his last decision and signed the documents, he politely took leave of his Secretary and made a sign, whereupon as if by magic the whole company vanished.

Since the King disliked dogs, especially barking dogs, it is surprising that he did not order these dachshunds to be removed out of earshot. It was a great pity that he was no dog-lover, for might he not perhaps have found in a dog the faithful friend that always eluded him in man?

In general, however, Ludwig was fond of animals. He had always disapproved of hunting and shooting, and it was not merely on account of the noise that no shot might be fired while he was visiting any of his so-called 'hunting-lodges'. He was devoted to his horses, and it is related that he once invited his favourite grey mare, Cosa Rara, to dine with him. Soup, fish, a roast and wine were served; Cosa Rara ate with hearty appetite and then, to mark her appreciation of the unusual honour shown to her, proceeded to smash the costly dinner-service to smithereens. Another story is told of the King's tolerance of anti-social behaviour on the part of an animal. One day while he was in the mirror room at Linderhof a wild chamois suddenly burst in and, taking fright, did considerable damage to the mirrors and furniture. A servant ran to eject the animal; but Ludwig cried, 'Let him alone! At least he doesn't

112

tell lies.' Kipling wrote a poem which would have pleased Ludwig; it begins:

> The beasts are very wise,
> Their mouths are clean of lies. . . .

But best of all Ludwig loved swans and peacocks: made, indeed, a cult of them. Once there were peacocks everywhere in the gardens of his palaces, and perhaps he had a fellow feeling for these proud, handsome and shy birds, in many ways so like himself.

The King knew all his rangers and their families by name and talked with them as though they were his equals. Sometimes he surprised them by an almost excessive informality, as for example by joining in their simple games or by seating himself on the grass beside a couple of young woodcutters as they took their midday meal. The peasants adored their romantic, friendly, warm-hearted, unpredictable King who would chat easily with them about the prospects of the coming harvest, discuss an agricultural problem, or knowingly appraise the merits of a newly-born calf; they called him the *Alpenkönig*, the King of the Alps. Yet this was the same man who in Munich was such a stickler for etiquette that he could rap the knuckles of a newspaper editor for referring to the King as 'he' rather than 'He', and who could write to his cousin Prince Ludwig:

> I observed on the occasion of Your Royal Highness's recent visit (as also on previous occasions) that Your Royal Highness converses with me in too free a manner, one which draws unsuitable attention to our cousinly relationship and which does not seem appropriate in the presence of the King. I am confident that Your Royal Highness will in future adopt that form of behaviour which all subjects must observe in the royal presence.

Even the Queen, to whom he now referred as 'the widow of my predecessor' or 'the Colonel of the 3rd Artillery Regiment' (an honorary title), was kept firmly in her place. 'I shall never cease to revere her,' he said to one of her ladies-in-waiting, 'because she has the honour of being the mother of the King. But there are times when she rather overdoes the mother and rather underdoes the King. I am the Sovereign; she is simply My mother, and at the same time My subject.'

The King could snub a prince and yet fraternize with a peasant; he might sometimes allow the friend of the moment to treat him with strange familiarity, though the licence to do so might suddenly be withdrawn; but it was quite exceptional for him to unbend, as he once did, in the company of a university professor previously unknown to him personally.

Felix Dahn, the distinguished historian and poet with whose work Ludwig was no doubt familiar, has left a most interesting, and one must presume reliable, account of a remarkable afternoon and evening which he spent with the King in August 1873 in the Schachen hunting-lodge, when they talked freely together for nearly six hours on a variety of subjects. Dahn was deeply impressed to find that this 'fanatical Wagnerian' was extremely well informed on international affairs and that he was a cunning dialectician.

At first he had of course addressed the King respectfully in the third person, though he had asked permission to speak to him 'as man to man, not as subject to King' – to which the King had answered, 'Of course, of course!' Soon, however, they both grew heated, and when Dahn, who though a Bavarian had settled in Prussia, showed himself to feel a mixed allegiance to the two countries, Ludwig sprang to his feet and began striding quickly up and down the room:

Naturally I too rose. Again and again he stopped suddenly right in front of me, his voice now very loud and shrill, his pale cheeks turning a deep crimson, the veins on his forehead swelling and his remarkable eyes sparkling with extraordinary excitement. Yet in spite of all this I would never have imagined that this quick-witted, lively and, as I have already said, shrewd and thoughtful intellect was to sink into the night of madness.

Soon the 'Your Majesty' was abandoned, and when Ludwig began to attack the Prussian Crown Prince, Dahn, now angry also, heard himself saying, 'No, you've got it wrong! You don't know your facts! It all comes from your blind hate!' When Dahn slipped into the impertinent, familiar 'du' and called Ludwig 'Sun King the Second', the King 'went purple in the face, and I thought he might be going to have a stroke'. But Ludwig would not let his guest leave, again and again crying, 'We've nothing like finished yet.'

There is no space to record much more of this astonishing audience – if such it can be called – than a few stray scraps. When told that the Prussians regretted that he was still a bachelor, Ludwig replied, 'I could get married any day I liked'. Of his tutors he said, 'I hated the lot', and passed on to such violent abuse of his parents that Dahn could not bring himself to write it down. Of Wagner he said that jealousy had been at the root of all the trouble in Munich: courtiers, officials and the nobility could never forgive him for preferring Wagner's company to theirs. When the Army was mentioned, the King said, 'I loathe and despise militarism'; and to Dahn's admission that he would

114

far rather have been a soldier than a poet, he cried, 'Bah! Absolutely incomprehensible!'

Dahn fought bravely to make the King see reason where Prussia was concerned; but except for a confession of his admiration for Bismarck Ludwig would not budge. He said he had recently been told by his great-uncle Prince Karl that the Crown Prince, on his way home from Munich after the victory parade in 1871, had said to his officers, 'Look, gentlemen – a fine country! Within a few years I shall have annexed it all.' 'That's not true!' cried Dahn. Ludwig stamped his foot: 'So you call my great-uncle a liar?'

It was half past nine before the King finally brought the session to a close. 'It's late,' he said. 'You can't go down (into the valley) now. You will be my guest for the night. Nobody has ever before spoken to me as you did, and I thank you. I won't ever forget it. May you prosper!'

'I was tremendously excited,' wrote Dahn. 'He had taken my blunt attack on his pet ideas like a true King.'

A graphic description of the King's appearance and gait is given by a young man named Felix Philippi, who came upon Ludwig by chance in August 1879 as he was walking between Garmisch and Partenkirchen. Philippi was lazily enjoying the beauty of the summer morning when firm steps suddenly disturbed his reverie, and turning his head he saw – the King! He just had time to conceal himself in some bushes from where he could observe what took place:

> Anybody who has once seen this man will never forget it! His appearance was as singular as his way of life and his actions. . . . It would have been impossible for him to have looked otherwise. Everything about him was so peculiar as to be almost grotesque . . . was theatrical . . . was totally abnormal. He had no idea that anyone was looking at him, so he was not acting a part or striving after effect, and yet – what studied pose and gait, what calculation in every movement and every expression! The unnatural had become for him the natural.
>
> He stopped a few paces from me and took off his hat . . . and I saw his remarkable head with its very artificially curled hair and the deliberately stylized beard. . . . For a while he stood there breathing heavily and with his head thrown back – a head borne on a body of unusual size and, for his age, of no less unusual girth. Then he walked slowly away. In spite of it being summer he was wrapped in a heavy winter coat. He did not walk as other men walk, but took the stage like an actor in a coronation procession in one of Shakespeare's historical plays, casting his thrown-back head first to

115

right and then to left ... and carrying his hat before him with sweeping gestures.

At the cemetery in Partenkirchen he stepped into a waiting carriage – a carriage upholstered in bright blue, ornamented with gold, and drawn by four richly caparisoned greys decorated with plumes like circus horses – and vanished from my sight.

Many stories are told of Ludwig's kindness and generosity, especially to the peasants for whom, when times were bad, he created work by ordering improvements to roads in summer or snow clearance in winter. One day a young shepherd lad, not recognizing the King, approached him and in his broad Bavarian dialect asked him the time. 'Haven't you got a watch?' said Ludwig. 'How should I come to have a watch?' replied the boy, who a few days later was amazed to receive a handsome silver timepiece from the King.

For Ludwig was never happier than when he was giving presents. Each year by November Hohenschwangau had become a regular bazaar, stored with jewellery, silks and satins, photographs, carved ivory trinkets, vases and bottles of scent destined as Christmas gifts; but everything had to be of a size suitable for placing on the gift-table, and thus Otto failed one year to get the horse he had openly hinted that he desired. Everyone was remembered: all the Bavarian princes and princesses, the Cabinet and Court Secretaries, the Court doctor, the faithful groom, Hornig, who accompanied him everywhere, and all his servants; even his unloved mother was not left out. He always enjoyed the happy astonishment produced by an unexpected and extravagant gift, such as that of a costly jewel to a humble coachman. Above all he loved giving flowers: Trauttmansdorff related in 1868 that the King's distribution of bouquets to society women and actresses, young and old, known and unknown to him, had developed into a mania.

Many, too, were the books that the King gave to his friends; for he himself was a voracious reader and would often read through the night until dawn. 'Reading is my greatest pleasure,' he told Wagner, '– one in which I really indulge to excess; for even when I am driving through the loveliest mountain valleys I cannot do without it.' And to Frau von Leonrod he wrote in 1874: 'In my dear, poetry-steeped Hohen-schwangau, in beloved Berg, on the shores of the lovely lake, on mountain peaks, in the remote hut or in the rococo splendour of my rooms at Linderhof, my greatest joy – and it is one which never palls – is to steep myself in the study of interesting books (chiefly historical ones); for in so doing I find consolation and a salve for all the bitter and painful things that this sad present, this nineteenth century that I so hate, brings with it.'

Though remarkably well read in the German classics, in travel,

116

history and religion, in time he turned more and more to books dealing with the life of the Court at Versailles. It fell to the lot of Cabinet and Court Secretaries to procure for him everything available on the subject, to search for works long out of print, and then to report on them in detail. Friedrich von Ziegler, when Court Secretary, found the task impossibly time-consuming and was obliged to enlist the help of his wife; merely the titles of these books, wrote Ziegler's son-in-law Walter von Rummel, would fill a volume. Rummel continues:

> All the French Louis, the fourteenth, fifteenth and sixteenth, their wives and mistresses, the Dauphins, the Prince de Condé, the duc de Berry, the comtes d'Artois and de Provence, were woken out of their sleep. The whole glittering Court life of the period at Versailles and Fontainebleau was conjured up – the *fêtes galantes*, cavalcades, tournaments, jousting, high masses, parades, illuminations, fireworks, concerts, allegories and pastoral picnics. Then the theatre: the thousand tragedies and comedies both lyrical and heroical, the *divertissements*, heroic ballets, fairy-heroic comedies, pantomime ballets, dramatized proverbs, tragi-pantomime ballets and pastorals. Not merely the names and titles, but also the plot and full contents of these pieces, had to be discussed in detail.

To this already long list Rummel added the innumerable religious, military and Court functions and ceremonies and all else that contributed to the greater glory of the Grand Monarque and his two immediate successors. The King, as he himself admitted, made 'a religious cult' of the memory of Marie-Antoinette, about whose life he 'could never read without emotion'.

So urgent did this worship of the *ancien régime* become, that in August 1874 the King decided to face the inevitable publicity and pay a second visit to Paris. He again travelled incognito, accompanied this time by Graf Holnstein, Generaldirektor Schamberger and four servants, and remained in the French capital for a week.

War wounds were still far from healed, and his ministers had done their best to discourage him from going; there was also an additional risk from an outbreak of cholera. But the King was not to be deflected from his intention, to which Bismarck had finally given his rather grudging approval. While in Paris the King was the guest of the German Ambassador, Prince Hohenlohe. Once again Ludwig proved an ardent sightseer and naturally a good deal of his time was devoted to Versailles, where the *grandes eaux* were turned on (at a cost to the State of 50,000 francs) to celebrate his twenty-ninth birthday. Since his first visit he had made a detailed study of the palace and the Trianons, and now astonished his guides by his immense knowledge of these buildings. He also went several times to the theatre, where he saw the great Coquelin act, and spent a day at Fontainebleau.

Ludwig's exceptional height and extraordinary gait, especially his manner of lifting his feet high like a horse and then bringing them down 'as if crushing a scorpion', made him very conspicuous wherever he went; it was hardly surprising, therefore, that he was soon recognized. It had been feared that if this happened he might be greeted with cries of '*A bas l'Allemand*!' or otherwise insulted; in fact the only unpleasantness came from a handful of youths at Versailles, who followed him in the street imitating his '*Königsschritt*' (King's step) and were promptly arrested. Mild umbrage was taken that he did not call upon the President, Maréchal MacMahon, who failed to appreciate that this sin of omission stemmed from unsociability rather than from discourtesy.

Even the Press behaved decently enough, though the *Evènement* regretted that, in view of the large indemnity that had been paid to Germany, the King had not taken '*quelques billets de mille sur cette forte somme pour fair jouer les grandes eaux à Ses frais*'.[1] It was generally realized that Ludwig was an inoffensive, peace-loving man who meant them no further harm; as the *Figaro* put it, 'He is not a wicked Prince, . . . he never accompanied his soldiers except on the piano. . . . One would think that the Bavarians had taken him from a fairy story.'

By 28 August the King was back at Berg, full of new ideas for his castles and soon once again immersed in his dream world. But for a very brief excursion a year later with Holnstein to Rheims, where in spite of his incognito he was as much gaped at by the crowds of pilgrims on their way to Lourdes as was the cathedral itself, he never again returned to France.

In 1872 there took place, in the Residenz Theatre, the first of the so-called *Separatvorstellungen*, or private theatre performances, attended only by the King and perhaps one or two special friends or the minion of the moment, who would sit in the box immediately below the King's. In all there were to be no less than two hundred and eight of these performances, the last taking place a year before Ludwig's death.

This idiosyncrasy of the King's was considered by many people to be a sign of mental instability. But it must be remembered that at that time the auditorium of a theatre remained brightly lit throughout the performance, and that when the public were present it was almost impossible for the King, in spite of specially contrived silk curtains in the royal box, to avoid the inquisitive and distracting stares of a fair proportion of the audience. 'I can get no sense of illusion in the theatre,'

[1] 'several thousand-franc notes of this large sum to cover the cost of working the fountains'.

the King once said to Possart, 'so long as people keep on staring at me and following my every expression through their opera-glasses. I want myself to look, not to provide a spectacle for the crowd.'

The majority of the pieces chosen for these private performances were plays, many of them dealing with life at the French Court under Louis XIV, XV and XVI. Sometimes long-outmoded dramas were resurrected, sometimes local playwrights (such as Karl von Heigel) were commissioned to produce suitable pastiches. The titles speak for themselves: *A Minister under Louis XIV, Madame Dubarry, The Boyhood of Louis XIV, The Pompadour's Fan*, and so on. Düfflipp, who had been invited to be present at the last-named of these, was asked his opinion of it by the King; he replied that he found it bad, and could not understand what the King saw in it. 'I too found it bad,' Ludwig answered; *'aber es weht doch die Luft von Versailles darin'* – 'but the air of Versailles blows through it'. In addition to these plays on Bourbon themes, works by Byron, Racine, Victor Hugo, Schiller, Grillparzer and others were also given. There were forty-four performances of operas by Wagner, Gluck, Verdi and Weber, and eleven evenings of ballet.

Heigel was one of those sometimes privileged to be present at a private performance, which usually began at 9 or 10 o'clock at night. He tells us that every light in the theatre, gangways and staircases included, burned brightly, and that the emptiness of the auditorium was no more depressing than 'the half-empty house when a modern tragedy is being performed'. He adds, 'The King was invisible to his guests but not to the actors, and anyone on the stage who had nothing to do and no lines to speak could exactly observe the impression the play was making on the King'.

In *A Tramp Abroad*, by the American humorist Mark Twain, there is a comic and fanciful description of one of these private performances in the Court Theatre. It deserves quotation because Heigel records that he showed and translated a part of it to the King, who 'laughed heartily':

In the enormous Opera House in Munich there is some sort of machinery which in case of fire can call an immense water power into play. This could, we are told, place the entire stage under water. On one occasion when the King was the sole audience a curious scene took place. In the piece a great storm is introduced; the theatre thunder rolled, the theatre wind blew, the noise of rain falling began. The King grew more and more excited; he was carried out of himself. He called from his box in a loud voice, 'Good, very good! Excellent! But I wish to have real rain! Turn on the water!'

The manager ventured to remonstrate: he spoke of the ruin to the decorations, the silk and velvet hangings, etc., but the King would not listen. 'Never mind, never mind! I wish to have real rain: turn on the cocks!' So it was done. The water deluged the stage, it streamed over the painted flowers and the painted hedges and the summer-houses; the singers in their fine costumes were wet from head to foot, but they tried to ignore the situation, and, being born and bred actors, succeeded. They sang on bravely. The King was in the seventh heaven; he clapped his hands and cried, 'Bravo! More thunder! More lightning! Make it rain harder! Let all the pipes loose! More! More! I will hang anyone who dares to put up an umbrella!'

But it was not merely in his reading, his play-going and his building that Ludwig indulged his passion for the *ancien régime*; he came in time to identify himself with the *Roi Soleil* and to people his palaces with the inhabitants of the Court of Versailles. One of the kitchen boys at Linderhof told how the King, in the last years of his reign,

> would have no one present while he ate. Nevertheless, dinners and suppers had always to be prepared for three or four persons, so that though the King always ate alone he did not feel lonely. He believed himself in the company of Louis XIV and Louis XV and their friends Madame de Pompadour and Madame de Maintenon, and from time to time even made conversation with them as if they had really been guests at his table.

For Ludwig's nightly drives in winter through the snowbound countryside in his golden rococo sleigh his coachmen, outriders and lackeys were obliged to wear dress of the period of Louis XIV, and sometimes the King himself would exchange the drab costume of the nineteenth century for a blue velvet cloak and a velvet hat trimmed with huge white ostrich plumes. Even the *Königsschritt* was in part modelled on what he believed to be the Sun King's royal tread, of which Voltaire wrote, 'He had a gait befitting only himself or a man of equal rank, and which would have been absurd in everyone else.'

The King had told Dahn, in the course of their memorable talk on the Schachen in 1873, that he could marry any day he liked. This was of course in a sense obviously true; but Ludwig had long since recognized the grave obstacle to his ever making a success of marriage.

Further light on the King's private life was thrown by the publication, in Liechtenstein in 1925, of a volume entitled *Tagebuch-Aufzeich-nungen von Ludwig II. König von Bayern*: the private diaries of the King, covering the period from December 1869 to within a few days of his death. Their editing, described by Newman as 'a deplorable exhibition of pseudo-psychiatry', is by 'Edir Grein', an anagram of

(Erwin) Riedinger. Publication outside Germany and the use of a pseudonym were no doubt wise precautions.

The history of the diaries is said to be as follows. In 1886 Minister-President Lutz, in his search for evidence of the King's unfitness to rule, obtained possession, no doubt through a suitably bribed royal servant, of two volumes of Ludwig's private diaries from which he proceeded to make certain transcripts. These transcripts, which should afterwards have been placed in the secret State Archives, were retained by Lutz when he retired from office, and it has been suggested that he could have done this in order to prevent a comparison being made with the original diaries – a comparison which might have revealed something to his discredit. Finally the transcripts found their way abroad, where they were published by Erwin Riedinger, Lutz's stepson.

Since the publication of Riedinger's book almost all biographers of Ludwig, including such eminent and careful scholars as Ernest Newman and Werner Richter, have treated the material in it as substantially genuine and have made more or less extensive use of it. It should, however, be mentioned that one or two distinguished German authorities on Ludwig express grave doubts about the accuracy of the transcription; this problem, however, can now never be decided as the original diaries are believed to have been burnt during the Second World War. Thus forewarned, the reader must decide for himself whether or not, in his opinion, the extracts that follow bear the stamp of truth.

Written in a chaotic hotchpotch of German and indifferent French spiced with a dash of Latin and a word or two of Spanish, the diaries tell the pathetic story of Ludwig's anguished struggles to restrain the homosexuality which as King he had no difficulty in satisfying: of his constant falls, his bitter self-reproaches and his vain resolves for the future. His guilt complex – for he was deeply religious and had a strong puritanical streak in him – prevented him from finding any pleasure in behaviour that many people would today accept as at all events understandable in one of his temperament. He had the worst of both worlds.

The printed transcript begins with this entry:

AU NOM DU PÈRE, DU FILS ET DU SAINT ESPRIT!

I lie in the sign of the Cross (the day of the Redemption of Our Lord), in the sign of the sun (*Nec pluribus impar!*)[1] and of the moon (Orient! Rebirth through Oberon's magic horn –). May I and my ideals be accursed if I should fall once more. Thank God this cannot again happen, for God's holy will and the King's august word protect me. Only spiritual love is allowed; sensual love is accursed! I call down a solemn anathema upon it. . . .

---

[1] Louis XIV's motto, which roughly means, 'A match for the whole world'.

And he proceeds, as often throughout the diaries, to fortify himself with a tag from one of Wagner's operas – on this occasion words of Wolfram from *Tannhäuser*.

In the extracts here given, the German text has been translated, the French and Latin being left, uncorrected, in the original language:

De par le Roy

Not again in January, nor in February! The important thing is as far as is *possible* to get out of the habit of it – with God and the King's help! . . .

Postscript: *D[e] p[ar] l[e] R[oy]*

No more pointless cold baths . . . [11 January 1870].

Solemn oath taken before the picture of the great King: 'To abstain from every kind of stimulation for 3 months'. 'Forbidden to approach closer than 1½ paces'. [29 June 1871].

It should be noted that the 'Richard' referred to in some of the quotations which follow is not Wagner but Richard Hornig, his equerry:

On the 21st, the anniversary of the death of the pure and noble King Louis XVI, symbolic-allegoric final *sin*, redeemed by the expiatory death and that catastrophe on the 15th of this month, cleansed from all impurity, a pure cup of Richard's love and friendship . . . = pure and holy kiss . . . just *one*.

    I the King

21 January 1872

    Vivat Rex et Richardus in aeternum –
    Pereat malum in aeternum. –

In January, Richard with me on three occasions . . .! singing Residenz Theatre (Louis XIV sets). Court ball on the 31st. Rode with R at Nymphenburg. On 28th Lohengrin! . . . [3 February 1872].

De par le Roy
Let it be sworn on our friendship,
no further fall before 3 June. . . .
    Ludwig   Richard
On 6 March 1872. In exactly 2 months it will be 5 years since that blessed 6th day of May when we first came to know one another, never to part until death. Written in the Indian pavilion. [6 March 1872].

De Par le Roy
Il est ordonné sous peine de désobeissance de ne jamais plus toucher au Roy, et defendu à la nature d'agir trop souvent. [22 April 1872].

Never again as on 12 May 1872 and otherwise as little as possible. . . .

Even kissing must be avoided. [13 February 1873; this entry is not in the King's hand].

Our final excerpt from the diaries treats of Baron von Varicourt (or de Varicourt), a young cavalry officer whom Ludwig appointed his aide-de-camp after only two days' acquaintance. Clearly the King was as charmed by his name, in which he thought to find Bourbon overtones, as by his person:

> On 21 March spoke to Freiherr von Varicourt for the first time. On the 23rd appointed him aide-de-camp. Hail to the bearer of such a name! About this time (3 April) with Frh. v. Varicourt to the Residenz Theatre: *The Pompadour's Fan* and *A Private Audience*, then supper with him in the Winter Garden (Grotto), 7-1 o'clock. . . . Beyond any possible doubt my friendship will endure. After the Easter festival supper again with him till 2 o'clock. On 27 April, *Leonhard the Wig-maker* at the Residenz Theatre. . . .
>   8 days at Berg. On the 15th with Frh. v. Varicourt in the Kiosk, then a ride along the shore by moonlight till 3.45 a.m. . . . [1873].

Letters also survive which tell of the King's infatuation for Varicourt. On 13 April Ludwig wrote to him: 'Your character is lofty and noble; your every word proved this yet again to me yesterday. There could be no more beautiful or desirable death for me than to die for you. Oh, could this but happen soon, soon! I desire such a death more than anything else this earth has now to offer.'

But, as so often with the King's passionate friendships, Varicourt's fall from grace was as sudden as his rise to favour. A week or two later he dropped off to sleep while the King was reading to him. 'Varicourt!' cried Ludwig angrily. 'You fall asleep in the presence of your King!' Ludwig never saw him again.

Few of those who served Ludwig can have known him better and over a longer period than Richard Hornig, who figures so prominently in the diaries. Hornig, who was four years older than the King, had accompanied him on his Franconian tour in 1866 and entered his personal service the following year. His assignment was a difficult and an arduous one. Böhm writes:

> In all weathers he had to dismount and, bare-headed, adjust the King's ermine rug or peel an orange for him. For whole nights on end he had to follow him on horseback and many a time his numbed fingers froze to the reins he held. Often he could only keep himself upright in the saddle by drinking plenty of spirits. It was not until 1878 that he was given permission to follow in a carriage. . . .

The King gave Hornig a small property on Lake Starnberg, and would sometimes take coffee with him there. But the friendship was punctuated by fairly frequent rows; in 1871 there was a period of sharp disgrace, followed by a reconciliation which led to Hornig adding to his other duties that of acting as a kind of personal assistant and secretary to the King. Hornig seems never to have been quite forgiven for getting married – something harder for him to bear, the King is reported to have said, than the whole of the Franco-Prussian War – and in August 1883 came an ugly scene at Herrenchiemsee when Hornig tried to prevent the King from smashing with his umbrella some sculpture which, contrary to his orders, had been carried out in plaster instead of marble. Two years later Hornig, after nearly twenty years in the King's service, was summarily dismissed.

Chance preserved the private diaries from destruction after the King's death; one is therefore tempted to ask whether other embarrassing material may not then have been deliberately destroyed. There is no evidence that this was so, though it is known that certain objects were disposed of by auction. Böhm alleges that marble portraits of some of the King's minions were piously broken up, but a search of the royal account books is said to show no record that any such statues were ever commissioned. If, however, they did exist, then it is sad that they did not survive, as did those busts in which the Emperor Hadrian immortalized the beauty of his Antinoüs.

Chapter Thirteen

BAYREUTH

In the spring of 1871 Wagner and Cosima had turned their serious attention to the planning of the Bayreuth Festival. Their immediate concern was the finding of suitable sites for the theatre and a house and, of course, the begging and borrowing of money to pay for them and for the production in due course of the *Ring*.

There was first, however, an embarrassing obstacle to be negotiated. The *Ring* belonged to Ludwig; would he agree to surrender his claims to it, or would he stand upon his rights and insist upon the production of both *Siegfried* and the *Götterdämmerung* in Munich? Wagner's ultimate victory over the King was not achieved without a good deal of chicanery and one or two downright lies on the composer's part – for example, his continued refusal to hand over the full score of *Siegfried*, of which the last note had already been written in February, on the pretext that it was not yet finished. As for the King, saddened though he was by lies that can hardly have deceived him, he showed his ever-forgiving and noble nature by yielding with no more than a sigh, and his habitual generosity by subscribing 25,000 thalers – a sum which he later agreed should be put at Wagner's personal disposal for the purchase of land on which to build his house.

In a moving letter, written from Linderhof on 3 January 1872, the King sent Wagner his best wishes for the year which was supposedly to see the completion of the 'divinely-inspired' *Ring*:

Never can my enthusiasm for you and your godlike work grow less. . . . In spite of all the storms that often seem to divide us, of all the cloud-racks that thrust themselves between us, our stars will yet find each other. Even if the profane eye cannot pierce the thick veil to see their radiant brightness, we two will recognize each other; and when at last we reach the holy goal we had set ourselves from the beginning, the life-giving, all-illuminating central sun of the eternal godhead for which we suffered and undaunted fought, we shall account for our deeds whose object and content were to spread that light over the earth, to purify and perfect mankind with its sacred flames and make it the partner of eternal bliss.

Meanwhile Wagner was endlessly busy visiting the larger German towns to enlist support for his Bayreuth venture and to institute '*Wagner-Vereine*' (Wagner Clubs) whose members subscribed jointly for vouchers for a certain number of seats at the Festival performances. There followed a series of concerts to draw attention to the Festival and to raise money – concerts which proved a great strain on the composer and a serious interruption to the progress of the *Götterdämmerung*. There were, indeed, moments when he even talked of throwing everything up and retiring with Cosima to Italy. But at last the land on which to build the theatre was decided upon and presented by the town council, and a plot purchased by Wagner for his own house, to be named Wahnfried. In April 1872 Wagner left Triebschen, his home for six happy years, and on 22 May, his fifty-ninth birthday, the foundation stone of the theatre was laid; the architect was Otto Brückwald of Leipzig, who incorporated certain features of Semper's project for the Munich Theatre.

All hopes of presenting the *Ring* in 1873, as Wagner had once with his usual optimism intended, had long since faded. He spent much of the spring of that year giving more concerts and making more propaganda, but though he was much fêted the financial returns were disappointing. He became moody again and depressed, and to cheer him Cosima secretly organized a concert and other celebrations for his sixtieth birthday; to preserve the element of surprise, she even went so far as to have special copies of the local papers printed for his use, from which all references to these festivities, already the talk of the town, had been deleted.

But it was money, not jollification, that the composer needed; and though he told the King in June that everything was going well, he was conscious that it was not. In spite of all his efforts, only 130,000 thalers – about a third of the total sum necessary – had so far been subscribed. In August, therefore, he was obliged to approach Ludwig contritely and hat in hand. Through Düfflipp, the Court Secretary, Wagner was informed that the King, who was now heavily involved in his own building activities, was unable to be of any further assistance.

Wagner was growing desperate. Early the following year (1874) he appealed to the Grand Duke of Baden to lay the matter before the Kaiser; but the Grand Duke was not prepared to help. Perhaps it now came to the ears of Ludwig that Wagner had turned to Prussia for aid; at all events he suddenly relented. 'No, no, and again no! It shall not end thus!' he wrote to Wagner on 25 January. 'Help must be given! Our plan must not fail.' (*Our* plan, be it noted.) 'Parsifal knows his mission and will do everything in his power to help.' A month later the King granted Wagner a loan of 100,000 thalers; the contract and terms of repayment were drawn up in a legal document, and Wagner was informed that the loan was to be considered the King's positively final contribution. But it was just enough; Bayreuth was saved.

Two years passed, two years of ceaseless toil and incessant worries for Wagner and Cosima; it was August 1876, and all was at last ready for the long-awaited première of the *Ring*. Ludwig had promised to come; but he had made certain conditions, or at all events certain requests:

> In Bayreuth I wish to dedicate myself wholly to the pleasure of the noble Festival performances. Oh, how I look forward to seeing you again, my dearly-loved one, my deeply revered friend, after so long a separation! I want to avoid anything in the way of an ovation from the people; I hope I shall be spared dinners and audiences, and from receiving calls from distinguished visitors: I absolutely hate such things. I am coming to feast myself enthusiastically on your great work and to refresh myself in heart and in spirit, not to be gaped at by the curious or to offer myself up as an ovation-sacrifice.

The citizens of Bayreuth had of course prepared a civic welcome; the streets were beflagged and illuminated, the station waiting-room was filled with flowers. But Ludwig was too cunning for them. At 1 o'clock on the morning of 6 August his train, by pre-arrangement, drew up at a wayside halt a mile or two short of the town, near the famous Rollwenzel inn where Jean Paul (Richter)[1] had written many of his extraordinary tales; it was a warm night and full of stars. The King, Count Holnstein (his Master of the Horse) and an aide-de-camp alighted, and Wagner, who was waiting, grasped the hand that Ludwig stretched out to him. Eight years had passed since they had last met, and both men had aged; but it was the King whom time had treated the less kindly. He was no longer the handsome boy whose beauty had once charmed Wagner: he was bearded now, his limbs had grown heavy and his features had coarsened, at thirty-one he looked already middle-aged; but his eyes had not lost their fire.

Then King and composer drove away together in a royal carriage to the Hermitage, the little eighteenth-century country palace of the Margraves of Bayreuth, where the King was to stay during his visit. There was so much to talk about that several hours were to pass before Wagner, worn out no doubt by the great load of his recent work, was allowed to return to Wahnfried.

The 'general rehearsals' of the four operas of the *Ring* – they were tantamount to performances – took place on 6, 7, 8 and 9 August; it was these that Ludwig was to hear, his pleasure unimpaired by the stares of the inquisitive or the chit-chat of inescapable royalty. *Rheingold* was due to begin at 7 o'clock, and long before that hour large crowds had lined the streets in the hope of catching at least a glimpse of their elusive King; but Ludwig made a détour and once again disappointed

---

[1] Till the advent of Wagner, Bayreuth's most famous citizen. His works, no longer read, were much praised by Carlyle and have such improbable titles as *Biographical Recreations under the Cranium of a Giantess, Some JUS DE TABLETTE for Men, A Jelly-Course for Young Ladies*, etc.

his loyal subjects. Wagner, who had driven with him from the Hermitage, led him to the royal box and sat with him during the performance. Richter, the young rebel who had roused the King to anger by his display of arrogance at the time of the *Rheingold* première in Munich in 1869, was conducting the cycle, and the Wotan was that same Betz who had joined in the rebellion; but no doubt Ludwig had forgiven, though he can hardly have forgotten, these troubles of earlier days.

The four evenings of ecstasy passed all too swiftly for Ludwig. All had gone well with the performances, though there had been one or two of those little technical hitches inseparable from a production of such magnitude, novelty and complexity. In particular, some of the difficult stage effects had miscarried: the Rhine had misbehaved in the closing moments of the *Götterdämmerung*, and there had been no visible dragon in *Siegfried*; made in London in three sections, its head and body reached Bayreuth safely, but the neck went astray – having, it is alleged, been misdirected to Beirut. Such trifles could not, however, spoil Ludwig's passionate enjoyment of the general rehearsals or impair the outstanding success of the first public performance of the cycle.

For the rehearsal of *Rheingold* the theatre had been virtually empty, as Ludwig had ordained. But suddenly he changed his mind: he wanted to hear whether the presence of an audience would improve the acoustics, and for the three remaining evenings the auditorium was packed. After the *Walküre* the fountains in the Hermitage gardens were turned on and illuminated by Bengal flares, while the King wandered up and down with Holnstein and his aide-de-camp, sometimes in his excitement singing snatches of the opera. It was after *Siegfried*, when the King was again walking in the gardens, that the shrubbery suddenly broke into song: Wotan, Alberich and the three Rhine maidens had hidden there to serenade him. Lilli Lehmann (Woglinde) related, 'The King was walking to and fro quite close to us . . . there was not another sound in the glorious garden, which was lit by a brilliant moon. . . . Then, as silently as we had come, we slipped away.' The King was delighted and sent the artists signed photographs of himself.

In the early hours of the morning after *Rheingold* Ludwig had written an interim letter of gratitude and congratulation to Wagner, but on his return to Hohenschwangau immediately after the final curtain of the *Götterdämmerung* he poured out his heart to the Friend. His burning thirst for the *Ring* was, he said, still unquenched: he must return to Bayreuth for the final cycle at the end of the month, by which time he hoped that the Kaiser and most of the other royal visitors would have returned home. But he begged Wagner to arrange protection for him, by means of a partition or a posse of police and in the intervals as well as during the performance, from any princes who might chance to turn up:

Last December I could not easily avoid the company of my mother, the Archduchess Elisabeth and her children at a performance of *Lohengrin*. It was horrible! And in proportion as the *Ring* surpasses *Lohengrin*, so will my torture be increased if I have to be with people with whom I am obliged to exchange silly chatter. . . . I envy the idly-curious princes who come just out of duty to the first two cycles; is there a single one among them who has longed for thirteen years, as have I, for these Festival days; a single one who from his earliest youth had clung to you, as I have done, in unshakable friendship and fidelity, with an enthusiasm that never has and never could falter?

So Ludwig returned to Bayreuth. Wagner had begged him this time to show himself to his people, who loved him and who knew how much the composer, indeed the whole world of music, owed to him. At the end of *Götterdämmerung* the King, though it must have cost him much, took the composer's advice and stepped to the front of the box to join in the applause as Wagner appeared before the curtain. Nor did Wagner fail his benefactor, for in his speech he warmly acknowledged his gratitude to his protector and the 'co-creator of his works'. The King did not even shun the ovation in the streets. Perhaps for the first time he was now fully conscious of what he had achieved at the cost of so much past unhappiness; perhaps never in his troubled life did he come nearer to true happiness than at that moment.

More than four years were to pass before the King and composer met again – and it was to prove their last meeting. In the autumn of 1879 Wagner's health had broken down and he had been obliged to exchange the inclement climate of Bayreuth for the warmth of Italy. A year later, on his way back to Bayreuth, he spent the first fortnight of November in Munich, mainly in order that Cosima and the children might hear one or two of his operas in performances specially put on for him at the Court Theatre. On the tenth came a private performance of *Lohengrin* during which Wagner sat with the King; and two days later an afternoon concert at the Court Theatre, for the King and a few invited guests, at which the Prelude to *Parsifal* was to be played for the first time, the composer conducting.

The painter Lenbach, who was among those privileged to be present at the concert, described to a friend what took place. First, the King was a quarter of an hour late and by the time he arrived Wagner was in an irritable mood and the orchestra restless. Nor was Wagner's temper improved when Ludwig, who had been overwhelmed by the music, insisted upon the Prelude being repeated; but when there followed a demand for the *Lohengrin* Prelude, so that the King might compare the two, Wagner handed his baton to the Theatre's regular conductor and angrily stepped down from the desk.

So Lenbach, as reported by his friend. But Newman begs leave to challenge the accuracy of this second-hand account. At all events the incident seems to have left no unpleasantness behind it either with the King or with Wagner, who continued to correspond as affectionately as before. Two years later, however, the King did do something which deeply hurt Wagner: pleading illness, he refused to come to Bayreuth for the première of *Parsifal*. On the King's birthday the composer telegraphed to him a four-line poem beginning, 'You scorn the Grail's solace'. Now it was Ludwig's turn to be angry: Wagner had expressed doubt as to the genuineness of the reason he had given for staying away. Whether the King was really sick or not we cannot know; more withdrawn now than ever from the clamour of the world, he may well have become ill at the mere thought of a repetition of the conditions of his last visit to Bayreuth. In any case he no doubt preferred to wait until *Parsifal* came to him.

And this it did, but not until after Wagner's death: in 1884 and again in 1885, when on each occasion Ludwig was present at three private performances in the Court Theatre in Munich. Bayreuth provided the production and the principal singers, and the scenery was brought by rail in twelve goods-wagons. Herman Levi, who had also conducted the premiere in Bayreuth, described the Munich performances as deeply moving.

Wagner had died in Venice on 13 February 1883. Though he had been ill for many months, death came suddenly and unexpectedly, and Ludwig was overwhelmed when the news was brought to him by Bürkel. 'Dreadful! terrible!' he cried. 'Let me be alone!' and there is a legend that in the intensity of his grief he stamped so heavily with his foot that a floorboard broke. When he had recovered from the first shock he sent again for Bürkel. 'Wagner's body,' he said, 'belongs to me. Nothing must be done without my orders as regards its transport from Venice.'

The coffin was brought to Bayreuth by way of Munich, where an hour's halt was made. The station was full of mourners; there were flowers, torches, mourning banners; the Beethoven funeral march and Siegfried's funeral march from the *Götterdämmerung* were played. Lerchenfeld, the King's aide-de-camp, had come with an enormous laurel wreath from the King, but Ludwig himself was not there; he was alone at Hohenschwangau – alone with his thoughts and his memories. He had given orders that all the pianos in his palaces were henceforth to be kept covered with black crape.

On 18 February Wagner's body was buried at Wahnfried, in a tomb that he himself had prepared. A few days afterwards, according to the two very reputable joint-authors of the article on the composer in the *Encyclopaedia Britannica* (eleventh edition), 'King Ludwig rode to Bayreuth alone, and at dead of night, to pay his last tribute to the master of his world of dreams.' Nowhere else, to the best of our knowledge, is this improbable story recorded.

There was no necessity for Ludwig to parade his sorrow: nobody could doubt it. When, a few days later, the King read of the world's grief, he said, 'It was *I* who was the first to recognize the artist whom the whole world now mourns; and it was *I* who saved him for the world.'

Chapter Fourteen

THE LAST ATTACHMENT

Ludwig's deep interest in the stage brought him into close contact not only with actresses and primadonnas whose voices charmed him, but also with actors and male singers. Emil Rohde and Albert Niemann, for example, had received many marks of his favour; so too had Franz Nachbaur and Ernst von Possart.

The King had first heard Nachbaur in the sixties in Darmstadt, where he was then engaged as principal tenor, and had succeeded in bringing him to Munich where he had sung the part of Walther in the première of *Die Meistersinger*. Soon Nachbaur found himself invited to private audiences and suppers with the King, who once said that he was the most amiable and amusing man of his acquaintance. The friendship continued for many years, and Nachbaur received a number of letters from Ludwig. There was a memorable evening in 1872 when the King invited him to be his guest in the Winter Garden. 'We stepped into a gilded boat, which a servant quickly loosened before disappearing into the bushes, and glided away over the shimmering blue waters. . . . The King stood very erect in the boat and was wonderful to behold: his eyes sparkled, his lips were tightly pressed together; his cheeks were now deathly pale, now flaming red. . . .' And once, on a wonderful moonlight night, the King had suddenly stooped to kiss the singer on the forehead. 'You see,' Nachbaur told Böhm, who relates these stories, 'he was half a head taller than I.' Incidentally Nachbaur was fifteen years older than the King.

Ernst von Possart, one of the most famous actors of his day, had been engaged by the Munich Court Theatre in 1864 and later became its director. He was much involved in the private performances, and corresponded at length with Ludwig on the correct historical and artistic presentation of the plays. The King showed him much kindness, and in 1885, after the last of the private performances, Possart wrote sadly to Ludwig lamenting that henceforth he would play only to the banal and often ill-informed general public.

But of all Ludwig's friendships with actors the most sensational was that with Josef Kainz.

A very remarkable photograph shows the King standing, looking tall and aristocratic, wearing a thick travelling coat and hat in hand, while beside him sits - yes, *sits* - a very commonplace, rather plain young man, dressed in a ready-made suit and looking ill at ease; no doubt his embarrassment comes from his being obliged to sit in the presence of his King. He is a young Austro-Hungarian actor, Josef Kainz: the last and, Wagner excepted, perhaps the most loved of all Ludwig's Friends.

Kainz had arrived in Munich in August of the year 1880 to seek his fortune. Though he had received one or two very favourable Press notices in Berlin and Vienna there had also been some sharp criticism, and he had not been offered any contract. 'So ugly a *jeune premier*,' the critic Laube had written, 'will never win the hearts of the Viennese public'; and another observer confessed later that Kainz's 'misshapen nose and lack of calves were at that time more in evidence than his latent genius'. Yet, strangely enough, there were others who found him *'auffallend hübsch'* (strikingly handsome) and, forgetting his nose, praised his fine eyes and his *'beauté du diable'*. There are, indeed, photographs which bear this out. One shows a good-looking young man with wavy hair like the King's, wearing a velvet jacket and broad bow-tie; it is hard to believe that this is the same man who sits so disconsolately beside his standing King.

How are we to account for this dual personality? There seems to be only one explanation that meets the facts. Kainz, when he was at the top of his form, became self-assured and sparkling; but when he was tired, embarrassed or bored – and, as we shall see, he was not infrequently all these at once – he relapsed again into the rather commonplace son of an extremely commonplace provincial railway employee.

After Vienna, Kainz found Munich rather dowdy. 'A tedious, uninteresting place,' he wrote home to his mother. 'At every corner there is a monument, and a museum that costs a mark to go into. Don't for a moment picture Munich as a big city; it's just a little provincial town – like Düsseldorf, for example.' But for that very reason he found Munich much less alarming than Vienna. His fellow actors at the Court Theatre, where he had been fortunate enough to have been given the part of Romeo for his début, proved to be simple, friendly people who wished him well as he stood in the wings waiting to make his first entry. Certainly it was one of Kainz's good days: 'For the first time in my life,' he told his mother, 'I felt myself an artist among artists.' His success was immediate, and at the close of the performance he was offered a contract for a three years' engagement.

Kainz's more favourable Press criticisms and a couple of carefully chosen photographs were submitted to Ludwig, who was impressed. He was in the middle of a Victor Hugo phase: *Ruy Blas* was already in production, and translations of *Cromwell* and *Marion de Lorme* were in hand; he was looking for a Didier for the latter, and Kainz appeared to be just the man. So on 30 April 1881 the King saw the young actor for the first time, in a private performance of *Marion de Lorme*. Alone in his box in the brightly lit, empty theatre he studied

Kainz. Here, undoubtedly, was a new star: never before had he seen such fire, heard so rich and resonant a voice. A sapphire and diamond ring was at once despatched to Kainz, and two more performances of the piece were commanded.

Kainz's future now seemed assured. A golden chain bearing the symbolic swan, a watch studded with diamonds, were the visible signs of continued royal favour, and the young actor was even accorded the rare privilege of attending two private performances of plays in which he was not taking part. On these occasions he was not of course admitted to the royal box. In fact, King and actor had not yet met, though gracious letters from the former and stilted replies from the latter had been exchanged; so formal, indeed, was Kainz's style that he was given the hint to cut down the honorific *Allerdurchlauchtigst, Allergnädigst, Alleruntertänigst* and *Allerhuldvollst* to a respectful minimum.

One morning while Kainz was rehearsing *Richard II* he found himself summoned to the director's office. Here Hesselschwerdt, the sergeant of the royal stud, awaited him with the command to set out on the following morning for a three-days' visit to Linderhof. The expedition was to remain secret; only at Kainz's urgent request was the Theatre director, Perfall, made a party to it, the actor's absence during important rehearsals requiring explanation.

Kainz has left a brief but lively account of the anxieties and embarrassments of his visit to Linderhof and his later experiences with the King. There was trouble from the very start. At some point on his journey he had the misfortune to run into one of his colleagues from the Theatre, and was obliged to return to Munich to put him off the scent; consequently it was not until seven in the evening that he reached Murnau station, where the royal coachman had been waiting in growing irritation since 10 a.m. to drive him to Linderhof. At two in the morning, weak from hunger, dog-tired and in a state bordering upon panic, he reached the palace; he was one of those unfortunate people who cannot do without quantities of sleep, and he wanted nothing so much as to go straight to bed for ten or twelve hours.

He was, however, conducted at once to the Grotto (blue-lit that night), where he found the King feeding his swans with scraps of bread. By now the whole affair seemed like some terrible nightmare to Kainz, who behaved exactly as was to be expected of him in the circumstances. 'Yes, Most Serene Highness,' 'Yes, Most Gracious Majesty,' 'Yes, Most Noble and Gracious Master;' not another syllable could he utter, and the stentorian voice that should have echoed and re-echoed through the Grotto faded away into barely audible whispers.

Towards midday the Court Secretary, Bürkel, was summoned by the King. 'Herr Kainz,' said Ludwig, 'is a pleasant and well-mannered young man, and I was much amused by his amazement [at the Grotto];

but I was utterly disappointed with his voice. He speaks quite differently off the stage. I find him completely uninteresting, and you must take him back to Munich at once.'

Bürkel, genuinely sorry for the young actor whose career would probably thus be ruined, begged the King to reconsider the matter. Ludwig hesitated; he did not want to be unfair. 'Very well,' he at last grudgingly consented, 'so far as I am concerned he may stay a day or two longer.'

The Secretary broke the news to Kainz. It was Didier, not Kainz, whom the King had invited to Linderhof, he explained; if only Kainz could become Didier, then he would triumph. So Linderhof became a stage – a stage upon which Kainz strutted and roared his way back into the royal favour. The three days were extended to twelve. There were drives together in the mountains, in a glittering coach drawn by six white horses. In the evening, and far into the early hours of the morning, the champagne flowed; the '*Sie*' became '*du*'; and Ludwig drank to the health of old Frau Kainz while her son intoned, hour after hour, immortal but interminable passages from Goethe, Schiller and Victor Hugo.

Ludwig was completely captivated. Here at last was the Friend whom, ever since Wagner had deserted him, he had been seeking. With Kainz, as with Wagner, it was the artist that he loved rather than the man. He believed in Kainz the actor; and time was to prove his judgment sound, for Kainz was to become one of the great names of the Viennese stage. Ludwig had rescued Wagner when all the world was against him; now he would enable Kainz to fulfil his high destiny. They would travel together so that Kainz might study the dramas of Schiller in the lands where they had been enacted. He had always wanted to visit Spain, and in Spain they would follow in the footsteps of Don Carlos. Then to Switzerland in search of Wilhelm Tell. To France; to Italy . . . and Ludwig began to build castles in the air more fantastic even than those that he had built in the Bavarian highlands.

One evening during supper the King propounded his plan for the Spanish journey. 'But Bürkel advises against it,' he added; 'he says it is too late in the season.'

'Bürkel is only your adviser,' answered Kainz. '*You* are King and Master.'

Ludwig sighed. 'Yes – but being a King is not always so easy.'

'Then why not abdicate?' suggested Kainz, his tongue dangerously loosened by the champagne.

How often he had wanted to! Ludwig recalled the lines of Louis XIII in *Marion de Lorme*:

Moi, le premier de France, en être le dernier!
Je changerais mon sort au sort d'un braconnier.
Oh! chasser tout le jour! en vos allures franches
N'avoir rien qui vous gêne, et dormir sous les branches!
Rire des gens du roi! chanter pendant l'éclair,
Et vivre libre aux bois, comme l'oiseau dans l'air.[1]

But Kainz must be taught his place. 'Never speak to me like that again!' he said severely.

From time to time the calm waters of their friendship were troubled by such sudden squalls. For Kainz was young and inexperienced; he found it difficult to gauge the precise admixture of intimacy and respect that Ludwig demanded of his Friends. He risked a good deal, for instance, when he told the King that he was moody; that he ought not to box the ears of his lackeys. But so far his slips had been venial – inviting sharp reprimand always, but soon forgiven and forgotten. The visit could certainly be considered to have been a success, and the young man returned to Munich not dissatisfied with the impression he knew he had made. He had but one complaint: he was completely exhausted by the late hours he had been obliged to keep. 'I could have endured anything,' he told his mother, 'absolutely *anything* – if only he had let me *sleep!*'

But then he remembered the presents he had received: three gold watches; a superb ivory cigar case engraved with a scene from *Parsifal*; four pieces of jewellery in the form of fleurs-de-lys, set with gems; two lapis lazuli clocks ornamented with jewels, and a lapis lazuli alarm clock; a goblet of beaten gold; a model gala coach, drawn by six horses, containing the figure of Louis XIV – all carved out of meerschaum; a wonderfully painted Nuremberg egg; a set of jewelled buttons in the form of lyres; two unspecified 'works of art', and a dozen pastels illustrating the story of Wilhelm Tell. Yes – the visit had certainly been worth while!

The difficulties in the way of a Spanish journey proving for the moment insuperable, and the heat of Spain refusing to abate even for kings, Ludwig embraced the lesser but more practicable project of a visit to Switzerland. This, as he explained to Kainz in a letter, was to be a mere 'preambulum' to a major excursion to Spain in the autumn. He had set his heart on a new production of *Wilhelm Tell* at the Court Theatre; with Kainz therefore he would tread the sacred soil associated with that immortal but legendary hero. He would make with Kainz

[1] The sense is: 'I am the first in the land, but as a human being I come last of all. How gladly would I exchange my lot for the care-free, open-air life of a poacher.'

the same journey that, sixteen years earlier, he had hoped to make with Kainz's predecessor, Emil Rohde.

The two friends set out together on the night of 27 June, accompanied by a retinue of six Court officials, three personal servants and two cooks; an equerry had been sent on ahead to make the arrangements for their stay. Ludwig, for some unknown reason, had persuaded himself that passports were necessary, and had obtained them for Kainz and himself in the names of Didier and the marquis de Saverny – the youthful, humbly-born genius and the generous, aristocratic patron of Victor Hugo's play; by travelling incognito he hoped to escape recognition, or at all events to avoid anything in the nature of an ovation. Vain hope! Within twenty-four hours all Switzerland knew the whole story.

Those who have a phobia about tunnels should not travel in Switzerland. Ludwig in a tunnel was invariably seized by childish panic; he feared assassination, he suspected dynamite everywhere. With the idea of getting the best possible service he had given orders that the locomotive was to be driven by the director of the railway in person – probably a man with little or no practical experience of the job – and it was further ordered that this man was to proceed at snail's pace through the tunnels. This merely prolonged the agony; by the time that the two travellers were approaching their destination, Lucerne, the one was in a bad state of nerves and the other completely exhausted.

In a vain bid to avoid publicity the King decided to leave the train at Ebikon, a wayside station on the outskirts of Lucerne, and to proceed by carriage to Kastanienbaum where the steamship *Italia* was to meet them. Unfortunately the boat was late, and while they waited on the landing-stage a large crowd collected. At last the *Italia* drew alongside. Her crew, doubled for the occasion, lined the deck in gala dress, and her captain, still more festively attired, invited 'His Majesty' to embark. Ludwig, anxious to escape as quickly as possible from the cheering crowds, stepped hurriedly on board. For a space peace returned and lunch was served. But as they approached Brunnen an ominous flutter of flags became visible on the quayside, a line of police and hurrying figures converging upon the landing-stage.

'I refuse to land!' announced the King. 'Proceed to Flüelen.'

As they were steaming past the Tell Chapel, Ludwig suddenly gave orders for the boat to draw alongside. He was told that there was no landing-stage. 'Then improvise one,' he said.

He himself declined to go ashore, but Kainz was despatched to examine and report on the chapel, which the painter Stückelberg was at that moment decorating with murals of the Tell legend. Stückelberg mistook the actor for the King, and Kainz did not disillusion him. On his return he told Ludwig, who was much amused until Kainz tactlessly added, 'It was awful being taken for a King.' 'Was it really so terrible?' replied Ludwig sadly.

Crowds had by this time stormed all the possible landing points, and Ludwig, who could not postpone disembarkation indefinitely, finally ordered the captain to put him ashore at Föhnhafen. Here a carriage was found to conduct the party to Axenstein, where arrangements had been made for their reception.

'Schloss' Axenstein, Ludwig always called it, and no one had dared to disclose to him the terrible truth: The Axenstein was – an hotel! It was a situation worthy of Tartarin or Don Quixote.

The carriage proved to be that great rarity – a genuine Swiss antique. Half way up the hill the main axle broke, a misfortune which gave opportunity for a new crowd to collect. And then came the culminating horror of the arrival at the hotel: the manager in his morning coat, files of bowing waiters, the gaping guests. . . .

'We leave tomorrow,' announced Ludwig.

'But, Your Majesty,' cried the disconsolate manager, 'we had hoped that Your Majesty. . . .'

Ludwig repeated his refusal to stay longer; he also refused to occupy the royal suite and insisted on changing rooms with Kainz.

At this critical juncture the situation was saved by a wealthy Swiss bookseller named Benziger, who came forward with the offer to put his country house, the Villa Gutenberg, at the King's disposal. Next day they moved in; 'and at last he is happy,' wrote poor Kainz, who had been bearing the brunt of the King's ill temper. In view of Ludwig's known rough treatment of his servants at home, it is interesting to read that Benziger's gardener found him 'touchingly affable and friendly' to his staff when at the Villa. He gave them handsome presents; and 'if a view caught his fancy he wanted his servants to enjoy it too, so he often took them all along with him. . . . Even the cook was not left out.'

Now the pursuit of Tell began in real earnest. Ludwig, an inveterate sightseer, was insatiable; Kainz was to be spared nothing. Every day, every night, the sites associated with Schiller's drama were visited and revisited; and everywhere the actor was obliged to declaim for hours at a stretch. Every scene was compared, rock by rock, with the poet's descriptions; and since Schiller had never been to Switzerland (he had relied on the rather vague recollections of Goethe for scenic advice), the descriptions proved to be highly inaccurate. Then the King developed a sudden craze for alp-horns. Alp-horn players were summoned from the neighbouring cantons and obliged to perform by night from selected crags. The King listened enraptured; nobody on Lake Uri could sleep a wink.

Kainz was rapidly approaching total collapse when the King suddenly had one of those brilliant ideas which caused inconvenience and discomfort to everyone but himself. Perhaps the most celebrated lines in *Wilhelm Tell* are those in which Melchthal describes the horrors of his journey across the Surenen Pass in midwinter:

> *Durch der Surennen furchtbares Gebirg',*
> *Auf weitverbreitet öden Eisesfeldern,*
> *Wo nur der heis're Lämmergeier krächzt....*

> Through the Surenen's fearful mountain chain,
> Where dreary ice-fields stretch on every side,
> And sound is none, save the hoarse vulture's cry....

Melchthal was to be Kainz's role; how could he play it unless he had suffered at all events a measure of what Melchthal had suffered? It was a pity that it was the height of summer, for though there was a glacier to cross there would be disappointingly little snow. Moreover, Melchthal had been hunted, hungry and alone, with nothing to quench his thirst but 'the coarse oozings of the glacier heights'; Kainz was to travel unharried and with four sturdy companions, a large picnic hamper, a dozen bottles of Moselle and half-a-dozen of champagne. But the best must be made of a bad job; Kainz should at least follow, step by step, the way that Melchthal had trod. Ludwig would of course play Heinrich von der Helden – that is to say, he would await Kainz at the village of Melchthal, a long but pleasant carriage-drive from the lake.

Kainz and his party set out at four in the morning, making, by the King's express wish, a detour to visit Walther Fürst's house near Attinghausen. At 11 o'clock the real ascent began. Kainz, who had never climbed a mountain in his life, started off at the brisk pace of all novices, but his enthusiasm quickly began to wane. A halt was made and the first bottle of wine broached. Thereafter the pace became slower; the sun beat down ever more fiercely; at increasingly short intervals the silence of the mountains was broken by the comforting sound of popping corks. It was nearly midnight when the footsore, exhausted party eventually reached the Pension Sonnenblick at Engelberg, where they were to pass the night.

The start on the following morning had been fixed for 5 a.m. in order that the travellers might cross the Jochpass and reach Melchthal by the early afternoon, but no power on earth could rouse Kainz before 11 o'clock. His feet were blistered, his knees ached; not another yard would he do on foot. If a carriage could be found to take him down to the lake he was prepared to go in it; if not, then he was going straight back to bed.

Meanwhile Ludwig was waiting with growing impatience at Melchthal, where he whiled away the tedious hours by distributing his portrait on twenty mark pieces to the delighted village children. At last he too returned to the lake, where Kainz had also just arrived. The moment was critical.

'Well,' asked the King eagerly, 'what was it like?'

'Horrible!'

Ludwig was deeply disappointed. Though his immediate anger was to some extent assuaged by Kainz's pathetic – and no doubt exaggerated – account of the miseries of the journey, he felt that the Friend had let him down. Well – he would give him the chance to make amends. Kainz, fresh from his soul-stirring experiences on the Surenen, must climb the Rütli that night by moonlight and recite once more the Melchthal scene.

Towards evening they embarked on the small steamer that had been chartered for the King's private use. Kainz of course wanted to sleep; Ludwig, on the other hand, wanted to try out the concerted effect of fourteen alp-horn players whom he had assembled on board. But even the King was forced to admit that at such close quarters the noise was no longer romantic, and the players and their instruments were put ashore at Brunnen. Then Kainz slept. He awoke suddenly to find someone standing over him. Panic seized him; he remembered that it was an unforgivable sin to fall asleep in the presence of the King. But Ludwig merely looked at him reproachfully. 'You were *snoring*,' he said, and turned on his heel.

While Kainz relapsed once more into deep sleep, Ludwig landed and climbed the Rütli alone; he saw that it was useless to try to drag Kainz with him. Tormenting doubts were surging in his mind: was this the long-sought Friend, or had he again been deceived?

A week later, on 11 July, the blow fell. Ludwig, still determined that Kainz should recite Melchthal's speech on the Rütli by moonlight, had dragged the young man up there at 2 o'clock in the morning after a long and exhausting day on the lake. The beauty of the summer night, the glittering waters spread below them, the moonlight upon the snow-covered peaks, had all combined to reduce the King to a state of romantic frenzy. He asked Kainz to begin at once.

Kainz said that he was too tired.

The King *begged* him to recite, but he again refused.

The King *commanded* him to recite. Kainz, completely worn out, refused yet again; within two minutes he was sound asleep.

Ludwig left him where he lay and returned to the Villa, determined now to break with him. Next morning he set out for Munich.

Kainz, as soon as he learned that the King had gone, started off in hot pursuit; now, when it was too late, he realized the full measure of his offence. At Lucerne he caught up with the King and, forcing his way into the royal presence, begged for forgiveness.

'It was of no consequence,' answered Ludwig; but there was little conviction in his voice.

The two men spent the afternoon buying antique watches for the King's collection. Finally, and at Ludwig's suggestion, they were photographed together by a local photographer. But the atmosphere remained strained: both knew that the honeymoon was over. Kainz was allowed to travel in the royal train as far as the frontier; then he continued his journey to Munich while Ludwig returned to Linderhof. When the moment for parting came, Ludwig embraced Kainz warmly and followed him long and lovingly with his eyes as he walked away down the platform.

It was not to be the end of their acquaintanceship, and indeed Kainz continued, until the King's death, to receive many marks of the royal favour. But Kainz had shown that he was not after all the long sought Friend. Once again Ludwig was alone.

Chapter Fifteen

THE CONSPIRACY

Ludwig's downfall was not the result of those *fadaises* and eccentricities of behaviour which conspirators made the principal pretext for a certification of insanity, but of his reckless extravagance and his neglect of the affairs of state; undoubtedly he was no longer fit to rule. How often during the last years of his life must his ministers have wished that their predecessors had encouraged him to abdicate when he talked of doing so; now he showed no desire whatever to oblige them, for without his throne and the Royal Treasury to which it gave him access he could not carry on with his building projects.

For some time past the King's financial position had been black, and each year it grew blacker. Though he received about four and a half million marks annually from the Civil List, by the spring of 1884 the Royal Treasury was seven and a half millions in debt. By Bavarian law creditors were allowed to sue the Royal Treasury, though it was doubtful whether they would dare to do so; to forestall the possibility of such a scandal, however, Emil von Riedel, the Finance Minister, raised from the Bavarian State bank a loan to clear the overdraft; it was to be repaid by annual instalments over a period of fifteen years. Meanwhile it was hoped that the King could be persuaded to 'cut down' on his castles. But economy was a word no more to be found in the royal vocabulary than it had been in Wagner's, and building continued more furiously than ever; by the summer of the following year the total debt had risen to nearly fourteen millions. To Ludwig the situation presented as yet no problem; he merely wrote to Riedel ordering him to arrange a further loan.

Riedel felt it his unpleasant duty to speak plainly. The Press was hostile, he said, the monarchy was threatened; the strictest economy was absolutely vital. The 'most truly obedient undersigned', as he styled himself, could not, he continued, 'with the best will in the world' obey; he could not raise the money. Ludwig was indignant that his command had not been instantly carried out. He wrote to the Minister-President, Lutz, that what was most urgently needed was a new Finance Minister.

Before the year was out the King was demanding the round sum of twenty million marks; he had one or two new palaces in mind and Neuschwanstein and Herrenchiemsee were still unfinished. The situation was rapidly becoming intolerable and there seemed a real possibility that Linderhof and Herrenchiemsee might be taken over by the creditors. To his faithful aide-de-camp, Graf Dürckheim, Ludwig wrote (on 28 January 1886) that if this happened he would either kill himself or 'leave for ever the accursed land where such a horrible thing had happened'. He continued:

I ask you, my dear Count, I urgently beseech you, to mobilize a body of people who are loyal to me, who will not be intimidated by anything and who, if the worst comes to the worst and the necessary money does not materialize, will throw out the rebellious rabble of duns. I rely upon your doing this discreetly and secretly, for ministers, police (whom one can't trust in this case) and secretaries (Klug, Schneider) must know nothing of it. These are officials who are frightened of the Chamber, the law, and public opinion; they are just a lot of old women, not the loyal subjects they ought to be.

At the same time Ludwig wrote to Feilitzsch, the Minister of the Interior, telling him that if he could no longer build, then he would be deprived of his greatest pleasure in life; he *must* have twenty millions immediately. Feilitzsch replied that there was nothing that he could do about it: a further State loan was completely out of the question, and 'rich people prepared to advance such a sum without any real security simply don't exist'.

Ludwig grew desperate. Hesselschwerdt relates that he was ordered to approach Prince Max von Thurn und Taxis (who had in fact been dead these fifteen years) for the loan, and to persuade Duke Ludwig in Bayern to use his influence with the Emperor of Austria. Soon the King's schemes for raising money grew even wilder. Aides-de-camp were to be sent to Stockholm to the King of Norway and Sweden, to the Sultan in Constantinople and the Shah in Tehran, to Brazil and to Brussels. In the last resort, men were to be recruited to break into the banks in Stuttgart, Frankfurt, Berlin and Paris. Ludwig was counting on at least four of his various enterprises succeeding; he felt as if he already had eighty millions in his pocket.

'In January or February 1886,' wrote Dürckheim, 'Hesselschwerdt came to me with an oral command from the King to go to England and raise ten millions from the Duke of Westminster.' Dürckheim pointed out how unwise such a step would be; he told Hesselschwerdt to inform the King that he had received the order and that he would write to His Majesty on the matter.

Hesselschwerdt replied that he could not give the message at present. 'You see,' he said, 'I'm in Naples at the moment.'

'What ever do you mean?'

'Yes – the King sent me to Naples; but there was no point in my going, so I stayed here. But I said I was going and that I would not be back till Wednesday, so I can't announce myself before then.'

Such being the situation, it was hardly surprising that the Minister-

President and the Cabinet felt obliged to take drastic action: the King must go. And since his brother was insane, his 65-year-old uncle Prince Luitpold, the next in order of succession, must be persuaded to act as Regent.

The King would have to be removed either by constitutional means or by a *coup d'état*, and the latter seemed the more practical way. For this purpose the first requirement was a medical pronouncement that he was incurably insane; for he was still popular, especially among the peasants, and public criticism must at all costs be forestalled. It was also necessary because without it Prince Luitpold, a retiring and unambitious man, would almost certainly refuse to fall in with their plan.

At least as early as January 1886 Lutz and his colleagues began to hatch their plot. Dr Bernhard von Gudden, the most eminent German alienist of his day, agreed to collect evidence, and after some initial reluctance Prince Luitpold said that, provided the medical report was conclusive, he would co-operate. Lutz also extracted, on no less than six different occasions, a pledge that he and his team would be kept in office under the new régime.

Gudden was soon at work discreetly collecting the tittle-tattle of lackeys and valets, especially of those who had fallen from favour with the King. In finding the kind of evidence he was looking for he was much assisted by Holnstein, the King's Master of the Horse – 'a brutal, reckless, unscrupulous adventurer', Newman calls him – who had himself incurred the royal displeasure and who in consequence now detested the Master who had once done so much for him. Since most of the staff in the castles were dependent on his good will his task was easy, and by the end of March the rough draft of the famous *Arztliches Gutachten*, or Medical Report, was completed.

The Report, a long document running in its final form to some five or six thousand words, consists chiefly of extracts from the depositions of past and present members of the royal household, especially servants. There is no smoke without fire; we cannot therefore doubt that most of the stories of strange goings-on in the castles, especially during the last two or three years of the reign, were at all events founded on fact. Some of them are confirmed by witnesses whose loyalty to the King was never in doubt. Hornig, though he might reasonably have borne a grudge for his dismissal in 1885, was at first very reluctant to testify and only did so from a sense of duty; it may therefore be presumed that what he told was true.

Gudden opened with an expression of deepest regret that this 'painful task' had to be undertaken. It must be remembered, he continued, that there was a strain of insanity in the royal family, and he instanced Princess Alexandra and, of course, poor Otto. Even as a boy the King had suffered from hallucinations and uncontrolled movements of the limbs, and from a neurotic shyness; for years past it had been almost impossible to persuade him to attend to State affairs. At Berg he had built his own little church so that he could hear Mass alone; and then there were his private theatre performances. His visits to his castles became each year more and more protracted, and even when he finally brought himself to a decision to return to Munich he would often walk for hours up and down the station platform summoning up the courage to board the train. Munich, he said, was 'a torment, a prison'; and as the train approached the town he would shout and scream with anger.

A torment, too, were the Court dinner-parties, which he often shirked or at the last moment ordered to be cancelled. For days beforehand and for hours on end he would excitedly discuss the list of guests, 'using the most extraordinary expressions', with anyone he encountered; on one occasion a minister who had come to report on important affairs of State was dismissed after two or three hours of such talk and without having had a chance to introduce the subject that had brought him there. When the King did attend a Court dinner-party he would steady his nerves with eight or ten glasses of champagne before 'mounting the scaffold', as he called it. At the table, quantities of flowers and épergnes had so to be placed that he was virtually cut off from his guests, and the loudest music was commanded in order to make conversation impossible. During the meal he would glare wildly through the barrage of flowers, or from time to time angrily bang his sabre on the floor.

Hornig, who had known the King for twenty years, reported that at first his master had felt a great need for company. On his nocturnal rides, which were generally made on moonlit nights, there were picnics in the woods to which young grooms and lackeys were invited. After tents had been pitched came carousing and children's games (the equivalents of our 'Hunt the Slipper', etc.) until the early hours of the morning. Later these picnics were discontinued; but still later came Turkish-style parties in the Schachen hunting-box to which troopers and stable-lads were invited and where everyone had to sit cross-legged on the ground, smoking hookahs and drinking sherbet. Oriental dress was normally *de rigueur*, but sometimes, rumour had it, young soldiers were made to strip and dance together naked. Similar parties were also held in the Hundingshütte, with the guests seated on animal skins on the floor and drinking mead from enormous drinking-horns. Yet though the King seemed to have plenty of time to entertain his servants, he virtually refused to give audiences to his ministers; according to Hesselschwerdt, towards the end of his reign the King saw his Cabinet Secretary perhaps twice a year and his Court Secretary not at all. Lackeys and barbers were entrusted with the task of finding new ministers and a new Cabinet Secretary.

It seemed uncertain whether the King still suffered from hallucinations. He often announced that he heard voices or footsteps, and when Hesselschwerdt could hear nothing he was told that he was growing deaf. When the King was alone he could sometimes be heard roaring with laughter and talking to himself so loudly that it sounded as if there was a party in progress. Ziegler, when he was with the King, was often reproached for looking at him 'with a strange and insolent expression on his face'.

Hornig mentions that when they were driving together the King would sometimes insist on their eating in the open in a blizzard or in a temperature well below freezing-point, assuring his shivering companion that they were at the seaside in the glorious hot sun. The King suffered from strange fantasies. To Hornig he once said, 'I dreamed I was breaking a large water-jug over the Queen's head, dragging her about on the ground by her hair, and stamping on her breasts with my heels'; and to Ziegler, 'I dreamed I was in the crypt of the Theatinerkirche, that I pulled King Max out of his coffin and boxed his ears'. He wanted to fly through the air in a car drawn by peacocks, and ordered the stage machinist, Brand, to construct a flying-machine in which he could pass over the Alpsee. Hornig was twice sent to Capri to check that the blue of the Grotto at Linderhof was of precisely the correct shade. Then there were the King's exaggerated friendships, suddenly begun and as suddenly terminated; after these friends had fallen from favour they could only be referred to by the first letter of their names.

One of the royal valets, a man named Mayr, testified that the King would tell him to 'take away that knife' or some other object, when in fact there was nothing there. Then the King would search for it for hours on end and ask where it had got to, why he had hidden it, and order him to put it back.

The King had what he called 'a holy tree', on the roadside between Berg and Ammerland, to which he bowed low whenever he passed that way. There was also a hedge which he greeted ceremoniously, and a pillar at Linderhof which he used to embrace at the beginning and the end of his visits there; but if he was only going away for a few hours he merely touched it.

The King often became highly excited, making strange dancing and hopping movements, pulling at his hair and his beard, or making faces at himself in the glass. During his outbreaks of temper, which sometimes lasted for hours at a stretch, he would prance round and round the room wringing his hands, then suddenly stop dead and stare fixedly at something. Sometimes he would play for hours with a single lock of his hair, or take a comb and ruffle it.

Hornig saw the King spit at a bust of his uncle the German Emperor

146

at Linderhof, while Hesselschwerdt received orders to collect together a band of thugs and take prisoner the Crown Prince, who was then at Menton, put him in chains in a cave and keep him on a diet of bread and water; he was not to be killed, because death would be too easy a way out. The King told Ziegler many times that he wished he could burn Munich to the ground – a disaster which in fact was very nearly to be realized sixty years later; he wished too, he told Hornig, that the people of Bavaria had only one head between them, so that it could be struck off by a single blow.

Towards the end of his life the King was constantly giving orders for his enemies to be imprisoned, flogged or driven into exile. He ordered his lackeys to seize Ziegler and one of his former aides-de-camp and put them to death. Two servants, Welker and Bieller, were to be transported to America, the former because he had failed to raise a loan of twenty-five million marks, the latter because he could not immediately catch a bird which had escaped from the royal aviary; Bieller was half throttled by the King when he dismissed him. The servants of course ignored these wild orders, but they took good care to assure the King that they had been punctually executed. Life was certainly difficult for the servants, for Ludwig's temper was more than unreliable; Mayr was obliged at one time to wear a black mask in the King's presence, and Buchner, a stupid man, a seal of sealing-wax on his forehead as a sign that his brain was sealed. Sauer was ordered to put on a specially designed dress and ride around Hohenschwangau on a donkey. Another servant, Marker, had orders to collect a band of men and blow up the Herreninsel.

Servants and stable-lads were often roughly handled by the King, and at least thirty cases were recorded of his striking or kicking them. Finally many of them feigned illness in order to escape from his service, and during the last year of his reign many were replaced by young guardsmen. A postillion named Rothenanger who was alleged to have committed some peccadillo was so brutally manhandled by Ludwig that one of the troopers had to come to his rescue; Rothenanger, a small and frail young man, died within the year, and it could not be ruled out that the treatment he had received might have been responsible for his death.

Sometimes the King left notes ordering the punishment of menials who had offended him; a number of these documents have survived, and though there is no mention of them in the report a characteristic example may be quoted here:

The wretch doesn't deserve to be allowed to come. Besides other misdemeanours he had the impertinence (and has long known it to be forbidden) to look up and to leave the room still looking up. He must be held down for a few seconds (it won't do him any harm) and have his head roughly banged against the wall. For three days, whenever he comes into My presence (except while serving at table) he must kneel with his head on the ground ... and remain kneeling until I give him permission to rise: this must be firmly drilled into him. For three hours of each of the three days when he is shut up, you must yourself tie his hands in order to bring home to him that he must submit to this humbly, otherwise it is all up with him and his life will be made a misery for him.

This kneeling with head on the ground, and other oriental gestures of servitude such as crawling on all fours, were the result of the King's study of a book dealing with the ceremonial of the Chinese Court.

Then there was Ludwig's passion for the absolute monarchy of the Bourbon Kings, Louis XIV, XV and XVI, and for their palaces. A former second lieutenant of the Bavarian Army received orders to establish absolute rule in Bavaria. At one time the King contemplated selling his kingdom for a vast sum to his uncle Prince Luitpold (who was in fact soon to get it for nothing), or else to Prussia, and with the proceeds buying another where absolute rule could more easily be established. A Privy Councillor named von Löher was sent, at considerable expense to the State, on several long but fruitless voyages in search of a country suitable for the purpose. Hornig reported that the King would secretly dress up as one of the Louis, and that sometimes when he drove by night he would wear his crown and carry his sceptre, both of which had to be fetched from a strong-room in Munich. Not content with Herrenchiemsee, the King talked of building a further Versailles in the Graswangtal. On the terrace at Linderhof was a bust of Marie Antoinette which Ludwig would greet by taking off his hat and whose cheeks he would stroke, and in the palace a picture before which he would kneel. Hesselschwerdt was obliged to do so too, and Welker had other and similar tales of the King's picture-cult.

After the dismissal in 1883 of Ziegler, once a royal favourite and the last man of education with whom the King had serious conversations on affairs of State, Ludwig lost all contact with the government of his country. Important documents and sealed despatches might be left unopened for days on end and finally be dealt with through servants; he was indeed now surrounded only by servants and lackeys, whose lot became increasingly difficult and hazardous. They were often obliged to speak to him through closed doors or communicate by scratching on them in accordance with an agreed code.

After a list of the abusive terms used by the King to describe his ministers – 'rabble', 'vagabonds', 'vermin' – there follows Hesselschwerdt's account, already quoted, of the King's wild attempts to raise money and his determination to carry on with his building in spite of his large debts. Then comes a general survey of Ludwig's physical condition – of the pains in the head and the insomnia from which he suffered, the latter driving him to an over-indulgence in chloral. The report closes with a disagreeable description of the King's table-manners, which had presumably been studied through key-holes or deduced from the state of his clothes after a meal:

> Valet Mayr testifies to His Majesty's slovenly, unappetizing and revolting manner of eating ... how His Majesty splashes the gravy and vegetables all over his clothes. According to Herr von Ziegler, His Majesty, having no teeth left fit to chew with, finds difficulty in digesting his food. . . .

Finally comes the summing up:

1. His Majesty is in a very advanced stage of mental disturbance, suffering from that form of mental sickness well known to alienists by the name of paranoia (insanity).
2. Suffering as he does from this form of disease, which has been gradually and continuously developing over a great number of years, His Majesty must be pronounced incurable and a further decay of his mental faculties is certain.
3. By reason of this disease, free volition on His Majesty's part is completely impossible. His Majesty must be considered as incapable of exercising government; and this incapacity will last, not merely for a full year, but for the whole of the rest of his life.

In connection with the last sentence, it should be mentioned that a clause in the Bavarian constitution authorized the deposition of a monarch who for any reason had been incapable of governing for more than a year.

Such was the Report. But even if its substance is accepted as true, the deductions made from the evidence are often far from convincing. Newman wrote that 'what seem to the casual observer crazy stigmas [in Ludwig] were nothing more than ordinary human characteristics that had been given extraordinary opportunities for exercise by the fact that he was a King with almost absolute powers, free alike of the prudent inner inhibitions and the severe restraint that keep the average man's indulgence in his desires within well-defined social bounds'. At the theatre he wanted, as we have already seen, to concentrate his attention on the play, not to be stared at by the audience; he therefore did what many people would like to be able to do but cannot: he commanded private performances. At State banquets, which he found as unutterably tedious as they no doubt were, he shielded himself from boring conversation by means of a screen of flowers and a barrage of loud music; indeed the time came when he escaped whenever possible from 'the whole conventional mountebankery of kingship'. Such eccentricities were adduced as evidence of the King's mental instability; in fact they were signs of extreme common sense. It could, however, reasonably be argued that he was, as it were, paid to do a job, and that in time he came to shirk not merely its fripperies but also its essential, though distasteful, obligations. He 'well remembered that he had a salary to receive, and only forgot that he had a duty to perform', as Gibbon wrote of a neglectful university don. But to be idle is not to be mad.

The charge against the King that he sometimes lost his temper and struck his servants is, if true, more difficult to explain away; but there are grounds for believing that reports in the *Gutachten* may have been much exaggerated. In 1887, when it was no longer a question of collecting 'evidence' to discredit the King, a former royal servant told Ziegler that except for boxed ears, which were always atoned for by the gift of a watch or a few thousand marks, he had never heard of or witnessed any rough handling of servants. As Ludwig von Bürkel, Court Secretary for many years, wrote, 'There were two souls in (Ludwig's] breast: the soul of a tyrant and the soul of a child', and servants who caught Ludwig's fancy were positively spoiled. Thomas Osterauer, a young trooper who entered the King's service in 1885 (and whose account of Ludwig's midnight adventure in a skittle-alley has already been quoted), received nothing but kindness from the King, who personally showed him all the wonders of Linderhof and its dependencies. It so happened that Osterauer's birthday fell while he was on duty at Hohenschwangau, but when Ludwig sent for him he did not associate the summons with that event:

I found His Majesty standing in front of a table which was decorated with flowers and on which were a cake half a metre in diameter, two pike with mayonnaise, two bottles of wine, two packets of cigars and several other things. . . . His Majesty said, 'Many happy returns of the day, my dear boy! Don't ever forget me, will you? All this is for you.'

I was completely bowled over, couldn't find a word to say and so had to send him my thanks in writing.

A retired cavalry officer, Paul von Haufingen, wrote in 1886:

During his last visit to Munich in April 1885 the King was woken one morning by the band of a passing regiment of Chevauxlegers. Going to the window he saw four soldiers who so attracted him that he sent for them and appointed them grooms of the chambers. He took them to the theatre with him, gave them jewels and other valuable presents; in short, nothing was too good for them and they were smothered with gifts and favours. One or other of the soldiers always had to play taroc with the King and the royal barber, Hoppe.

Soldiers suddenly preferred were often as suddenly dismissed and returned to their regiments, where the strange spectacle might sometimes be witnessed of a trooper with a splendid diamond and sapphire ring on his little finger, polishing a pair of his officer's boots. Ludwig has been compared to William Beckford, the millionaire dilettante and builder of Fonthill, England's Neuschwanstein. But Ludwig could not compose music or paint; still less could he have written a *Vathek*. However, Ludwig's castles did at least remain standing, whereas Beckford's folly collapsed. Eccentric though Beckford was, no one ever attempted to have him locked up; and the King, in spite of what Bismarck called his *Schrullen* (crotchets), would as a private individual probably never have been certified. He would very likely have been declared a bankrupt; he might, if the stories of his striking his servants are true, have been charged with assault and fined or even briefly imprisoned; but his sanity would never have been seriously called in question. Among the English and Irish peerage at that time there were not a few men whose eccentricity was as pronounced as Ludwig's, but who none the less continued to circulate freely under the discreet surveillance of a trusty manservant.

The meretricious *Gutachten* seems, however, to have satisfied Prince Luitpold, and all was proceeding according to plan when, at the beginning of April (1886), Ludwig took the surprisingly sensible step of consulting Bismarck. The Chancellor, who as late as 1883 had remarked that Ludwig understood government better than any of his ministers, and who had never ceased to be grateful to him for writing the *Kaiserbrief*, advised the King to appeal to the Bavarian Diet for a loan, and on 17 April Ludwig instructed his ministers to do this. Lutz was horrified when he heard; Ludwig's insolvency was one of the Minister-President's strongest cards, and it was more than possible that the Diet might loyally come to the King's rescue. 'The Chancellor has done us a bad turn,' he cried. 'I don't see how we are going to get out of this.'

A copy of the Report was immediately shown to Bismarck by Lerchenfeld, the Bavarian Ambassador in Berlin, who was in league with the conspirators. The Chancellor at first admitted that some of the evidence it contained was disturbing; later, however, he referred to it contemptuously as 'rakings from the King's wastepaper-basket and cupboards'. But he at once put his finger on the weak spots of the document, doubted the wisdom of a *coup de main* and recommended that the case for deposition should be submitted openly to the Diet. Could the evidence of lackeys under the thumb of Holnstein, a man notorious for his hatred of the King, be considered impartial? What conviction would be carried by a report signed by a single doctor who had never even examined his patient? (After Ludwig's death, when ministers and doctors found themselves exposed to some angry criticism, Gudden's son-in-law naively offered in explanation that 'an examination would have meant postponing action'!)

Lerchenfeld replied to Bismarck's criticisms with 'a tissue of evasions, sophistries and chicaneries', till the time came when the Chancellor sadly washed his hands of the whole sorry business. The conspirators, anxious at all costs to act before the Diet had met, wasted not another moment. The Report was augmented and modified in the light of Bismarck's comments, and on the night of 7–8 June it was signed, not only by Gudden but also by his son-in-law, Dr Hubert von Grashey, and two other medical men. Meanwhile the support of the public had been wooed by ministerially-inspired articles in various Bavarian newspapers which hinted openly that the King was no longer responsible for his actions. It seemed that every possible precaution had been taken when, on the afternoon of 9 June, a State Commission set out for Neuschwanstein to arrest the King.

Chapter Sixteen

THE CURTAIN FALLS

The commission set up by the crafty Lutz to apprehend and certify the Monarch consisted of five officials and a small medical contingent. It was headed by Baron von Crailsheim, the Foreign Minister and Minister of the Household, who was supported by two Councillors – Count Törring and Dr Rumpler, and by Lieutenant-Colonel Washington and Count von Holnstein. On the medical side, Dr Gudden was joined by his assistant, Dr Müller, and several asylum warders. It was a serious error of judgment to have included the recently disgraced and embittered Holnstein.

The party arrived about midnight at Hohenschwangau, where arrangements had been made for them to spend the night, and settled down at once to a previously ordered seven-course supper, the menu of which has survived. With almost incredible lack of taste it bore the title *Souper de Sa Majesté le Roi*, and records show that during the meal forty quarts of beer and ten bottles of champagne were drunk. After supper was over, Holnstein went round to the stables to organize the transport of the King to Berg. Finding one of the royal coachmen, a man named Osterholzer, getting a carriage ready for the King's nightly drive, Holnstein told him to unharness the horses because another carriage and a different coachman would be fetching the King. Osterholzer refused, saying that he was carrying out His Majesty's orders; Holnstein replied, 'The King gives no more orders from now on, only His Royal Highness Prince Luitpold'.

Osterholzer was loyal and quickwitted; he understood the danger to the King and acted promptly. Slipping away unobserved he took the footpath to Neuschwanstein, where he arrived breathless and was admitted at once into the presence of the King, who was just being dressed by one of his lackeys, Weber, for his drive. Osterholzer threw himself at Ludwig's feet and poured out his alarming story in so incoherent a spate of words that Weber was obliged to interpret them. Then they both implored the King to escape while there was still time; Osterholzer would be able to find another carriage.

Ludwig did not at first appreciate the full gravity of the situation. 'Why should I go?' he asked. 'If there were any real danger, Karl would have written to me'; he did not yet know that Karl Hesselschwerdt had deserted to the enemy. But he agreed that certain precautions should be taken. The local police and fire brigades were summoned, the castle gates closed and orders issued that no unauthorized person was to be admitted. Then he telegraphed for his aide-de-camp, Dürckheim, whose loyalty could not be in doubt, to come immediately.

Meanwhile at Hohenschwangau news of Osterholzer's disappearance had been brought to Crailsheim who, rightly surmising that the coachman had betrayed them, saw that they would have to act at once. So he roused his companions, and soon after 3 a.m. the weary and slightly absurd party (they had now changed into formal dress) drove off in mist and heavy rain up the winding road through the dark dank fir forests to Neuschwanstein; only Rumpler, whose function it was to advise on protocol, remained behind.

At the castle gates they were confronted by a posse of police armed with fixed bayonets, who were as little impressed by Court dress and glittering uniforms as they were by the information that the King was insane and had been deposed. There was no opportunity for Crailsheim to produce in confirmation the pompous document he had brought with him from Munich, for the police were openly hostile. 'Another step, and we fire!' cried the sergeant. 'These are the King's orders and we obey them.' The remainder advanced threateningly, and the butt of a rifle struck a bottle in the pocket of one of the warders and broke it. Immediately there was a strong smell of chloroform: the commissioners had evidently come prepared for any eventuality.

At this juncture an element of farce was briefly introduced into the tragedy by the precipitate arrival of a distraught old lady menacingly brandishing a parasol. This was Baroness Spera von Truchsess, by birth a Spaniard but brought up in Russia, the wife of the one-time Bavarian Ambassador in St Petersburg.

The Baroness was very amiable and immensely rich; but she was also very unstable, and a not infrequent inmate of Gudden's mental establishment. When not under restraint she entertained on a vast scale in Munich, where she knew and was known by everyone. For years she had been infatuated with the King, and had built herself a country villa at Hohenschwangau with the sole object of catching an occasional glimpse of him as he drove by. Everything that went on at the two castles was known to the Baroness almost before it had happened, and no doubt her spies had informed her of the preparations that had been made for the reception of the commissioners. At dawn she was woken with the news that a strange cavalcade had been seen on its way up to Neuschwanstein; she therefore promptly gave orders for her landau to be got ready, said her prayers and, armed only with her parasol, drove swiftly with her maids and her lap-dog to the rescue of her beloved King.

The commissioners saw with alarm the arrival of this Fury, who immediately began counting on her fingers the twelve 'traitors' and roundly abusing each in turn. 'You, Graf Törring – your children must be ashamed of you! Minister Crailsheim, I shall never play piano duets with you again!' Then, using her parasol as though it were a sword of Toledan steel, she succeeded where the traitors had failed and forced her way into the castle.

Ludwig was in his bedroom, dressing again after a short nap, when he heard a commotion in the adjoining room. A moment later the old lady burst in on him and, curtseying low, fell on her knees at his feet; she had come, she said, to carry him off to Munich and safety. The King helped her up and assured her kindly that he had no immediate need of her services; might he not summon her husband to take her home? To Dürckheim he said later, 'Had the situation not been so critical, I should really have had a good laugh over the old Baroness'; and an eye-witness of the scene reported that of the two it was not the King who seemed to be the lunatic. But when Ludwig learned from her that the commission included among its members Crailsheim, who was still his minister, and Holnstein who for so many years had been one of his closest friends, he broke into a rage and ordered the immediate arrest of the whole party.

Meanwhile a crowd of peasants – men, women and children, who had scrambled up the hillside from Hohenschwangau and the nearby villages – had arrived at the gates of Neuschwanstein where they began to threaten and harass the disconsolate commissioners. Angry, humiliated, soaked to the skin, Crailsheim and his team now realized that they had no choice but to cut their losses and return to Hohenschwangau. But hardly had they regained the old castle when the police arrived to arrest them and take them back to Neuschwanstein. This time they were obliged to make the journey on foot, running the gauntlet of hostile, jeering peasants, one of whom was heard to cry to her child, 'Take a good look at them! When you are grown up you will be able to say that you once saw traitors'.

Back at the new castle the prisoners were conducted to the servants' quarters and locked up separately in sparsely-furnished rooms. Holnstein tried to assert his authority by loudly ordering a good breakfast to be brought to him immediately. But no one took any notice of him; it was for him to obey, not to command. Even visits to the lavatory could only be made by permission and under armed escort.

Holnstein, no coward, was to say later that in his day he had fought two duels but that he would rather fight ten more than relive the hours that followed. They were all genuinely frightened; and not without cause, for at that very moment Ludwig, storming and raging, a medieval monarch in his mock-medieval castle, was said to be ordering his minions to put out the eyes of the prisoners and flog them till the blood flowed. Two days later the King denied ever having given such an order, and in any case Holnstein was in a position to know that the royal servants only pretended to carry out Ludwig's more outrageous commands. But Crailsheim was sufficiently scared to bribe a servant to smuggle to Rumpler a hastily scribbled note which read, 'Extreme speed is necessary; we are in mortal peril. The King has ordered us to be put to death; send help as soon as possible'.

In the event it proved a false alarm. As suddenly as it had broken out the King's anger abated, and at midday the commissioners were released, one by one and still intact, to make their own way back to the old castle and thence to Munich. The curtain had fallen on the first act of the drama.

The routing of the commission, which was followed soon after by the arrival of Dürckheim post-haste from Munich, had gained for Ludwig a valuable counsellor and valuable time; it was not Dürckheim's fault that his counsel was rejected and the time wasted.

Dürckheim's very sensible advice was that the King should go at once to Munich and show himself to his people. But Ludwig was weary now and seemed no longer capable of action; 'Eight white elephants' (as he liked to say) could not drag him to his unloved capital, and in any case the trouble was simply one of money: a few million marks, and all talk of his insanity would cease. Munich having been eliminated, Dürckheim begged him to fly to the Tyrol; but once again he was met with a flat refusal: 'I'm tired; I can't travel. And what on earth should I do in the Tyrol?'

Ludwig agreed, however, that Dürckheim should despatch telegrams from Hohenschwangau and Reutte to the Commander of a Battalion of Chasseurs at Kempten and to various persons who might rally round him, among them Bismarck. The telegram to Kempten was intercepted; but that to Bismarck reached its destination. To it the Chancellor replied with the advice given to Ludwig by Dürckheim: the King must go at once to Munich. 'I argued thus,' he later told a newspaper reporter: 'Either the King is sane, in which case he will do as I suggest, or he is really mad, and then he will not be able to overcome his dread of appearing in public. The King did not go to Munich. He took no decision; he no longer had the strength of will. He abandoned himself to his fate.'

As soon as it became known in Munich that Dürckheim had joined the King at Neuschwanstein, the War Ministry sent a telegram ordering his immediate return to the capital. Dürckheim replied that he could not leave the King. A further telegram arrived from Munich, this time in the name of Prince Luitpold and threatening the young officer with arrest on a charge of high treason if he persisted in disobeying orders.

Now Ludwig took a step which, though at first sight it seemed of little significance, must have shown Dürckheim that his master had ceased to fight, that he had surrendered to the enemy: 'Send a telegram to my uncle,' he said, 'and ask him if I may keep you here with me.' So it had come to that! Ludwig was *asking* the usurper of his throne – the Prince-Rebel, as he called him – for permission to keep his own aide-de-camp at his side!

But from Luitpold came no comfort; the order of the War Ministry must be obeyed. Dürckheim told Count Eulenburg later:

> I had to inform the King of the contents of this telegram and his appeal to me not to abandon him was heart-rending. But finally he said, 'I realize that you must go back, or your career and your future will be ruined.' Then he asked me to procure poison for him, and the more I refused the more he implored me. How could I get poison, I asked – even supposing that I was willing to agree to doing anything so criminal? The King replied, 'From the nearest chemist; you can get poison anywhere. I cannot go on living!'
>
> It was a terrible moment. But in the end I left: I saw that there was nothing more to be done.

Dürckheim presumably left Neuschwanstein early on the morning of 11 June. On his arrival in Munich he was arrested on the station platform, and at first there was talk of a charge of high treason. (It was alleged that he had been party to, if not the author of, a broadsheet challenging another that proclaimed Prince Luitpold as Regent.) But the charge was dropped and a few days later he was set free. His military career did not suffer from his loyalty to the King, and he became in due course General-in-Command of the 2nd Bavarian Corps.

Yet even now there was still hope. The peasants, who adored their King, were ready and eager to rescue him and escort him under an armed guard – for the Chasseurs were still loyal to him – across the Austrian border. Their emissaries, Osterholzer and Weber, came to Ludwig and implored him to give his consent: he had only to say the word and they would come for him. But the King would not agree: he would do nothing, he said, that might lead to bloodshed. Was it not really, however, that he was no longer capable of taking any active step? He would not help himself; he would not allow others to help him: he was lost. And soon the chance was gone. Like rats abandoning a sinking ship, most of his lackeys went over to the enemy and left the castle. The police at the gates were replaced by Luitpold's men; the fire brigades were dispersed, and on the walls of Hohenschwangau bill-stickers were pasting notices proclaiming the establishment of the

Regency. But for two or three still loyal servants Ludwig was alone – alone with his terrible thoughts.

Suicide was constantly in his mind. To the faithful Weber he said, 'Tell Hoppe that when he comes tomorrow to shave me he should look for my head in the waters of the Pöllat.' Again and again he asked Mayr for the key of the tower, but Mayr, guessing his intention, as often replied that it could not be found. Then, hour after hour, the King strode up and down the still unfinished throne room, now and then stepping out on to the balcony to gaze, calmly and silently, at the glorious panorama as if he were saying farewell to it.

A servant – usually it was Weber – was always at hand at a discreet distance, and sometimes Ludwig would turn and, as though thinking out loud, address him. 'Do you believe in the immortality of the soul?' Weber assented. 'So do I,' replied the King. 'I believe in the immortality of the soul and in the justice of God. I have read much about materialism. There is no satisfaction in it; it is not noble, for it makes man no better than the beasts.' Another time he said: 'They hurl me from the highest summit down into nothingness, they destroy my life; while I live they call me dead, and that I cannot endure. Had they deprived me of my crown, that I could have survived. But to deprive me of my reason, take my freedom from me and treat me as they treat my brother – no, that is intolerable. From that fate I will escape. They are hounding me to my death.'

'Drowning,' he said suddenly to Weber, 'is a fine death: there is no mutilation. But to jump from a height. . . .' It was no doubt with the intention of drowning himself that, during the afternoon, this man who had earlier shown himself incapable of action announced that he was going to walk down to the Alpsee; he was told that it was impossible for him to leave the castle. As dusk fell he grew even bolder and ordered Osterholzer to be sent for; he would after all agree to escaping to the Tyrol. But it was now too late: Osterholzer, threatened with instant arrest if he disobeyed the command of Luitpold's minions, had left Hohenschwangau.

'Won't my people come to rescue me?' Ludwig asked.

'The peasants, Your Majesty, have no arms.' Presumably the support of the Chasseurs could no longer be counted upon.

Ludwig strode once more up and down the room. 'I was born half an hour after midnight,' he said, 'and half an hour after midnight I will die.'

Throughout the long and terrible hours of daylight the King had remained relatively calm; but with the coming of night he began drinking heavily – a whole bottle of spiced rum and a bottle of champagne – and the drinking made him, as in excess it always did, not drunk but wild and excited. He knew that it was only a matter of time before *they* – the underlings of the Prince-Rebel – came to take him away. He needed Dutch courage to face the ordeal.

Weber was with him; his loyalty should be rewarded. Going to his study he took 1,200 marks in gold from his writing-table drawer; then he called Weber to him. 'This is all I have left. You have earned it; you were the most faithful of them all. Take it; I shall not need money any more.' The boy burst into tears and Ludwig, deeply moved, took a diamond and sapphire clasp from one of his hats and gave him that also. Then – and it is surely evidence that his mind was not wholly unhinged – he wrote a note to the effect that if the clasp had to be returned to the Treasury, Weber was to receive 25,000 marks in compensation.

Meanwhile a second commission had left Munich in the course of the afternoon, reaching Neuschwanstein about midnight. Gudden had from the first wanted a medical rather than a State commission, and this time he got his way: the new body consisted of two doctors (Gudden himself and Müller), several asylum warders and a senior police officer. Müller has graphically described what followed:

> Hardly had we alighted at [Neu]schwanstein when the valet Mayr, for many years a faithful servant of the King, came running towards us and begged us to hurry to the King's apartments; if we did not go at once, then the King, who was in a very excitable state, might throw himself out of the window. He knew that a plot was hatching and he was showing strong suicidal tendencies. He had many times asked for the key of the tower. . . .
>
> We acted immediately. The carriage [to take Ludwig to Berg] had been ordered for 4 a.m. and we had to protect the King from himself until it arrived. Gudden quickly decided what to do. . . .

His plan was to send Mayr to the King with the key, saying that it had just been found. Meanwhile the commission, supplemented by a small posse of the local constabulary, were to be divided into two groups: several of the warders would then climb a short way up the spiral staircase of the tower to prevent the King reaching the top, while the rest of the party concealed themselves where they could cut off his retreat.

The King, who trusted Mayr, fell into the trap:

> The servant took the key in to the King, while we waited outside in a state of the greatest suspense and excitement. I myself had never seen the King.
>
> Suddenly we heard firm footsteps, and a man of imposing stature stopped by the entrance to the corridor and spoke in short discon-

nected phrases to a servant who was bowing low. From above and below, we and the warders advanced towards the door and cut off the King's retreat. Then warders swiftly seized the King by the arms, while Gudden came forward and said, 'Your Majesty, this is the saddest task that I have ever had to perform. Four alienists have given their opinion on Your Majesty's condition, and as a result of their decision Prince Luitpold has taken over the government. I have orders to conduct Your Majesty to Schloss Berg this very night. If Your Majesty commands, the carriage will leave at 4 o'clock.'

The King uttered no more than a sharp, agonized '*Ach*!' then repeated again and again, 'What do you want? What does this mean?'

The warders now led him back to his bedroom. . . . In the anteroom there was a strong smell of arrack, which the patient had previously been drinking in fairly large quantities. One could smell it too in the bedroom, where the warders quickly secured the windows. . . . The King was swaying slightly, backwards and forwards and from side to side, and his speech was rather blurred; but it must not be forgotten that the patient had naturally been deeply shocked by what he had been told, and this could equally have accounted for the symptoms mentioned.

In the bedroom Gudden presented his colleague and each of the warders in turn to the King and mentioned that he had had the honour of an audience with His Majesty in 1874. Ludwig replied, 'Yes, I clearly remember it,' and proceeded to enquire about his brother Otto's condition. Then, abruptly, he said, 'How can you declare me insane? You have never even examined me.'

It was a very pertinent question. Gudden answered that it had not been necessary: there was ample documentary evidence.

'Indeed! Prince Luitpold seems to have managed very successfully so far. But there was no need for so much craftiness; he had merely to say the word and I would have abdicated and gone abroad. Well, how long do they expect my "treatment" to take?'

'Your Majesty, according to the Constitution, if the King is for whatever reason prevented from governing for a period of more than a year, then a Regency is established. So it would seem that a year is now believed to be the shortest possible time.'

'No,' Ludwig replied, 'it won't take as long as that. They can do what they did to the Sultan; it's quite easy to end a man's life.'

'Your Majesty, my honour forbids my answering.'

The warders, who had been seeing to the King's personal requirements for the journey, now began to ask various questions. Ludwig turned to them, 'Why can't you go away? I want to be alone; all this is so disagreeable.' The answer came pat: they had their orders.

Shortly before 4 o'clock the King, looking deathly pale, took leave of his few remaining servants and thanked them graciously for their loyalty to him in the past. To Mayr, whose treachery he still did not suspect, he whispered a pathetic request for poison. To another he was heard to say, 'Goodbye, Stichel. Preserve this room as a sanctuary; don't let it be profaned by the inquisitive, for in it I have passed the bitterest hours of my life....' Yet before the year was out the first tourist was to desecrate that sanctuary, and ever since then they have filed in their thousands through the private apartments of the King. Perhaps it is fortunate that Ludwig did not live to know how soon his last request was to be disregarded.

Schloss Berg had been chosen, in preference to Linderhof, for the King's incarceration as being more easily accessible to Gudden, whose asylum was in Munich. The eight-hour drive to the castle, all the way in pouring rain, passed without incident. It had been decided that the King might sit alone, in the second of the three carriages, but its inner door-handles had been removed, and there was an asylum warder beside the driver on the box and another at the back. At Seeshaupt, at the head of Lake Starnberg, where the last change of horses was made, the King asked for a glass of water. It was brought to him by the wife of the owner of the posting establishment, who afterwards preserved the glass as a family heirloom.

At midday the carriages reached the castle gates, where Ludwig paused a moment to say a friendly word to Sergeant Sauer, who was on duty there; then he entered the castle and, as was his wont, walked through the rooms inspecting everything with a critical eye. To Dr von Grashey, Gudden's son-in-law, had been entrusted the task of preparing the King's apartments for the reception of a mental patient, and Ludwig cannot have failed to notice the spy-holes that had been cut in the doors or the holes drilled in the window-frames for iron bars that were still to come. But he made no comment; back in the castle he had always so much loved he seemed calm, resigned, icily courteous.

Lunch was served to the King with small gold fruit-knives replacing steel ones. 'Surely I'm not starting with fruit?' he asked. The servant replied that he was only obeying his orders; he had also been told strictly to ration wine and spirits. For Gudden was determined that the King should be brought to lead a more normal life: to live soberly, see more people, and sleep by night rather than by day. When the King retired to bed at 3 o'clock saying that he was to be woken at midnight, the order was countermanded.

Ludwig woke of his own accord in the early hours of the morning and asked why he had not been called; once again he was told that there had been 'orders'. He wanted to get up and be dressed; but his clothes had been taken away (more orders), and after he had wandered for some time up and down his room in his nightshirt he felt cold and agreed to go back to bed.

What was to prove the last day of his life opened tranquilly enough. If he resented the absence of all but one of his former servants – Zanders, his head chef, alone remained – he concealed his displeasure and allowed himself to be shaved and his hair to be crimped by an unfamiliar barber. He raised no protest when he was told that although it was Whit Sunday he might not go to Mass. He ate an excellent breakfast and, the rain having at last stopped, asked Gudden whether he might take a stroll in the grounds.

The two men set out, with two warders following at a discreet distance. Though Gudden returned rather exhausted mentally by the King's endless questioning, he had to admit that the experiment had been a success; when over their lunch the doctors exchanged notes about the patient's behaviour, he was full of optimism. The King seemed to be perfectly rational, perfectly normal: he was not going to present any difficulties. But Müller was far less confident, and Washington, who was lunching with them, recalled a favourite phrase of the King's, '*Den müssen wir einseifen*', which literally translated is 'We shall have to lather this one' – in other words, trick him, take him in. 'Yes,' Gudden admitted, 'His Majesty certainly lathered me very thoroughly; but I shan't let him *shave* me!' And he added: 'He is just a child.'

During the afternoon the King had a long talk with Zanders, then sent for Müller; he was now submitting everybody within reach to an unending catechism, and Müller related that in the course of three-quarters of an hour he had been asked more questions than in his entire State examination. At 4.30 the King, in spite of Gudden's efforts to dissuade him, insisted upon being served with another enormous meal, which he washed down with a glass of beer, two glasses of spiced wine, three glasses of Rhine wine and two small glasses of arrack; Gudden's instructions in the matter of alcohol do not seem to have been very strictly carried out.

A little after 6 o'clock the King sent for Gudden to accompany him on another walk, as had been arranged earlier in the day. Gudden was far from eager; to Washington he said, 'I do wish His Majesty would give up his walk; one gets absolutely worn out by his ceaseless questions.' Then he despatched a telegram to the Minister-President, 'So far everything going splendidly here', and with an 'I'll be back for supper at eight' he went off to join the King. So confident was Gudden of the tractability of his patient that he gave a whispered order that no warders were to accompany them; the two men therefore set off alone. Both were wearing overcoats and carrying umbrellas because another storm threatened.

When 8 o'clock came and there was no sign of the King and Gudden, Müller at first imagined that they might be taking shelter from the rain, which was now falling heavily. He sent a policeman to look for them, and shortly afterwards two more; he was worried, but not as yet seriously alarmed. Then, as the time passed without news, apprehension gave way to panic and the search was intensified until every available man was out, with lamp or torch because night had fallen, scouring the undergrowth.

The path which the two men were presumed to have taken passed in places close to the lake, and at 10 o'clock someone observed a black object in the water, not far from the shore. It proved to be the overcoat and jacket of the King, and within half an hour the bodies of both men had been found, floating in shallow water about twenty yards from the bank. They had been dead for several hours, for the King's watch had stopped at 6.54; Gudden's showed 8 o'clock – but it was a standing joke that he never remembered to wind it up.

The Dream King was dead. But to the dreams that he dreamed he gave substance, and so his memory lives on. Each year more than half a million people visit his castles, above whose doors might well be inscribed the words of W. B. Yeats, 'Tread softly, because you tread on my dreams'. Each year thousands go to hear the later operas of Richard Wagner – operas that would very likely never have been written had not Ludwig come to the composer's rescue at the most critical moment of his career. It is not always the conscientious rulers, the 'good' kings of the history books, who contribute the most to the enrichment of the spiritual life of mankind.

* * *

Much ink has been spilled in an attempt to reconstruct exactly what took place on the shores of Lake Starnberg that wet and tragic Whit Sunday evening, and even within the last few years new but still inconclusive evidence has come to light. A premeditated attempt to escape, or to commit suicide, which Gudden bravely tried to prevent? The deliberate murder of Gudden, whom Ludwig doubtless hated and despised, followed by suicide or possibly by a heart attack? The mystery remains, and it can never now be solved; but any reader who wishes to play the amateur detective will find copious material, together with plans and diagrams showing the foot-prints of the King and Gudden, in Hacker (pp. 395–424) and in other biographies of Ludwig.

That a strong swimmer should be able to commit suicide in shallow water is hard to believe, and certainly the heart attack theory has much to commend it. But Ernest Newman came to a different conclusion.

163

'To us today,' he wrote, 'the murder-and-suicide explanation seems the correct one, but it surely proves not the King's madness but his complete sanity. He knew that life, for him, was over ... And so, I imagine, he had resolved to end it all there and then.' Newman was an ardent champion of the theory that Ludwig was never insane, and he has the support of perhaps the only contemporary of the King who really understood him. The Empress Elisabeth was visiting her mother at Possenhofen when news of her cousin's death was brought to her. She cried out in her grief, 'The King was not mad; he was just an eccentric living in a world of dreams. They might have treated him more gently, and thus perhaps have spared him so terrible an end.'

Chapter Seventeen

LUDWIG AND THE ARTS

By Dr Michael Petzet

King Ludwig II embodied the last, glorious epoch of Bavaria's long history.

His ideas about art were not specifically Bavarian, but part of the world-wide revival of interest in earlier artistic and architectural forms, which were given their particular character by the King's personality. This art, once discredited, today can be understood only through the laws of its age; Ludwig, too, can only be understood as a child of his time. For example his withdrawal is a trait also found in his princely contemporaries – Queen Victoria fled from public life for years after Prince Albert's death; Pius IX withdrew from mundane affairs to become a 'prisoner in the Vatican'.

Heinrich Kreisel, the first to recognize the importance of the royal castles in connection with the history of nineteenth-century German art and mentality, divides Ludwig's buildings into three groups. He believes the King saw the whole universe in terms of one or other of these groups: the Grail, which symbolized the 'medieval' castles (Neuschwanstein and Falkenstein); the Sun, which symbolized buildings in the late-baroque and rococo styles (the royal apartments in the Munich Residenz, Linderhof with the Hubertuspavilion and the theatre project, and Herrenchiemsee); and the Moon, which symbolized buildings in oriental styles (Schachen, the Moorish kiosk and the Morocco house near Linderhof). In Ludwig's own words, 'the symbol of the Sun (*nec pluribus impar*) and the Moon (Orient! rebirth by Oberon's miraculous horn) . . .' he uses two of these symbols.

Even before his first meeting with Wagner Ludwig had known the world of the Middle Ages at Hohenschwangau, the ancestral seat of the lords of Schwangau, which his father, Maximilian II, had acquired in 1833 in order to 'restore it to its original medieval state' after plans by the stage designer Domenico Quaglio. As a child Ludwig had made a sketch of this castle. By the age of twelve he was reading *The Ring of the Nibelung* drifting 'on the mirror of the Alpsee' at the foot of the castle, and long before his first fateful encounter with Wagner's *Lohengrin* the legend was familiar to him through the murals in his father's castle. In 1864 and 1865, when he had moved from the princes' suite into his father's apartments, he transformed the royal bedchamber, which was decorated with murals of Rinaldo and Armida, into a miniature artistic ensemble (the additions were subsequently removed). Even at this early stage he revealed the characteristic features of his later vast artistic enterprises, which always had theatrical or operatic associations. On the ceiling the stage technician Penkmayr created 'a nocturnal illumination representing the moon', to which stars and a rainbow machine, a rock cascade and three artificial orange trees were later added. But at Hohenschwangau, 'this Paradise on earth, which I populate with my ideals and thus feel happy', he soon found himself ill at ease. The cause of this was the presence of his 'prosaic' mother, and to escape from her he had planned, as early as 1868, a building 'in the style of the old German knights' castles' on the ruins of Vorderhohenschwangau. This typically late-romantic idea of reconstruction, which recurred in 1883 in the plans for the castle of Falkenstein, was combined with the idea of a new castle of the Swan-knight. The knight's heraldic bird had appeared in Maximilian's castle (which in many respects prepared Ludwig for his own castle) in a vast number of artistic forms – it was his favourite bird as well.

The 'New Castle of Hohenschwangau', which was first made accessible to the public, together with the other castles, on 1 August 1886 after the King's death, and which was then called Neuschwanstein, was altered according to Ludwig's wishes from a small robber-knight's castle with a stylistic resemblance to the late-Gothic details of Nuremberg models, to a monumental 'Romanesque' castle. Its five-storeyed *Palas* reminds us of the *Palas* of the Wartburg, which the King visited in 1867 when preparing for the new production of *Tannhäuser*. Neuschwanstein appears to us today a typical 'medieval' castle; however, it is not a copy of any particular medieval building, but a curious original invention of the nineteenth century. Ludwig's rejection of the idea of employing a painter to reconstruct a castle in the older romantic style, with parts copied from different medieval buildings, is significant: 'According to His Majesty's Most High Will, the new castle is to be built in the Romanesque style. As we are living in 1871, we have for centuries progressed beyond that period when the Romanesque style was created; surely, therefore, the present building must benefit from achievements in the spheres of art and science. . . . I should be similarly reluctant to suggest that we should put our minds back and reject knowledge which most certainly would have been turned to account had it existed at an earlier time.'

The King's criticism of Julius Hofmann's drawing of the canopy over the bed in the bedchamber shows that he paid great attention to correctness in interior decoration as well: 'The workmanship is not delicate enough. His Majesty imagines the wood-carvings much more elegant and dainty, more like filigree. The canopy should reach its apex in the centre, and the ornament should slope down at the back and front as well as on both sides.' The 'late-Gothic' style, with furniture which, in its comparatively 'historical' forms, is clearly contrasted with

Hohenschwangau's Biedermeier neo-Gothic that had 'not yet entered into the spirit of the style', is seen only in the bedroom and the adjoining chapel; the rest of the interior decoration, with a *leitmotif* of swans, was conceived in the 'Romanesque' style. Julius Hofmann, who in his youth had worked with his father for Archduke Maximilian in the Palace of Miramare near Trieste and in 1864 had received the commission to change the town hall of Mexico City into a residential palace for the future Emperor, proved himself in Neuschwanstein to be a master-designer in every conceivable style. A group of historical painters working in collaboration with Dr Hyazinth Holland, a literary historian and a learned specialist in medieval iconography, were to complete the programme. Naturally, very few subjects other than those taken from Wagner's operas were intended for the castle, which was originally conceived as a 'temple' dedicated to Wagner – a temple which the composer was never to enter; in accordance with an order the King gave in 1879, the paintings were, however, to follow the ancient legends and not Wagner.

Ludwig, in contrast to his grandfather, purchased only one painting of any importance, namely Anselm Feuerbach's 'Medea'. He did not want painters with a strong individuality, but only such 'as had carefully studied medieval poetry', historical painters who exactly reproduced Ludwig's own ideas, based on literary studies. His first aim was a real or imagined 'historical truth', enhanced by poetry. At a time when the great naturalistic artist Wilhelm Leibl was painting in Bavaria, it appears from Ludwig's instructions and criticisms, which seem only to touch externals, that the King was concerned with content rather than with form; however, a definite style does result. Because he wanted to see exactly what was represented, he refused any inexact reproduction, criticized paintings done in a superficial manner as being slipshod, and condemned every exaggeration as caricature. Of course there was no room for anything common in this kind of historical painting, which was made no easier for the artists by the demands of the King, so conscious of his own dignity, for an exalted and at the same time natural manner of portrayal. On top of everything else was the King's most exacting demand of an unreasonably short time for the completion of the work – a limit set 'because of the well-known dilatoriness of artists'. The painters Hauschild, Spiess, Piloty, Aigner, and Ille, working desperately day and night in the living rooms of Neuschwanstein, managed to finish on the first day of the Christmas holidays of 1881.

The creations of this group of painters, second-rate as they were, are important only within the framework of the 'total work of art' (*Gesamtkunstwerk*) of Neuschwanstein, whose exterior was first designed, not by a historical painter, but by a scene painter, Christian Jank. This total work of art, created by a host of artists and craftsmen

167

under the direction of the architect Eduard Riedel, his successors Georg Dollmann (after 1874), and Julius Hofmann (after 1884), is based on imaginary stage-settings for Wagner's operas which interested the King. The settings were so familiar to the King that at times he even came into conflict with the Master over the new productions of *Lohengrin* and *Tannhäuser*. Ludwig, who subsequently used to enjoy dressing up as Lohengrin, in 1865, some years before the foundation-stone of Neuschwanstein had been laid, had staged on the Alpsee at the foot of the old castle the Swan-knight's arrival 'on the banks of the Schelde'. The décor of the second act of *Lohengrin*, the 'court of the castle at Antwerp', was then used by Christian Jank for his sketches for the courtyard, which are ostensibly derived from those done by Angelo II Quaglio for the Munich *Lohengrin* production of 1867. The sketch of a bedroom, the bridal chamber of the third act, was transformed for the Neuschwanstein women's apartments.

In accordance with the wishes of its builder, the new castle was, however, to be not only the castle of Lohengrin but also that of Tannhäuser. The King wanted his castle to rise from the rugged rocks of the Pöllat gorge in the magnificent scenery of the Bavarian mountains like the historically correct model of the Wartburg against the background of the Wartburg valley, which Heinrich Döll, the landscape specialist among the Munich scene painters, had made from stage properties. Originally a singers' hall was also planned, copying the festive hall of the Wartburg, which had been completed only in 1867. Its plan had already served for the scenery of the second act of the Berlin première of *Tannhäuser* in 1858, expressly ordered by King Friedrich Wilhelm IV. When Wagner wanted the Paris designs, which were in accord with his ideas, for the Munich production, Hofrat Düfflipp warned him of the King's doubts: 'The hall of the Wartburg was in the Gothic style, which His Majesty regards as an unjustified anachronism because at the supposed time of the legend of Tannhäuser it was not the Gothic, but the Byzantine style that was current'. The King gave in over the question of the setting because Wagner insisted on using the singers' hall of the Paris première, built in a kind of English Gothic. But when Ludwig commissioned Christian Jank to design a new singers' hall in Neuschwanstein it was to be adapted from the Wartburg festive hall and the singers' bower in the Wartburg singers' hall. It is significant that this new hall was the model for future settings of *Tannhäuser*.

Originally the King wanted to complete his combination of all *Lohengrin* and *Tannhäuser* settings in Neuschwanstein with a large rock bath instead of the little grotto which was later attached to the King's study. Maximilian had built a most original red marble bath, like a rocky cave, on the ground floor of the Lions' Tower of Hohenschwangau. For want of a suitable site the plan for a large grotto in Neuschwanstein, by a decree of 15 December 1875, was transferred to a grotto planned by Karl von Effner, the director of the Court gardens, in the park of Linderhof. The work was finally carried out in 1876–7 by the landscape gardener August Dirigl. Here Ludwig intended the grotto of the Hörselberg from *Tannhäuser* to be combined with the Blue Grotto, which was presented to him at the same time as a stage setting in the 'private performances' (*Separatvorstellungen*). The King's delight in the Blue Grotto was typical of the general enthusiasm for grottoes shown at that time in exhibitions, and in the building of large aquariums. Richard Hornig, the equerry, was sent twice to Capri to memorize the precise shade of blue. The combination of stage-set, nature, architecture, and the special features of contemporary exhibitions and conservatories (as in Ludwig's Winter Garden in Munich) produced a typically nineteenth-century grotto, which reveals many facets of a taste that was not exclusively Ludwig's. This 'total' theatre afforded the solitary visitor the complete illusion of stage and auditorium in one, the ultimate improvement on the nineteenth-century peep-show stage; it did not separate the onlooker from the stage by the dark abyss of an empty auditorium, as in the private performances. Gliding in his boat over the lake in the middle of the stage, or sitting on various raised seats at the side, the King experienced an 'action' that consisted only in the change of lighting effects and the change of scenery viewed from different points. The Hörselberg grotto, shedding a red radiance on August Heckel's backdrop of the Venusberg scene, could be transformed into the Blue Grotto with a waterfall. Through a peep-hole framed by the grotto wall, the King could even see the real scenery and a nearby castle outside.

Behind the illusion of the artificial rocks, supported by a skeleton of ironwork, there was the modern technical machinery: a complex of water-pipes to feed the lake and cascade, a machine to produce waves, a heating device for keeping a constant temperature of 16 degrees Réaumur, and one of the first electric power-stations in Bavaria, equipped with a number of the recently invented dynamos which worked the arc-lamps and a rainbow machine. The King, however, was never quite happy about the results achieved by his stage painter, Otto Stoeger, whom he often drove to the verge of despair. Sometimes he demanded the impossible: Friedrich Brandt, the stage technician and producer, was commissioned to construct a flying machine in the shape of a peacock-carriage to fly over the Alpsee. The Court Theatre was provided with the most modern machinery for lighting and changing scenery; and his old-fashioned carriages and sleighs and his castles were also equipped with the latest technical devices. It is typical that he even negotiated a commission for the Bavarian government with the otherwise little-appreciated inventor of the submarine, Wilhelm Bauer.

In 1876 another rural stage-setting was erected in the woods near Linderhof – the Hundinghütte. This was to be 'a room of rough-hewn wood similar to the décor of the first act of *Die Walküre*', for which Christian Jank's set, used at the Munich première, and not the Bayreuth set, was taken as a model. The King, a great lover of trees himself, selected the gnarled tree-trunk around which the room was to be built. In the Linderhof forests this had to be a beech tree, so 'a double beech covered with the bark of an ash' is recorded on the building plans. This was where the King liked to retire to read in solitude on his bearskin couch. He is supposed to have brought his visions to life with 'a drinking bout with mead in the old Germanic style', staged by his servants. In order to be carried back into the world of the *Ring* – which in 1864 he had commissioned Michael Echter to paint as murals in the 'passage of the Nibelung' in the Munich Residenz – he needed no further scenery. Nature herself liberally provided him, on his walks and drives in the neighbourhood of Neuschwanstein and Linderhof, with his beloved mountains for the décor of the second and third acts of *Die Walküre*, the 'wild rocky range of mountains', the 'summit of a rocky mountain' and the other landscapes of the *Ring*.

The King tried to outdo nature by fireworks, the illumination of cascades and scenic displays on the Alpsee, and he did not strive for a banal naturalism in the stage-sets of his Court Theatre, transplanted occasionally into natural settings. What he wanted was 'the realization of the highest ideal, mirroring, so to speak, nature in a fairylike radiance', an ideal in which history and nature meet.

Not far from the Hundinghütte another stage-set was created in 1877, the hermitage of Gurnemanz from the third act of *Parsifal*. The first draft of *Parsifal* was directly inspired by a letter from Ludwig to Wagner in 1865. In his hermitage the King wished to be steeped in this poetic work, near the 'lawns plentifully strewn with flowers' representing the 'flowery Good Friday meadow', one of the Court gardener's creations. The décor of *Parsifal* was constantly in Ludwig's mind years before the performance, and in 1876 he had a hall of the Grail designed by Eduard Ille in Byzantine style, a copy of St Sophia. From this hall of the Grail he developed the idea of a throne room in Neuschwanstein, for which Julius Hofmann's designs did not take their final shape until 1881. Thus the 'Wartburg', designed for the young King, was converted into Parsifal's 'castle of the Grail', in which the ageing King pleaded for his redemption. For Ludwig the six canonized kings in the apse were the intercessors for, and the prototypes of a veritable monarchy by God's grace. Their deeds are portrayed principally by Wilhelm Hauschild, and among them is St Louis IX, whom

King Ludwig also had represented in the chapels of Neuschwanstein and Linderhof. The adjoining singers' hall, which had been planned differently, was now to become a preparation for the throne room and was decorated in 1883–4 with murals depicting Wolfram von Eschenbach's *Parzival*. In the singers' bower Parzival appears as the King of the Holy Grail, and the departure of his son, Lohengrin, is on the opposite wall. Thus the concept of Neuschwanstein is united at start and finish in the saga of the Swan-knight.

The throne room of Neuschwanstein, which was to have been completed in the year of Ludwig's death, but which never received its throne, is the only one of the King's Byzantine projects to be realized. As early as 1869 he had commissioned Dollmann to design a great Byzantine palace in which, as later in Herrenchiemsee, his monarchy by God's grace was to be manifested, and in 1885, towards the end of the King's life, Hofmann was given a further Byzantine commission. One of the last projects was the late-Gothic robber-knights' castle of Falkenstein, which was originally designed for the King by Christian Jank and then, after 1884, by Max Schultze of Regensburg, the chief architect of the Princes of Thurn und Taxis; this, too, was to have contained, as a kind of sanctuary, a bedchamber in the style of the throne room of Neuschwanstein. As funds were diminishing, the King demanded only the completion of this one room's constantly increasing dimensions. Eugen Drollinger's unfinished design of it remains; it was lying on the drawing-board when news arrived of the King's death.

'Thousands of people will come from far and wide to the national festival,' the King exclaimed enthusiastically, thinking of festival plays in Semper's never-to-be-built theatre on the green heights above the Isar – the same King who, at the end of his life, watched *Parsifal* only as a private performance. These performances, to which visitors were as unwelcome as they were to the castles, are perhaps the most significant evidence of the deflection of an art destined for the general public to one reserved for the King alone. At the same time they show his temporary abandonment of Wagner and the medieval world for those 'other ideals'. These had occupied his mind ever since early youth, though he had never mentioned them in his correspondence with his 'divine friend' the composer, who completely lacked any understanding of them.

Ludwig himself chose the very original repertoire of his private performances, which usually took place in April, May and November in order to alleviate his much-hated forced sojourns in his capital. From 1872 onwards there were 209 private performances, among them (after 1878) 44 operas, and not only Wagner's but also those of Verdi, Meyerbeer, Auber and others. The principal theme, however, was always the age of the Bourbons. The King, for whom reading was a great delight, was familiar with every historical work, memoir and travel book in this field, and wanted to see all the most famous French and German plays on the subject. His favourite piece was Albert Emil Brachvogel's *Narziss*, the only play to be performed twelve times. It was always performed on 9 May, the anniversary of Louis XV's death. The King had already given the play, which had been in the repertoire for some time, a new production, and each year he chose a different guest actress for the role of Madame de Pompadour. The title role was always played by the famous actor Ernst Possart, subsequently the manager of the Munich Court Theatre, who used to correspond with the King about the correct interpretation, for which he prepared by careful historical studies.

If Ludwig found a historical theme particularly suitable he had it adapted for the stage by one of his court poets, August Fresenius, Hermann von Schmid, Ludwig Schneegans or Karl von Heigel. Ludwig's first principle was fidelity to history; he checked historical sources used by the poets, and occasionally even demanded original engravings to provide an authentic original for action on the stage. He commissioned some dramas solely for their sets; indeed, certain sets were constructed without a play, and were shown before or after performances, frequently with varied lighting effects such as were used in the Linderhof grotto. His stage designers, Angelo Quaglio, Christian Jank and Heinrich Döll, had to study history very carefully and were often sent to the places in question – Rheims for *The Maid of Orleans*; Switzerland for *Wilhelm Tell*, and above all to Versailles. Only Duke Georg von Meiningen, with whom Ludwig occasionally corresponded, made similar efforts to get historically correct scenes for his theatre, and elsewhere, even in larger theatres, many sets were simply made up from properties in the store.

Ludwig intended temporarily to transfer his private performances to the palace of Linderhof; but in 1875, in view of his critical financial position, he gave up the plan of a theatre combined with the palace and instead had the far less expensive circular temple built. The pastels of figures from the French Court, which appeared continually in the private performances, were to be placed in the small oval rooms of the palace, which were already provided for, according to the instructions of the King on 30 September 1870 for the enlargement of the *Königshäuschen*, on the first ground-plan sketched by the equerry, Hornig. 'Try by all possible means to get hold of a picture of the Marquise de Créqui,' the King writes to Hofrat Düfflipp in 1871; 'I badly need a pastel portrait of her for Linderhof as I am just reading her very interesting memoirs in seven volumes.' Naturally Madame de Pompadour could not be left out of Ludwig's sequence of pastels; and for this purpose he ordered that 'the costume of Fräulein Ziegler from the play *Narziss* be procured as a pattern, and that this be copied exactly in the picture by the painter Heigel'. In the dining-room the *Tischlein, deck' dich* allowed Ludwig to be alone even when eating in the company of the royal personages, represented by their pastel portraits in the adjoining small rooms. It is quite understandable, therefore, that the King himself occasionally wished to wear the historical costumes designed by Franz Seitz for private performances. The order, 'Would Your Excellency at once send from the theatre wardrobe, without causing a stir, and only for a short time, a few hats and a fine complete costume of the later period of Louis XV', bears this out, as does also the fact that a splendid Louis XIV robe was sold out of Ludwig's estate.

Franz Seitz, technical director and costumier of the Munich Court Theatre, who had already played a part in constructing Ludwig's rooms in the Munich Residenz, completed in 1869, supplied costumes for the King and also a number of designs for the interior decoration of Linderhof; so too did Christian Jank, who specialized in the rococo interiors for the private performances. Linderhof, partly designed by scene painters under the direction of the architect Georg Dollmann as a kind of stage-set, became as incomparable an invention of the nineteenth century as Neuschwanstein, which was similarly allied to certain conceptions of stage scenery. What was planned here and carried out by highly competent craftsmen – the carvings by Philipp Perron and the stucco-work by Theodor Bechler – is the completely original rococo style of Ludwig II, not to be mistaken for Viennese neo-rococo. Ludwig's rococo is derived from late-Bavarian rococo, still alive in nineteenth-century peasant art, but surpasses its various models by its inexhaustible fantasy, for example in the motif of the mirror room, so characteristic of German palace-building in the eighteenth century, in the hall of mirrors. This style, developed for Ludwig II, later revealed definite models of the rococo period, yet it does not fall into mere imitation. Examples are the Hubertuspavilion near Linderhof, designed by Julius Hofmann in 1885 after Cuvilliés' Amalienburg, and the final enlargement of the bedroom at Linderhof, which was to be redesigned by Eugen Drollinger from Cuvilliés' bedroom in the so-called *Reichen Zimmer* of the Residenz. Even the designs for the frames of the mirrors and candelabra from the Meissen porcelain factory, which had its own traditional rococo style, had to be drawn in Munich and passed by the King.

Life and art at the Court of the Bourbons, the main subject of the private performances, also featured in the King's scheme for pictures in the palace. The scheme's execution was as critically supervised by the King as were the designs, made at the same time, for a porcelain dinner-service with scenes from the age of Louis XIV and XV, both destined for Linderhof. In a marginal note on a design for a coffee-pot with a picture of *Louis XIV et Molière* by Joseph Watter, Ludwig writes: 'The picture should be executed more carefully; in particular, the details of the bed should be treated with more precision, the faces made to look nobler; in general, the engraving is to be followed more closely'. Again and again it is the figure of Louis XIV who 'in his attitude and his whole personal appearance should be represented as nobler and more imposing'. Purely formal mistakes, for example false perspective or inappropriate colours, were also censured. At Linderhof there was no place for painters with too much originality, so the murals are, as such, just as second-rate as those in Neuschwanstein. But they, too, cannot be separated from the total work of art created by the will of the King, which, in its picture-arrangement as well as in the play of architecture and colours, should only be regarded as an eighteenth-century palace. Appropriate surroundings were created by Karl von Effner in the autumn of 1877: a park which is undoubtedly one of the most important garden designs of the nineteenth century. It leads from the formal French gardens on the main and side axes of the palace, through spacious landscape gardens into the wooded slopes above. At Linderhof, as at Neuschwanstein, the positioning of the windows has taken nature into consideration; for example, the King could look out from his bed on to the waterfall. Like an eighteenth-century landscape garden with ornamental buildings, Linderhof and Neuschwanstein appear as the key points in the King's huge natural park which, with the variously executed or merely planned schemes, extended from Garmisch by way of the Plansee and Füssen to Falkenstein in the eastern Allgäu.

This is the realm through which the King passed on his frequent and mostly nocturnal drives in golden Louis XV coaches or sleighs befitting such a palace. Franz Seitz designed suitable costumes for the grooms, the equerry, and the King himself, and also the coaches and sleighs, which were made by the court coach-builders, Franz Gmelch and Johann Michael Mayer. An oil-painting of 1880 by Wenig shows the King driving in his sleigh from Neuschwanstein by way of the Schützensteig to Linderhof. In the snowy night landscape golden cupids bear a crown, magically lit (by means of an electric battery), above the head of the King, who never seemed to feel the cold even during a drive of many hours. Although he already possessed the big state coach as well as a smaller golden coach, which could be changed into a sleigh in winter, in 1873 the King was dreaming of yet another. One of the lackeys reports: 'Last night His Majesty dreamed of a splendid state coach. . . . In the middle and on the front goddesses supported a crown; it was fantastically carved and decorated with palms, goddesses and cupids, giving the impression that it was carried by goddesses and cupids.' Of this royal dream, however, there remain only a sketch and a model which, like many later projects of coaches and sleighs, was never executed.

But there was one other dream, the greatest of his life, which he wanted to make a reality: his new Versailles, which, under the secret name of 'Meicost-Ettal' – '*L'État c'est moi*' – he first intended to build in the neighbourhood of Linderhof; but after long years of exhaustive preparations the foundation-stone for the new castle was eventually laid in 1878 on the Herreninsel in the Chiemsee. For Ludwig the equestrian statue of Louis XV, which he placed in the vestibule of Linderhof, had a particular significance, for he could trace his name to the Bourbons: Ludwig I was his godfather, and none other than Louis XVI of France was Ludwig I's godfather. Ludwig's journey to conquered France in 1874, and his plans for a new Versailles, might, when seen from the German national perspective of the empire founded jointly by Bismarck and Ludwig (although against the latter's wish), be politically misinterpreted. But the King was planning Meicost-Ettal principally as a memorial to Louis XIV, his 'inherited godfather' – less as a memorial to a French King than one to the creator and unique embodiment of the principle of absolute monarchy, jeopardized by Louis XVI's and Marie Antoinette's deaths which had deeply affected him. Whereas the 'royal villa' of Linderhof, comparatively modest in scale, was planned only as a dwelling for the King, Meicost-Ettal was to represent, according to Dollmann's plans of ever-growing dimensions, a kind of renaissance of absolute monarchy. Ludwig had had to renounce it, but he could conjure it up in those vast halls, empty of court society, and live in this memory as a true king, far from the bourgeois world of the nineteenth century.

According to Ludwig's final plan, Herrenchiemsee was to have the vastness and grandeur of Versailles. He did not want simply to copy a particular *style*, as he had at Linderhof, but a particular *building*. He intended to build an imitation on a scale unparalleled even in the imitative nineteenth century, to make a unique attempt at a compendium of all possible copies, but within the limitations peculiar to architectural copies rather than the customary copies of sculpture and painting. For the prototype had to be understood as a homogeneous whole, although the non-homogeneous image of Versailles – begun by Louis XIII, rebuilt and added to in several stages by Louis XIV, and continually altered down to the end of the eighteenth century – could hardly be matched to Ludwig's image of a Louis XIV Versailles. He therefore created 'in the spirit of the style', which, however, always betrays the spirit of the nineteenth century even in the few parts which seem to be accurately copied. In this way the historic prototype, often discovered with difficulty, has become in execution merely the starting point of a design which develops its own laws; the ground-plan may approach the Versailles prototype closely, and yet it is regulated by a strict nineteenth-century symmetry. The King could expect from Dollmann an exact copy of the Versailles garden façade; the Versailles court façade of Louis XIII's palace had to be recreated in Louis XIV style. The park, inseparably allied to the concept of Versailles, was not simply to be copied from the existing grounds but to be resuscitated in its original splendour. Herrenchiemsee's particular charm is its unique island position, with the long canal flowing into the lake. Long before the foundation-stone of Herrenchiemsee had been laid the palace and park of Versailles and the fountain of Latona (with jets playing) were seen on the stage in the play *The Way to Peace*, which Schneegans wrote from Ludwig's directions for a private performance (première on 6 May 1874). He also made stage-sets such as the *salon de l'oeil de boeuf*,[1] the royal bedchamber, the conference room and the mirror gallery. That the King felt even the completed palace to be a sort of stage-set is proved by his order to let some historically important personages from Louis XIV's Court 'true to their portraits' look out in 'accurately copied costumes' from the windows of the north wing, which had only just been finished in the rough.

In the same way as the singers' hall was linked with Neuschwanstein, two rooms were linked to the planning of Herrenchiemsee, two rooms which were the real purpose for building the palace: the *chambre de parade* and the gallery of mirrors. From the first design of a small Versailles limited to a single wing, to the three-wing project, the *chambre de parade* remained unchanged on the east side, in its characteristic Versailles combination with the gallery of mirrors on the west side. Together they form the central axis which continues via the east-west axis of the garden to the canal. The *chambre de parade*, honoured as a sanctuary by the court ceremonial of absolute monarchy, could not serve Ludwig II for a bedchamber as at Linderhof; it remained the state bedchamber of Louis XIV, and as such the room appeared to the King of Bavaria as a ' "writing on the wall" for the chimera of his own monarchy, for which he was born too late'. And yet the state bedchamber certainly could not be called a copy of the much simpler *chambre de parade* in Versailles. From the earlier designs by Franz Seitz to the final elaboration worked out by Julius Hofmann the appetite of the King, which even in the nineteenth century was unparalleled, demanded more and more gorgeous furnishings (the cost rose to more than 384,000 gulden). The valuable textiles of the state bedchamber were commissioned in 1875, three years before the foundation stone of the palace was laid. The Munich ateliers of Jörres and Bornhauser worked for seven years on the curtains of the bed of state alone.

[1] A room with an oval window.

Like the state bedchamber, the gallery of mirrors was first shown on the stage in the private performances. Whereas on the stage the King only demanded the perfect illusion, for Herrenchiemsee he demanded a copy to scale, including the component corner rooms, the hall of peace and the hall of war. He reproached Dollmann, who had given a measurement differing by only six feet on the whole length, and said that he should 'on no account work according to his own ideas'. The ceiling, an enormous copy, could only be completed by a whole group of 'conscientious painters', all of whom were sent to Versailles in 1879 'to study carefully the character of the paintings there'. At the end of September 1881, after the King had examined the completed gallery and subsequently compared it with the engravings, he noticed that two of the pictures had accidentally been interchanged: 'As two of the pictures were interchanged, His Majesty assumes this might well be the case with other pictures too; this would indeed be a terrible thing for His Most High Majesty, and he could never forgive it'. Nor was the King quite happy about the colours of the gallery of mirrors. As he usually turned night into day, he lived in his apartments in artificial light and, as in the theatre, greatly enjoyed unexpected lighting effects. His favourite colour was blue, the colour his mother had attributed to him as a child (red was his brother Otto's colour); he also wanted vivid reds and greens, but usually disliked yellow. 'The colour scheme in the great gallery of war and in that of peace is far too pale,' we read in the report to Hofrat Bürkel. 'His Majesty had already stated that His Most High Majesty could not bear light colours.'

After the gallery of mirrors the other state apartments were added continuously until 1883, beginning with the staircase of the south wing, a copy from the Versailles *escalier des ambassadeurs*, which had been demolished in 1752. This reconstruction, copied from contemporary engravings, is nevertheless typically nineteenth-century because of its modern glass roof, which bathes the vivid colours of the marble and the whiteness of the stucco-work in an evenly glaring light. When the staircase was transformed with thousands of lilies and roses, as happened whenever the King was there, it looked like a Hans Makart painting. Next to the Louis XIV apartment a Louis XV apartment was created in the rococo style developed at Linderhof, which had little in common with the corresponding Louis XV apartment in the upper storey of the north wing of Versailles. The most original rooms, designed by Eugen Drollinger for this suite, were the light blue salon and the pink salon, whose mirrors turn the carvings intertwined with garlands of flowers and birds into endless pergolas. The small bedroom reserved for Ludwig II, like the bedrooms at Neuschwanstein and Linderhof, was in the King's favourite colour, in contrast to the red state bedchamber. Otto Stoeger, who had contrived the lighting of the Linderhof grotto, had to experiment for a year and a half until the King was satisfied with the final solution: a blue globe to bathe the room in an even blue light.

In 1885, when building had to stop, the north wing was finished in the rough; the south wing had not progressed beyond the foundations. Despite this, Herrenchiemsee has not remained an unfinished dream. Ludwig's idea of Versailles embraced only a certain group of apartments which were nearly all completed, embedded in the gigantic caves of rough brickwork which played no part in the King's vision and whose completion was therefore not vital. On his first visit in 1881 Ludwig complained that the rough brickwork ought to have been disguised, if only temporarily, in the rooms adjoining the state bedchamber. To the visitor today, however, who emerges from the gorgeous apartments into the unfinished north staircase, the rough brickwork appears as attractive as does the world behind the theatre curtain to a spectator who enters it for the first time. Probably the only visitors who were permitted to inspect the palace in Ludwig's lifetime were Prince and Princess Ludwig Ferdinand. In Hofrat Bürkel's report on their visit we read: 'By Sunday their Royal Highnesses could no longer suppress their longing and at half past eight visited the illuminated palace. During this inspection, which lasted for two and a half hours, Her Royal Highness kept on exclaiming "Oh! how beautiful it is, how glorious, how uplifting", and His Royal Highness Prince Ludwig Ferdinand graciously remarked that for him the palace of Versailles seemed by comparison almost like a desolate ruin in its pallid splendour, its paintings coated with smoke and dust.'

In the hall of Herrenchiemsee as well as in the Moorish kiosk at Linderhof the peacock motif appears. It was one of Ludwig's favourite birds, and it also appears, though only incidentally, in the realm of his other much-favoured bird, the swan, as a symbol of eternal bliss and immortality, in the arched bowers of the singers' hall. The peacock combines Ludwig's two interests which, besides Wagner and the Middle Ages, determined his concept of the universe: the age of the Bourbons and the world of the Orient. The latter, familiar to him from books, had a tremendous attraction for the King and for many of his contemporaries. It was not chance that besides the Hindu Kush, among other possible kingdoms suggested to the King by the archivist Löher, the most acceptable seemed to be Egypt and Afghanistan, 'particularly because . . . only in these countries the unfolding of a wider seigniorial glory seemed to be possible'. Wagner even planned an opera, *The Victors*, with an oriental theme, for whose completion the King hoped in vain: 'In a very captivating work on India, Brahmanism and Buddhism, I found to my great astonishment that simple and therefore very moving and heartrending story which you wanted to use for *The*

Victors.... Believe me, in time it will be counted among the most glorious of your works. India and Buddhism have something inexpressibly appealing to me, evoking nostalgia and rapture.'

India is the country in which Jules Massenet laid the scene for his opera *The King of Lahore*, which had acquired fame through its great success during the Paris Exhibition. After the dress-rehearsal in 1879 the King immediately demanded two private performances. In the years that followed Jank, Döll and Quaglio staged the oriental operas included in the private performances in the same opulent manner, among them Mozart's *The Magic Flute* (1879), Karl Goldmark's *The Queen of Sheba* (1880), and Weber's *Oberon* (1881)in a new arrangement by Franz Wüllner, specially commanded by the King. He took particular delight in the décor for Felicien David's *Lalla Rookh*, adapted from Thomas Moore (1867). For this opera in 1876 he had painted the still extant model of the Kashmir valley, and wanted to transfer it to the Linderhof grotto to be interchangeable with the *Tannhäuser* backdrop. He also had Kalidasa's Indian drama, *Sakuntala*, translated and arranged by Karl Heigel, as well as another of Kalidasa's works, the Indian story of *Urvasi*, which was put on at the last of the private performances on 12 May 1885. The King had ordered that the décor should be designed 'not in the usual way, but true to pictures of the Himalayas'. The report of the stage-technician Karl Lautenschläger throws an interesting light on the King's ideals, for he valued truth to nature on the stage as much as true historical scenes: 'The King wishes to feast his eyes on this primeval forest, enlivened by birds of paradise, parrots, song-birds, elephants and other animals. I had already finished the design, and the drawing was shown to His Majesty just after he had returned from an outing on which he had seen "grazing stags". His Majesty now wanted also to see the peaceful sight of grazing stags in the Indian primeval forest, so the stags were added.' After the performance, which completely satisfied the King, Lautenschläger was informed 'that the King had made the following observation: "Herr Lautenschläger lets the animals in the Indian forest go hungry. Animals do not just wander about in the forest; they go there to find food. Therefore in the second performance Lautenschläger must not let the animals simply wander about. Furthermore, the Indian sun, whose rays enliven the forest, must be painted more intensely, to bring out a different and more lively play of colour." '

The King wished to be transported to this same Indian fairyland in his Winter Garden, which had been built on top of the north wing of the Munich Residenz in 1867. This bold glass and iron construction, which far surpassed his father Maximilian's old Winter Garden at the south-east corner of the Residenz, was created in the tradition of the palm houses which played such an important part in nineteenth-century architecture, to which the iron palm house of King Friedrich Wilhelm IV on the Island of Peacocks near Potsdam also belongs. Ludwig's delight in the tropical vegetation which Karl von Effner grouped round a lake in front of the view of the Himalayas, painted on the back wall by Jank, was typical of his time; tropical arrangements of plants and oriental furnishings were fashionable and the well known 'Makart-bouquet', first used by the painter Hans Makart, decorated the houses of the well-to-do.

The King soon began to transfer several 'oriental' buildings, for which he had formed a taste at the time of his visit to the Paris Exhibition in 1867, to his Bavarian mountains, which in his imagination were sometimes transformed into the Kashmir valley with the Himalayas behind. His first building in the oriental style was a luxuriously furnished Turkish hall, built about 1870 on the Schachen, externally a simple wooden mountain hut. 'Here Ludwig II, wearing a Turkish costume, used to read,' Louise von Kobell reports, 'while his crowd of servants, dressed as Muslims, lay around on carpets and cushions, smoking tobacco and sipping mocha coffee. For this had been commanded by the Royal Sire who, with a superior smile, frequently let his eyes rove above the edge of his book over his artistically grouped retinue. Incense burners emitted their scent, and large fans were swung to and fro in order to enhance the illusion.' In 1876 Ludwig had a Moorish kiosk erected at Linderhof, although he possessed similar kiosks in his Winter Garden and in the park of Schloss Berg. In the middle of the kiosk, which he had acquired from Schloss Zbirow in Bohemia, was the peacock throne designed by Franz Seitz and executed according to his directions in Paris. Georg Dollmann, the architect, was sent to the Paris Exhibition in 1878 to report on the oriental houses at that time fashionable all over Europe the Algerian, Persian, Egyptian and Chinese houses – and to choose the most magnificent of them, the Moroccan house, for the King. It was set up in the same year at Linderhof, where His Majesty desired to use it 'only to read there, undisturbed for a few hours'. Further oriental projects, for example a Moorish hall in Neuschwanstein, were never carried out. In 1886, after the King had procured for himself several views of the Imperial Winter Palace in Pekin, Julius Hofmann also designed a 'Chinese' palace, to be built on the lonely shores of the Plansee. Here the King, who was interested in Chinese Court Ceremonial, might have played for the last time the role of an absolute monarch.

In the long line of the Wittelsbachs, Ludwig II was the greatest Maecenas of the theatre and one of the most distinguished builders; his works gained their individual quality from their connection with the theatre – Neuschwanstein from Wagner's operas, Linderhof, Herrenchiemsee and the oriental buildings from the private performances. In an age of architectural revival he considered, in contrast to the builders of earlier centuries, not only the setting and the theme, but also the style. To the styles of his father and grandfather he added the neo-baroque and a neo-rococo, known in Germany from the furnishing of the Viennese Palais Liechtenstein and in France from the creation of the Louis-Philippe style. He turned from the neo-Gothic of his father to the neo-Romanesque of Neuschwanstein, and came to feel the general predilection for the Orient which had grown up since Romanticism. Ludwig, who never went to Italy, could not share his grandfather's enthusiasm for Italy or for Greece, a country which he also never visited and which was utterly alien to him: 'I imagine the plains of Hellas, scorched by the glaring sun, to be repulsive rather than attractive,' he once wrote to Wagner. He would build a copy of Versailles, but not of Greek and Italian buildings as his grandfather had done. Ludwig I knew how to overrule his architects' objections, but he liked to argue with them personally. His grandson Ludwig II, on the other hand, issued his orders to the artists – orders which often contained minute details of form and content – after solitary meditations based on his own spiritual conception, through the court secretary. In this way Ludwig II was both builder and creator; he would not tolerate the personal preferences of his often very skilful but second-rate painters, sculptors and poets. Wagner alone could find in Ludwig an ideal Maecenas, because Ludwig had little theoretical knowledge of music, which appealed to his emotions only, and accepted Wagner's poetry with quite uncritical admiration. Semper, too, was able to win over the young King to his concept of the Festival Theatre, which was undoubtedly the most significant theatre design of the second half of the nineteenth century, and which failed not so much because of public opposition as from Wagner's half-hearted attitude.

Ludwig, one of the greatest builders in an age of historic revival, demanded before all else historical truth based on his own scientific and literary studies. But even when the King asked for nothing more than a straight copy, the result was often an unmistakable independent achievement. For example, designs intended to be in Louis XV style merged into Ludwig II's individual rococo. It is significant that here nineteenth-century naturalism is occasionally associated with *art nouveau*, foreshadowed in an amazing way not only in the striking *objets d'art*, designed in strangely personal colours by Adolph Seder and Franz Brochier, but also in the various contrivances for Neuschwanstein, the 'Romanesque' chandeliers of the throne room, or Jank's marvellous 1870 arcade designs for the knights' house. The latest technical achievements were employed in the royal castles – for example metal-casting of ornaments and figures for the superstructures on the roof – and, always in the cause of illusion, astonishingly modern devices were created, such as window-panes without crossbars, or the sliding door of the Winter Garden at Neuschwanstein which consisted of a single pane of glass. But at the same time the eighteenth-century Bavarian traditions of handicraft were preserved in Ludwig's buildings as nowhere else in Germany. Franz Seitz' son and collaborator, Rudolf Seitz, became the first director of the restoration workshop, from which the *Landesamt für Denkmalpflege* (Board of Preservation of National Monuments) emerged. By his innumerable commissions to various workshops in Munich, Ludwig turned his capital into a European arts and crafts centre, which could hold its own with Vienna and Paris.

While Maximilian II and Ludwig I built principally for the public, Ludwig II's castles and palaces were so exclusively reserved for the King himself that he could cherish the idea of their destruction after his death. After 1870, when the order was given 'not to speak of politics any more, unless His Majesty asks a question', the King, who at the beginning of his reign showed rare political gifts, had increasingly lost interest in politics, but he displayed tremendous activity in his artistic work. For him the theatre and his castles were more than a mere illusory world into which he withdrew in protest against the bourgeois world which showed no understanding of him: they were his very life, in which dream and reality were blended and history lived again – not merely on a stage. Here the King acted with an extreme skill and energy which he completely lacked in political matters; in no way did he ruin the State Treasury by his undertakings, as is often alleged, but paid everything out of his own private purse.

But when the privy purse ran heavily into debt and building had to stop, the King's life lost its purpose. Thus Ludwig, whom Verlaine was to call the 'only true king of the century', despairing of the vocation of a monarch within a constitutional monarchy, finally had to perish because in an 'ideal, monarchical, poetical solitude' he had tried to create an art in harmony with his wide view of the universe.

CHRONOLOGY OF LUDWIG'S LIFE

Ludwig's age	*Year*	*Events*
	1845	25 August: Prince Ludwig, later King Ludwig II, born at Nymphenburg.
2–3	1848	20 March: King Ludwig I abdicates and is succeeded by King Maximilian II: Prince Ludwig becomes Crown Prince.
		27 April: Ludwig's brother Otto born.
15–16	1861	2 February: Ludwig hears his first Wagner opera, *Lohengrin*.
18–19	1864	10 March: death of King Max II: Ludwig II succeeds to the throne.
		4 May: first meeting of Ludwig and Wagner.
19–20	1865	10 June: première of *Tristan*.
		19 October: Ludwig goes to Switzerland.
		11 November: Wagner visits Ludwig at Hohenschwangau.
		10 December: Wagner forced to leave Munich.
20–21	1866	10 May: Ludwig orders mobilization for 22 June.
		22 May: Ludwig visits Wagner at Triebschen.
		27 May: Ludwig opens the first Diet of his reign.
		16 June: German Confederation declares war on Prussia (Seven Weeks' War).
		25 June: Ludwig visits Army Headquarters at Bamberg.
		3 July: Austrians defeated at Königgrätz (Sadowa).
		22 August: peace treaty with Prussia.
		November–December: Ludwig's tour of Franconia.
21–22	1867	22 January: Ludwig announces his engagement to his cousin Sophie, daughter of Duke Max in Bayern.
		31 May : Ludwig visits the Wartburg.
		20 July: Ludwig visits France.
		10 October: Ludwig's engagement broken off.
22–23	1868	29 February: death of ex-King Ludwig I.
		21 June: première of *Die Meistersinger*.
		First plans for Neuschwanstein.
23–24	1869	5 September: foundation-stone of Neuschwanstein laid.
		22 September: première of *Das Rheingold*.
24–25	1870	26 June: première of *Die Walküre*.
		19 July: start of the Franco-Prussian War.
		25 August: Wagner and Cosima von Bülow marry.
		1 September: Battle of Sedan.
		30 September: first plans for Linderhof.
		30 November: Ludwig invites King Wilhelm I of Prussia to become German Emperor.
25–26	1871	18 January: King Wilhelm I of Prussia proclaimed Emperor at Versailles.
		10 May: peace signed at Frankfurt.
		21 May: Prince Otto put under mild restraint.
		16 July: victory parade in Munich.
26–27	1872	22 May: foundation-stone of Bayreuth Opera House laid.

Family tree of the Bavarian Royal Family

This is a simplified chart, leaving out what is not essential to the story. Bavarian kings are in capital letters.

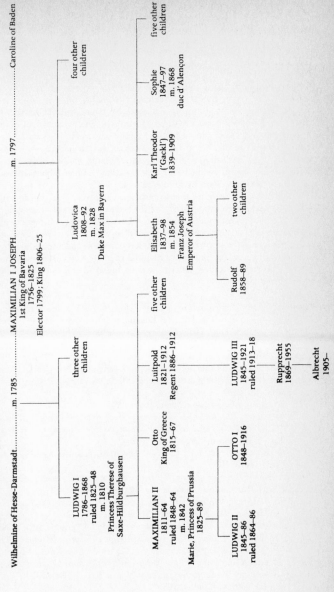

Wilhelmine of Hesse-Darmstadt............m. 1785............MAXIMILIAN 1 JOSEPH............m. 1797............Caroline of Baden
1st King of Bavaria
1756–1825
Elector 1799; King 1806–25

LUDWIG I
1786–1868
ruled 1825–48
m. 1810
Princess Therese of
Saxe-Hildburghausen

three other
children

Ludovica
1808–92
m. 1828
Duke Max in Bayern

four other
children

MAXIMILIAN II
1811–64
ruled 1848–64
m. 1842
Marie, Princess of Prussia
1825–89

Otto
King of Greece
1815–67

Luitpold
1821–1912
Regent 1886–1912

five other
children

Elisabeth
1837–98
m. 1854
Franz Joseph
Emperor of Austria

Karl Theodor
('Gackl')
1839–1909

Sophie
1847–97
m. 1868
duc d'Alençon

five other
children

LUDWIG II
1845–86
ruled 1864–86

OTTO I
1848–1916

LUDWIG III
1845–1921
ruled 1913–18

Rudolf
1858–89

two other
children

Rupprecht
1869–1955

Albrecht
1905–

Bibliography

The standard biography of Ludwig II is Gottfried von Böhm's *Ludwig II. König von Bayern* (see below). This long and admirable book – it runs to 800 pages – has been extensively drawn upon, with varying degrees of acknowledgment, by all subsequent writers on the subject. An excellent and more recent biography is that by Werner Richter. An English translation of this, by William S. Schlamm, was published in Chicago under the title of *The Mad Monarch* (Henry Regnery, 1954); it is now out of print, and there appears to be no copy of it in the British Library. Rupert Hacker's anthology, and of course Otto Strobel's five volumes of Ludwig-Wagner correspondence, were also invaluable to me. The literature dealing with Ludwig is very large, and the bibliography given below includes by no means all the books I have consulted; fuller bibliographies will be found in the works therein listed by Richter, Hacker and Petzet.

It is greatly to be regretted that Ernest Newman never found time to write his intended life of Wagner's friend and patron; but the last two volumes of his magnificent biography of Wagner are indispensable reading for Ludovicologists, and there is also a brief but brilliant sketch of 'the mad Ludwig' in Henry Channon's *The Ludwigs of Bavaria*. Major Chapman-Huston's book, though it is unreliable and also unduly stresses Ludwig's homosexuality, contains interesting material from the secret archives of the Wittelsbachs.

A wealth of illustrative material will be found in the works of Sailer, Petzet and Rall/Petzet given below.

Baedeker, Karl: *Munich and its Environs*, London, 1950; New York, 1956
————— *Southern Bavaria*, London and New York, 1953
Bainville, Jacques: *Louis II. de Bavière*, Paris, 1900
Biermann, Christoph: 'Leiden eines Königs', *Deutsches Arzeblatt*, vol. 45, 1973
Böhm, Gottfried von: *Ludwig II. König von Bayern*, Berlin, 1921 and 1924
Channon, Henry: *The Ludwigs of Bavaria*, London and New York, 1933
Chapman-Huston, Desmond: *Bavarian Fantasy; the story of Ludwig II*, London, 1955; New York, 1956
Des Cars, Jean: *Louis II de Bavière*, Paris, 1977
Gerard, Frances: *The Romance of Ludwig II. of Bavaria*, London, 1899
Grein, Edir (editor): *Tagebuch-Aufzeichnungen von Ludwig II. König von Bayern*, Schaan/Liechtenstein, 1925
Gutman, Robert W.: *Richard Wagner: The Man, His Mind and His Music*, London and New York, 1968
Hacker, Rupert: *Ludwig II. von Bayern in Augenzeugenberichten*, Düsseldorf, 1966
Heigel, Karl von: *König Ludwig II. von Bayern*, Stuttgart, 1893
Herzfeld, Friedrich: *Königsfreundschaft, Ludwig II. und Richard Wagner*, Leipzig, 1939
Hierneis, Theodor: *Der König speist*, Munich, 1953
    English translation, *The Monarch Dines*, London (Werner Laurie), 1954
Kobell, Louise von: *Unter den vier ersten Königen Bayerns*, Munich, 1894
————— *König Ludwig II. von Bayern und die Kunst*, Munich, 1898
Kolb, Annette: *König Ludwig II. von Bayern und Richard Wagner*, Amsterdam, 1947
Kreisel, Heinrich: *Die Schlösser Ludwigs II. von Bayern*, Darmstadt,
    English translation, London, 1955
McIntosh, Christopher: *Ludwig II of Bavaria*, London, 1982
Mayr-Ofen, Ferdinand: *Tragic Idealist: Ludwig II of Bavaria*, London, 1937; New York, 1939

Newman, Ernest: *The Life of Richard Wagner* (vols 3 and 4), New York, 1941, 1946

———— 'The Strange Case of King Ludwig II of Bavaria', in *The Saturday Book*, no. 4, London and New York, 1944

Oberdorfer, Aldo: *Il Re folle, Luigi II di Baviera*, Milan, 1935
(French translation, Paris, 1937)

Petzet, Michael: *König Ludwig II. und die Kunst*, Munich, 1968

Petzet, Detta and Michael: *Die Richard Wagner-Bühne König Ludwigs II.* Munich, 1970

Pourtalès, Guy de: *Louis II de Bavière ou Hamlet-Roi*, Paris, 1928

Rall, Hans, and Petzet, Michael: *König Ludwig II.*, Munich, 1968

———— 'Die politische Entwicklung von 1848 bis zur Reichsgründung 1871', *Handbuch der bayrischen Geschicte*, ed. M. Spindler, vol. IV, 1974

———— *König Ludwig II. und Bismarcks Ringen um Bayern*, Munich, 1973

Richter, Werner: *Ludwig II. König von Bayern*, Erlenbach, 1939 and Munich, 1950
(English translation, Chicago, 1955)

Röckl, Sebastian: *Ludwig II. und Richard Wagner*, Munich, 1913 and 1920

Sailer, Anton: *Bayerns Märchenkönig*, Munich, 1961

Strobel, Otto: *König Ludwig II. und Richard Wagner, Briefwechsel*, 5 volumes, Karlsruhe, 1936-9

Tschudi, Clara: *König Ludwig II. von Bayern*, Leipzig
(English translation, 1908)

Wolf, Georg Jacob: *König Ludwig II. und seine Welt*, Munich, 1922

There are also excellent pocket guidebooks to the three principal castles.

INDEX

grandfather), 3, 12, 39, 54, 76, 97, 175, 181;
abdicates, 4; his career, 4; and Lola Montez,
4, 15; on Prince Ludwig, 4; at *Tristan*
première, 33; and Ludwig's 'follies', 39; and
Ludwig's duties as King, 52; and the Dahn-
Hausmanns, 63; and Ludwig and Sophie
engaged, 67; his death (1868), 95, and the
new Munich, 95; his public buildings, 182
Ludwig II (King of Bavaria 1864–86, *formerly*
Prince Ludwig Friedrich Wilhelm
(Wittelsbach), *originally named* 'Otto' (p. 3)
Ludwig III (King of Bavaria 1913–8, Ludwig's
cousin), 109
Ludwig Ferdinand, Prince (Sophie's brother
and Ludwig's cousin), 61, 69, 114, 178
Ludwig Ferdinand, Princess, 178
Ludwig in Bayern, Duke, 143
Luitpold von Bayern, Prince (Ludwig's uncle
and *later* Prince Regent of Bavaria
1886–1912), 90, 92, 144 *bis*, 151, 153,
156–60 *passim*
Lutz, Freiherr von (Minister of Justice and
later Minister-President), 142; at Versailles
Conference (1870), 90; and Ludwig's private
diaries, 121; and Ludwig decide Ludwig
must go, 144; his conspiracy, 144, 151, 153;
his Commission to arrest Ludwig, 152, 153
(*see also* Commission)
Lutz, Johann (Cabinet Secretary), 39, 41, 45

MacMahon, Maréchal (President of France
1873–9), 118
Maid of Orleans, The (a play), 172
Maier, Matilda (a friend of Wagner), 15
Maintenon, Madame de, 120
Makart, Hans (artist), 177, 180
Mallinger, Mathilde (operatic singer), 63, 78
Maria de la Paz (Spanish Infanta), 61; *quoted*
61–2
Maria Stuart (Schiller), 59 *ter*
Marie Antoinette, 59, 117, 148, 175
Marie the Queen Mother (*formerly* Crown
Princess *and* Queen of Bavaria, Ludwig's
mother), 20, 66; personal details, 6; gives
birth to Ludwig, 3; on Ludwig, 4; her second
son (Otto), 4; and the young princes feeding
swans, 5; at Hohenschwangau, 5; and her
husband, 5; and Bavarian peasant costume,
6; and Wagner, 26; and Lila von Bulyowsky,
60, 61; and Ludwig and Sophie, 65; and
Ludwig's matrimonial intentions, 72; and
Sedan victory celebrations in Munich, 89;
Ludwig and, 89, 114, 116, 129, 166; at the
Victory Parade (16 July 1871), 93
Marie, Queen of Naples, 65–6
Marion de Lorme (Victor Hugo), 163, 135–6
Mary Queen of Scots, 59
Massenet, Jules, 179
Max in Bayern, Duke (Ludwig's great-uncle)
7 & n, 15, 18, 33, 72; his 'ultimatum' to
Ludwig, 72

Max Josef I (Elector and *later* King of Bavaria
1799–1825), 3, 7n
Max, Prince, *see* Maximilian II
Max von Thurn und Taxis, Prince, 36, 107,
143
Maximilian II (King of Bavaria 1848–64,
formerly Prince Max, Ludwig's father), 3,
10 *bis*, 12, 24, 37, 76, 95, 99, 179; becomes
King, 4; and the Siegestor, 4; and
Hohenschwangau, *q.v.*, 5, 95, 96, 103, 165,
166, 168–9; and the swans, 5; and Queen
Marie, 5; 'an intellectual *manqué*', 5; and a
'Spartan upbringing', 6; his sanity, 6; as a
father, 6, 7; and Schleswig-Holstein (1864),
9; his rheumatism, 9; his death, 9; and Schloss
Berg, *q.v.*, 15, 95, 97; his public buildings,
182
Mayr (a royal valet), 146, 147, 149, 158, 159
ter, 161
'Meicost Ettal', 100, 175
Meilhaus, Fräulein Sybille (Ludwig's
governess, *later* Baronin von Leonrod), 5, 7,
100
Mein Leben (Wagner's autobiography), 48
Meistersinger von Nürnberg, Die (The
Mastersingers of Nuremberg) (Wagner), 11,
15, 23, 47, 54–5, 56, 71, 80; cast of, 78; dress
rehearsal, 78–9; première, 79, 132
Melchtal (character in Schiller's *Wilhelm Tell*),
139
Melchtal (Swiss village) 139 *ter*
Metz, capitulation of (27 October 1870), 89–90
Military review (August 1875), 108, 109
Minister under Louis XIV, A (a play), 119
Mohl, Robert von (Baden Ambassador), 66 *bis*,
75–6
Moltke, Feld-Marshall Helmut, Graf von, 54
Montez, Lola (*alias* Mrs Eliza Gilbert), 4, 21,
33, 44, 60, 67
Moorish house, Ludwig's, 103
Moorish kiosk, the, 103, 178
'Morning Prayer of a Modest Man', 44
Moy, Baron, 37
Mozart, Wolfgang, 16
Müller, Dr, 153, 159, 162 *bis*, 163; *quoted*,
159–60
München, see Munich
Müncheners (the people of Munich, *see also*
Munich), 9, 11, 30, 57, 58, 76–7, 84; their
impressions of Ludwig, 11; and Wagner, 25,
44–5; their cultural education, 23; and von
Bülow's Schweinehunde, 30, 33; and
Ludwig's neglect, 53, 54; and his engagement
to Sophie, 66, 72
Munich (*München*, capital of Bavaria, *see also
Müncheners*), 3–9 *passim*, 11, 12, 20, 24–6
passim, 28 *bis*, 29, 30 *bis*, 56, 58, 61, 66, 70,
72–89 *passim*, 92, 94 *bis*, 108, 125, 129–30
passim, 140, 141, 154, 155–6; the
Frauenkirche, 4, 109; intellectuals of, 5; the
English Garden. 7, 67; Karl-Theodor

197